THE UNITED STATES
AND THE CARIBBEAN

THE UNITED STATES AND THE CARIBBEAN

TRANSFORMING HEGEMONY AND SOVEREIGNTY

Anthony P. Maingot
and
Wilfredo Lozano

ROUTLEDGE
New York • London

Published in 2005 by
Routledge
270 Madison Avenue
New York, NY 10016
www.routledge-ny.com

Published in Great Britain by
Routledge
2 Park Square
Milton Park, Abingdon
Oxon OX14 4RN U.K.
www.routledge.co.uk

10 9 8 7 6 5 4 3 2 1

Library of Congress Cataloging-in-Publication Data

Maingot, Anthony P.
    The United States and the Caribbean : transforming hegemony and sovereignty / by Anthony P. Maingot and Wilfredo Lozano.
        p. cm.
    Includes bibliographical references and index.
    ISBN 0-415-95044-9 (hb : alk. paper) — ISBN 0-415-95045-7 (pb : alk. paper)
    1. Globalization. 2. Caribbean Area—Relations—United States. 3. United States—Relations—Caribbean Area. 4. Caribbean Area—History—1945–.
5. United States—History—1969– . I. Lozano, Wilfredo, 1950– . II. Title.
F2178.U6M332 2004
327.729073—dc22
                                                            2004011023

Table of Contents

Preface

The transition from authoritarian rule to constitutional government
The continent-wide economic depression of the 1980s and the subsequent shift toward more open market-conforming economies
The end of the Cold War in Europe
The transformation of relations with the U.S.

Each of these major events and processes was an epochal change in the history of Latin America and the Caribbean. More striking is that all four changes took place within the same relatively short time, though not all four affected each and every country in the same way. They became interconnected, with change on each dimension fostering convergent changes on other dimensions. Thus, by the beginning of the new millennium, we had witnessed an important transformation and intensification in U.S.–Latin American relations.

This book is part of a series of ten books on U.S. relations with Latin American and Caribbean countries. Each of these books is focused on the fourth of the four transformations mentioned—namely, the change in U.S. relations with Latin America and the Caribbean. Our premise is that the first three transformations provide part of the explanation for the change in U.S. relations with its neighbors in the Americas and for the changes in the foreign policies of Latin American and Caribbean states. Each of the books in the series assesses the impact of the epoch-making changes upon each other.

The process of widest impact was the economic transformation. By the end of 1982, much of North America, Western Europe, and East Asia launched into an economic boom at the very time when Latin America plunged into an economic depression of great severity that lasted approximately to the end of the decade. As a consequence of such economic collapse, nearly all Latin American governments readjusted their economic strategies. They departed from principal reliance on import-substitution industrialization, opened their economies to international trade and investment, and adopted policies to create more open market-conforming economies. (Even Cuba had changed its economic strategy by the 1990s, making its economy more open to foreign direct investment and trade.)

The region-wide economic changes had direct and immediate impact upon U.S.–Latin American relations. The share of U.S. trade accounted for by Latin America and the Caribbean had declined fairly steadily from the end of World War II to the end of the 1980s. In the 1990s, in contrast, U.S. trade with Latin America grew at a rate significantly faster than the growth of U.S. trade worldwide; Latin America had become the fastest growing market for U.S. exports. The United States, at long last, did take notice of Latin America. Trade between some Latin American countries also boomed, especially within subregions such as the southern cone of South America, Venezuela and Colombia, the Central American countries, and, to a lesser extent, the Anglophone Caribbean countries. The establishment of formal freer-trade areas facilitated the growth of trade and other economic relations. These included the North American Free Trade Agreement (NAFTA), which grouped Mexico, the U.S., and Canada; the MERCOSUR (southern common market) consisting of Argentina, Brazil, Paraguay, and Uruguay; the Andean Community, whose members were Bolivia, Colombia, Ecuador, Peru, and Venezuela; the Central American Common Market (CACM); and the Caribbean Community (CARICOM). U.S. foreign direct and portfolio investment in large quantities flowed into Latin America and the Caribbean, financing the expansion of tradable economic activities. The speed of portfolio investment transactions, however, also exposed these and other countries to marked financial volatility and recurrent financial panics. The transformation in hemispheric international economic relations—and specifically in U.S. economic relations with the rest of the hemisphere—was already far-reaching as the 21st century began.

These structural economic changes had specific and common impacts on the conduct of international economic diplomacy. All governments in the Americas, large and small, had to develop a cadre of experts who could negotiate concrete, technical trade, investment, and other economic issues with the U.S. and with other countries in the region. All had to create teams of international trade lawyers and experts capable of defending national interests, and the interests of particular business firms, in international, inter-American, or subregional dispute-resolution panels or court-like proceedings. The discourse and practice of inter-American relations, broadly understood, became much more professional—less the province of eloquent poets, more the domain of number-crunching litigators and mediators.

The changes in Latin America's domestic political regimes began in the late 1970s. These, too, would contribute to change the texture of inter-American relations. By the end of the 1990s, democratization based on fair elections, competitive parties, constitutionalism, and respect for the rule of law and the liberties of citizens had advanced and was still advancing throughout the region, albeit unevenly and with persisting serious problems, Cuba being the principal exception. In 2000, for example, for the first time since their revolution, Mexicans elected an opposition candidate, Vicente Fox, to the presidency, and Alberto Fujimori was compelled to resign in Peru, accused of abuse of power, electoral fraud, and corruption. In each instance, the cause of democratization advanced.

Democratization also affected the international relations of Latin American and Caribbean countries, albeit in more subtle ways. The Anglophone Caribbean is a largely archipelagic region, long marked by the widespread practice of constitutional government. Since the 1970s, Anglophone Caribbean democratic governments rallied repeatedly to defend constitutional government on any of the islands where it came under threat and, in the specific cases of Grenada and Guyana, to assist the process of democratization in the 1980s and 1990s, respectively. In the 1990s, Latin American governments also began to act collectively to defend and promote democratic rule; with varying degrees of success and U.S. support, they did so in Guatemala, Haiti, Paraguay, and Peru. Democratization had a more complex relationship to the content of specific foreign policies. In the 1990s, democratization in Argentina, Brazil, Uruguay, and Chile contributed to improved international political, security, and economic relations among these southern cone countries. Yet, at times, democratic politics made it more difficult to manage international relations over boundary or territorial issues between given pairs of countries, including Colombia and Venezuela and Costa Rica and Nicaragua. In general, democratization facilitated better relations between Latin American and Caribbean countries, on the one hand, and the U.S., on the other. Across the Americas, democratic governments, including the U.S. and Canada, acted to defend and promote constitutional government. Much cooperation over security, including the attempt to foster cooperative security and civilian supremacy over the military, would have been unthinkable except in the new, deeper democratic context in the hemisphere.

At its best, in the 1990s, democratic politics made it possible to transform the foreign policies of particular presidential administrations into the foreign policies of states. For example, Argentina's principal political parties endorsed the broad outlines of their nation's foreign policy, including the framework to govern much friendlier Argentinean relations with the U.S. All Chilean political parties were strongly committed to their country's transformation into an international trading state. The principal political parties of the Anglophone Caribbean sustained consistent long-lasting foreign policies across different partisan administrations. Mexico's three leading political parties agreed, even if they differed on specifics, that NAFTA should be implemented, binding Mexico to the U.S. and Canada. The George H. W. Bush and Bill Clinton administrations in the U.S. followed remarkably compatible policies toward Latin America and the Caribbean with regard to the promotion of free trade, pacification in Central America, support for international financial institutions, and the defense of constitutional government in Latin America and the Caribbean. Both administrations acted in concert with other states in the region and often through the Organization of American States. Democratic procedures in these and other cases establish the credibility of a state's foreign policy because all actors would have reason to expect that the framework of today's foreign policy would endure tomorrow.

The end of the Cold War in Europe followed the accession in 1985 of Mikhail Gorbachev to the post of General-Secretary of the Communist party of the Soviet Union. The end accelerated during the second half of the 1980s, culminating with the collapse of communist regimes in Europe between 1989 and 1991 and the breakup of the Soviet Union itself in late 1991. The impact of the end of the U.S.–Soviet conflict on the hemisphere was subtle but important: the U.S. was no longer obsessed with the threat of communism. Freed to focus on other international interests, the U.S. discovered that it shared many practical interests with Latin American and Caribbean countries; the latter, in turn, found it easier to cooperate with the U.S. There was one exception to this benign international process. The U.S. was also freed to forget its long-lasting fear of communist guerrillas in Colombia (who remained powerful and continued to operate nonetheless) in order to concentrate on a "war" against drug trafficking, even if it undermined Colombia's constitutional regime.

The process of ending the Cold War also had a specific component in the Western Hemisphere, namely, the termination of the civil and international wars that had swirled in Central America since the late 1970s. The causes of those wars had been both internal and international. In the early 1990s, the collapse of the Soviet Union and the marked weakening of Cuban influence enabled the U.S. government to support negotiations with governments or insurgent movements it had long opposed. All of these international changes made it easier to arrange for domestic political, military, and social settlements of the wars in and around Nicaragua,

El Salvador, and Guatemala. The end of the Cold War in Europe had an extraordinary impact on Cuba as well. The Cold War did not end the sharp conflict between the U.S. and Cuban governments, but the latter was deprived of Soviet support, forcing it to recall its troops overseas, open its economy to the world, and lower its foreign policy profile. The U.S. felt more free to conduct a "Colder War" against Cuba, seeking to overthrow its government.

Two other large-scale processes, connected to the previous three, had a significant impact in the international relations of the Western Hemisphere. They were the booms in international migration and cocaine-related international organized crime. To be sure, migration and organized crime on an international scale in the Americas are as old as the European settlement begun in the late 15th century and the growth of state-sponsored piracy in the 16th century. Yet the volume and acceleration of these two processes in the 1980s and 1990s were truly extraordinary.

Widespread violence in Central America and Colombia and economic depression everywhere accelerated the rate of emigration to the U.S. Once begun, the process of migration to the U.S. was sustained through networks of relatives and friends, the family-unification provisions of U.S. legislation, and the relatively lower costs of international transportation and communication. By the mid-1990s, over 12 million people born in Latin America resided in the U.S.; two thirds of them had arrived since 1980. The number of people of Latin American ancestry in the U.S. was even larger, of course. In the 1980s, migrants came to the U.S. not just from countries of traditional emigration such as Mexico but also from countries such as Brazil that in the past had generated few emigrants. As the 20th century ended, the U.S. had become one of the largest "Latin American" countries in the Americas. The U.S. had also come to play a major role in the production and consumption of the culture, including music, book publishing, and television programming, of the Spanish-speaking peoples. All of these trends are likely to intensify in the 21st century.

Had this series of books been published in the mid-1970s, coca and cocaine would have merited brief mention in one or two of the books, and no mention in most of them. The boom in U.S. cocaine consumption in the late 1970s and 1980s changed this. The regionwide economic collapse of the 1980s made it easier to bribe public officials, judges, police, and military officers. U.S. cocaine supply interdiction policies in the 1980s raised the price of cocaine, making the coca and cocaine businesses the most lucrative in depression-ravaged economies. The generally unregulated sale of weapons in the U.S. equipped gangsters throughout the Americas. Bolivia and Peru produced the coca. Colombians grew it, refined it, and financed it. Criminal gangs in the Caribbean, Central America, and Mexico transported and distributed it. Everywhere, drug traffic-related violence and corruption escalated.

The impact of economic policy change, democratization, and the end of the Cold War in Europe on U.S.–Latin American relations, therefore, provide important explanations common to the countries of the Americas in their relations with the U.S. The acceleration of emigration, and the construction and development of international organized crime around the cocaine business, were also key common themes in the continent's international relations during the closing fifth of the 20th century. To the extent pertinent, these topics appear in each of the books in this series. Nonetheless, each country's own history, geographic location, set of neighbors, resource endowment, institutional features, and leadership characteristics bear as well on the construction, design, and implementation of its foreign policy. These more particular factors enrich and guide the books in this series in their interplay with the more general arguments.

As the 1990s ended, dark clouds reappeared on the firmament of inter-American relations, raising doubts about the optimistic trajectory that seemed set at the beginning of that decade. The heavy presence of the military on civilian society was significantly felt in Colombia, Venezuela, and Peru (until the end of Alberto Fujimori's presidency in November 2000). In January 2000, a military coup overthrew the constitutionally elected president of Ecuador, although the civilian vice-president soon reestablished constitutional government. Serious concerns resurfaced concerning the depth and durability of democratic institutions and practices in these countries. Venezuela seemed ready to try once again much heavier government involvement in economic affairs. The U.S. had held back from implementing the commitment to hemispheric free trade that both presidents George H. W. Bush and Bill Clinton had pledged. Only the last of these trends had instant international repercussions, but all of them could affect adversely the future of a Western Hemisphere based on free politics, free markets, and peace.

This Project

Each of the books in the series has two authors, typically one from a Latin American or Caribbean country and another from the U.S. (and, in one case, the U.K.). We chose this approach to facilitate the writing of the books and ensure that the books would represent the international perspectives from both parts of the U.S.–Latin American relationship. In addition, we sought to embed each book within international networks of scholarly work in more than one country.

We have attempted to write short books that ask common questions to enable various readers—scholars, students, public officials, international entrepreneurs, and the educated public—to make their own comparisons and judgments as they read two or more volumes in the series. The project sought to foster comparability across the books through two conferences held at the Instituto Tecnológico Autónomo de México (ITAM) in Mexico City. The first, held in June 1998, compared ideas and questions; the second, held in August 1999, discussed preliminary drafts of the books. Both of us read and commented on all the manuscripts; the manuscripts also received commentary from other authors in the project. We also hope that the network of scholars created for this project will continue to function, even if informally, and that the Web page created for this project will provide access for a wider audience to the ideas, research, and writing associated with it.

We are grateful to the Ford Foundation for its principal support of this project, and to Cristina Eguizábal for her advice and assistance throughout this endeavor. We are also grateful to the MacArthur Foundation for the support that made it possible to hold a second successful project conference in Mexico City. The Rockefeller Foundation provided the two of us with an opportunity to spend four splendid weeks in Bellagio, Italy, working on our various general responsibilities in this project. The Academic Department of International Studies at Instituto Technológies Autónomo de Mexico (ITAM) hosted the project throughout its duration and the two international conferences. We appreciate the support of the Asociación Mexicana de Cultura, ITAM's principal supporter in this work. Harvard University's Weatherhead Center for International Affairs also supported aspects of this project, as did Harvard University's David Rockefeller Center for Latin American Studies. We are particularly grateful to Hazel Blackmore and Juana Gómez at ITAM, and Amanda Pearson and Kathleen Hoover at the Weatherhead Center, for their work on many aspects of the project. At Routledge, Melissa Rosati encouraged us from the start; Eric Nelson supported the project through its conclusion.

Jorge I. Domínguez Rafael Fernández de Castro
Harvard University ITAM

Acknowledgments

Any book written by two authors of such different national and intellectual backgrounds and covering as many societies as this one does clearly owes much to many more people than can be acknowledged in a short note.

We do wish to express our sincere thanks to the two General Editors of the Series, Jorge I. Dominguez and Rafael Fernandez de Castro. Their repeated written and verbal comments and critiques were simply invaluable in helping us sharpen the books, focus by bringing us time and again back to the central theme, the tension between hegemony and sovereignty in the Caribbean.

Wilfredo Lozano received splendid intellectual support from his many colleagues and friends at FLACSO in Costa Rica and in his native Dominican Republic. Anthony P. Maingot was fortunate to have exceptional collaboration from the many graduate students from the U.S. and around the Caribbean at Florida International Universitys, Latin American and Caribbean Center.

To all these colleagues, students, and friends, our heartfelt thanks and gratitude.

Finally, both authors benefitted enormously from the editing and translating skills of their wives, Julia Castillo de Lozano and Consuelo Stuntz Maingot. Along with their patience and dedication went a pair of razor-sharp critical eyes which more often than not we had to acknowledge as being right on the mark. To both Julia and Consuelo, our thanks, admiration, and love.

Anthony P. Maingot and Wilfredo Lozano

CHAPTER 1

The Special U.S.–Caribbean Relationship

1.1   An Historical Hegemonic Relationship

No other region of the world has had a relationship with the U.S. similar to that of the Caribbean. For one, the dramatic asymmetry in power, accompanied by geographic proximity, made the region easily accessible to a variety of U.S. designs. Because these two factors, power and proximity, have not changed, there has been a substantial degree of continuity in the fundamental nature of U.S.–Caribbean relations. To be sure, there have been changes in the global context and changes in U.S. domestic politics, both of which have brought about changes in the content and style of U.S. foreign policy. Seen from a broad perspective, U.S.–Caribbean relations have been shaped by, and in turn, have given shape to some very special characteristics.

The Caribbean has been second only to Mexico as an area of U.S. geopolitical and geostrategic concerns in the hemisphere. With the waning of Manifest Destiny by the end of the 19ᵗʰ century, U.S. elites turned their sights towards islands, Hawaii in the Pacific, to be sure, but also those in the Caribbean. But, as Frederick Merk has persuasively argued, this new expansionism lacked a fundamental characteristic of the Manifest Destiny: a sense of mission to bring what was best in U.S. society to other peoples. The Caribbean version of Manifest Destiny was outright imperialism wrapped in a thick ideology with geopolitical and neoDarwinian racism. "Imperialism," says Warren Zimmerman, "is inherently racist."[1] Aside from this self-aggrandizing function, imperialism had other psychological benefits. "Islands . . . ," wrote Merk, "were restoratives of youth and preventatives of premature old age."[2] Like the youthful paramour, however, they were not to be invited home for tea. The islands were never perceived as worthy of integration into American civilization.

U.S. geopolitics, based largely on the Alfred Mahan principle of controlling the commercial sea lanes, went hand in hand with what Dana G. Munroe called "dollar diplomacy": military intervention to promote and secure economic expansion.[3] As a young aspirant to the U.S. Senate put it during the Spanish–American War: "We will establish trading posts throughout the world as distribution points for American products. We will cover the ocean with our merchant marine. . . ."[4] And, certainly, the U.S. Marine Corps kept the Caribbean safe for these purposes.[5]

In the post–Cold War era, when the concept of globalization is so universally cited and yet so variedly defined, it gives us pause to note that in the Caribbean there has always been a convergence between hard-headed economic interests and the export of American values in support of those interests. William Appleman Williams has argued that since the opening of the age of U.S. imperialism in the 1890s, the central thrust of U.S. foreign policy has been the "open door": opening markets everywhere is good for the U.S. and good for people overseas. What Williams terms the "internationalization of business" was essentially a globalizing effort sustained by the expansion of the U.S. corporation with U.S. government support and protection. In other words, for the Caribbean as for the U.S. government, being "in business" did not begin with the present age of globalization.[6] As Lester D. Langley has so well documented, the marriage of business and government in the Caribbean has a long history.[7]

In addition to all this, however, in the Caribbean being in business meant, for decades, outright military interventions to protect U.S. corporate interests. The term "banana republic" accurately described a situation in which U.S.-owned banana companies determined the fate of many a Central American administration. It was President Herbert Hoover who, after noting that between 1898 and 1924 the marines had landed 21 times on Caribbean shores, decided to shift away from intervention as the manner in which U.S. business would be promoted. President Franklin Delano Roosevelt carried the Hoover idea into a new form of Pan-Americanism, treating U.S. neighbors with more respect. The "good neighbor policy" promised self-determination and national sovereignty as well as the peaceful settlement of disputes involving U.S. property. This policy was more likely, in other words, to win friends and influence nations at a time when other international forces (communism and fascism) appeared menacing.[8]

Being in business, thus, could be, and has been, accomplished by the U.S. through a variety of means. The Caribbean region lent itself, at socially and politically acceptable costs in lives and capital, to an array of U.S. strategies that ranged from encouraging emulation and using co-optation to threats and outright use of force, or any combination of these.

Although little studied, being in business also had a Caribbean side: the ability and opportunity of local elites to engage the U.S. and the world in trade and finance. Whether it was through island trade with merchants in such U.S. ports as Charleston, New York, or Boston, or through native banks that financed everything from trade to revolutions, the Caribbean has never been far removed from world and American economic and financial affairs. Significant parts of this linking was assisted by two groups: the Sephardic Jews, who had Dutch Curaçao and Danish St. Thomas, Virgin Islands, as their original bases, and Freemasonry, which was Caribbean-wide and had intimate links with British, French, and American counterparts. In particular, the financing of trade and politics before the military arrival of the Americans in the 1890s was done by Sephardic Jews, who had ample financial contacts in European banking circles.[9]

But, being in business has always coexisted with a profound and sustained sense of the geopolitical importance of the Caribbean on the part of the U.S. From concerns over the safety of the Panama Canal and the battles to contain and defeat communism to the present-day War on Drugs, the U.S. has used every strategy available to ensure that its governing definition of national interest is upheld. It has not, however, always been able to pursue these strategies in a seamless and undisputed manner.

Despite the U.S.'s geopolitical and economic capacity to exercise hegemonic influence, two characteristics of the special U.S.–Caribbean relationship later exercised a restraining influence on the hegemonic, unilateralist tendency: the region's multinational and multiethnic complexity and its role in U.S. domestic politics. The multinational nature of the region is fundamentally due to the fact that the European colonial presence, with the exception of that of Spain, was left undisturbed even after the Monroe Doctrine was added to the U.S. foreign policy arsenal. True, its articulation did contribute in 1867 to the French withdrawal from Mexico and that of the Spaniards from the Dominican Republic in 1865, and in 1895 Great Britain was pressured into negotiating with (rather than bombarding) Venezuela over the Guiana boundary. Despite Secretary of State Richard Olney's bravado in 1895 about the U.S. being "practically sovereign on this continent," the British, French, Dutch, and Danes (up to 1917) kept their possessions in the region. This helps to explain the region's unique, and often perplexing, multinational and multicultural mix. Any book on the region has to begin by outlining this complexity, and U.S. policymakers have to take it into account. To understand the legacy of Spanish, British, French, Dutch, and American imperial influences is to understand the present balkanization of the region.

Politically, the colonial past, and the decolonization process that followed, resulted in 16 new independent states representing 87% of the region's population. The other 13% of the population still lives on the 12 islands that retain some form of constitutional–political attachment to a metropolis. Let us be clear, however. To refer to these arrangements with the conventional term "colonialism" would be quite inappropriate. In every one of these still-dependent territories, there are democratic electoral opportunities for changing their status. Those distinct French, British, Dutch, or American statuses are maintained by what can only be called "sovereign consent," not imperial imposition. In addition, the fact that the dependent territories have six times the per capita gross domestic product (GDP) of the independent Caribbean states has a great deal to do with their determination to maintain the metropolitan links. Puerto Rico, with 42% of the region's GDP, is a particularly complex case of strong and growing cultural–linguistic assertions of identity in the midst of economic dependence. It certainly is not the only one, as anyone who is acquainted with the vibrant culture of negritude of the French Antilles will attest.

Language, being the most important part of culture, is definitely a major centrifugal force. The English-speakers (West Indians or "cricket Caribbeans") invariably claim the term "Caribbean" for themselves. But they represent only 17% of the region's population. Even the French speakers, at 21%, can claim to be more representative, if we include the many million Creole or Patois speakers of Haiti, Martinique, Guadeloupe, and St. Lucia in that number. Dutch speakers represent a mere 2% of the population in the region and, besides, to walk the picturesque streets of Curaçao, Aruba, Bonaire, or Suriname is to be mostly exposed to the dulcet tones of Papiamentu in the first three and Sranang in the last. So, what do the other 60% speak? Spanish. Somewhat belatedly, the largest of the region's islands, Cuba, the Dominican Republic, and Puerto Rico, are today asserting a Caribbean identification with force and verve. Their influence is augmented by the various Caribbean-oriented populations of the Central American and northern South American coasts.

There are several consequences of this historical and geopolitical reality. First, these recently decolonized societies are turning to their former metropolitan masters for continental "colonial" status or for assistance in a whole range of areas, from relief from their sense of economic vulnerability in the context of globalization and the North American Free Trade Agreement (NAFTA), to assistance in law and order operations.

Despite the fact that—at least since World War II—the European powers have been reconciled to the reality that this is truly an American sphere of influence,[10] these powers have not completely abandoned their present territories and former colonies. By promoting the interests of the

African, Pacific, and Caribbean (APC) countries through treaties such as Lômé, and more recently the COTONOU Agreement, the Europeans have made sure that many U.S.–Caribbean–European concerns are often settled by the World Trade Organization (WTO). Indeed, in the WTO text there are 147 provisions that address the concerns of small states.

Adding to this multinational mix, there is an ethnic dimension to U.S.–Caribbean relations comparable only to the Mexican case. Migration to the U.S. from a dominant racial group in a region has forced the U.S. to trim its foreign policy toward the region in terms of its domestic racial politics. How radical a change this is, and how fundamentally it has modified the relationship with the U.S., is made clear by the following explanation Merk gives of the past history of racism and foreign policy in the age of U.S. imperialism. The appearance of a demand for overseas colonies, according to Merk, coincided in time with a revival of racism in the U.S. As in the 1840's, expansionism synchronized with racism. In each period the postulates were the superiority of the Anglo-Saxon peoples over all others and the obligation of the superiors to give leadership to the inferiors. In the 1840s, racism had crossed party lines. But it had infected the antiexpansionist Whigs more than it had the Democrats. In the 1880s and 1890s it was especially virulent among Republicans, the party of the expansionists.[11] On that score, the link between U.S. colonialism and racism shows strong parallels with the case of Victorian Britain.[12]

The situation, since at least the maturing of the Civil Rights movement in the U.S. in the 1960s, has been the exact reverse of this racist past. Race and ethnicity are now bridges that contribute to better understanding and relations. Be this as it may, nothing ever stands still. This special relationship with the predominantly Afro-Caribbean islands is in relative decline as the U.S. racial and ethnic composition has changed. Specifically, the rise of Hispanic political mobilization and the relative decline of black political power has meant the relative decline of Afro-Caribbean influence. A U.S. city such as Miami, a veritable gateway to the Caribbean, as we shall see, is essentially a Latin city.

All these characteristics listed point to a fundamental of U.S.–Caribbean relations, not as conjuncture but as an ongoing structural reality characterized fundamentally by asymmetry. But even structural realities do not remain static. In the final analysis, policy is based on perceptions, or as Jarvis points out, misperceptions, and these certainly change. We have seen U.S. policy go from Manifest Destiny to outright imperialism, and from Pan-Americanism to the more permissive "sphere of influence" approach of the end of the 20th century.

Meanwhile, sociological and political processes continue to give shape to a new Caribbean with its own regional dynamics. As complex as the evolving U.S.–Caribbean relations are, there are some identifiable underlying intra-Caribbean characteristics that can help in its study. First, rather than being purely secondary or derived versions of superpower rivalry, many of the conflicts and confrontations in the Caribbean are the result of independent Caribbean actors pursuing their perception of national interests as well as of their own survival in power in an area that has changed dramatically since World War II. There are now some 15 new, politically independent actors with highly developed senses of national honor shaped by a very complex combination of traditional ideas of sovereignty as well as of racial and cultural solidarity on a global scale. Many more potential actors are waiting in the wings of the Caribbean stage. The final resolution of the political status of islands such as Puerto Rico, the Virgin Islands (American and British), the Netherlands Antilles, and the "overseas departments" of France (Martinique, Guadeloupe, and French Guyana) lies in the future. There are also cases of rediscovered Caribbean identifications such as that of the Dominican Republic. Then there is Cuba, which has attempted to solidify its Caribbean presence through the Association of Caribbean States.

Second, race and ethnicity will continue to be central to the Caribbean's definition of itself, an emphasis that will contribute to the retention of the archipelago's already strong, distinct identity. This identity will have broader implications for the area's international relations because this concern with race is not purely psychological; it relates to a fundamental dimension of Caribbean ideology. Nearly all the leaders of the new nations of the Caribbean came to power on platforms of social justice and condemnation of any form of racial discrimination.

Third, globalization and the internationalization of the region will provide new challenges to that regional sense of identity and perception of vulnerability. The area is a battleground of ideas, souls, and affiliations. Radio and TV programs blanket the area, as do traveling representatives of every religious, political, and trade union organization conceivable. Students educated abroad return to govern and administer, and membership in Intelsat guarantees that they will stay in touch with their colleagues around the globe. None of this is necessarily bad. Caribbean people have historically been able to adapt productively to changing circumstances, and to adjust their identifications at home or abroad.[13]

Having said this, however, there can be no doubt that the waters of the Caribbean Sea are much more turbulent than ever before. The fear is that geography will again deal the islands a dirty hand through their use as stepping-stones or conduits of the astronomical amounts of illegal drugs flowing from South America to the U.S. The return flow is of laundered dirty monies finding havens in the offshore banking systems of the Bahamas, the Caymans, the Netherlands Antilles, and Panama, to mention just a few "financial paradises." The threat lies in that, as traditional economic sectors shrink or disappear, they will be replaced by a whole network of activities related to the perfidious trade.

Fourth, from the political-institutional point of view, a general distinction can be made between those systems that have essentially solved the problem of transition or succession of power and those that have not, even given that stability is never guaranteed. In the former category are the large number of parliamentary systems with relatively stable electoral methods of succession. In the latter category, there are two types of situations that remain unsettled. First, there are the essentially "personalistic" systems where the passing of the caudillo will most probably lead to a period of uncertainty, if not outright turbulence. Cuba and Haiti fall in this category. The second type of uncertainty stems from what might be called the issue of uncertain status. Precisely because they are democratic systems, it is unclear which direction the people of Puerto Rico, the U.S. Virgin Islands, and other self-governing but not sovereign territories (see Table 1.1) will decide to take. There are also cases of potential secession such as that of Nevis threatening to leave the St. Kitts–Nevis union or Sint Maarten breaking with the Netherlands Antilles and adopting an Aruba-type *status aparte* within the Dutch kingdom.

The point is that the Caribbean is still in evolution, and U.S. perceptions of it will also evolve. No one should assume that the end of the Cold War is equivalent to the "end of history" in this region. No one should assume that U.S.–Caribbean relations have matured to a point of stasis. In fact, as in international relations generally, it is always safer to assume that there is always change. The unintended and unexpected, the contingent, and even the accidental all play their parts.

Be all this as it may, there is some order to these otherwise unpredictable processes. In the final analysis it is good to begin the study of U.S.–Caribbean international relations with the assumption that any foreign policy initiative—be it of a large or a small state—involves a trade-off between basic ideological assumptions, preferred policy outcomes, realistic assessments of the environment, and national capabilities. Successful policies are those that, of course, eventually pay off, that is, maximize benefits and minimize costs to any part of the overall state agenda through wise trade-offs. What gives this presumably logical process some degree of predictability in U.S.–Caribbean relations is, to reiterate, the enormous asymmetry that exists therein. This, in the final analysis, means that the key question for the Caribbean in this post–Cold War period is the same as it was before that era ended: how will the U.S. exercise its enormous advantage in power? The answer will tell us much about the kind of trade–offs that the small

Table 1.1 The Insular Caribbean: Basic Statistics

Independent States[a]	Population (in 1000s)	Area (km²)	GDP (1998) per Capita	Language
Cuba	11,000	114,500	—	Spanish
Dominican Republic	7,600	49,000	1,799	Spanish
Haiti	7,000	28,000	208	French and C
Jamaica	2,500	11,000	1,559	English
Trinidad and Tobago	1,290	5,000	4,618	English
Bahamas	272	13,900	12,944	English
Barbados	261	430	7,894	English
St. Lucia	153	620	3,907	English and C
St. Vincent/Grenadines	127	390	2,635	English
Grenada	108	340	3,347	English
Antigua/Barbuda	92	440	8,559	English
Dominica	96	750	3,310	English
St. Kitts/Nevis	48	270	6,716	English
On Mainland				
Guyana	760	215,000	825	English
Suriname	457	163,000	710	Dutch and C
Belize	211	23,000	2,725	English
Dependent Territories[b]				
Guadeloupe (F)	413	1,710	12,287	French and C
Martinique (F)	371	1,100	14,524	French and C
French Guiana (F)	135	90,000	13,044	French and C
Netherland Antilles (Netherlands)	197	800	11,698	Dutch and C
Aruba (Netherlands)	77	90	16,186	Dutch and C
Cayman Island (U.K.)	33	264	23,966	English
British Virgin Islands (U.K.)	17	150	14,010	English
Turks and Caicos (U.K.)	14	417	7,061	English
Montserrat (U.K.)	11	102	3,846	English
Anguilla (U.K.)	10	90	6,937	English
Puerto Rico (U.S.)	3,700	8,900	9,815	Spanish
U.S. Virgin Islands (U.S.)	104	347	12,038	English

Note: C = Local creole language.
[a] Norman Girvan, Paris: UNESCO Discussion Paper No.17 (August 1997), Table No.1.
[b] Victor Bulmer-Thomas, *Integration and Trade* Vol. 15 (2001), Table 10.

states of the Caribbean will have to carry out to derive any advantages from a relationship engendered by geography and history. Neither the U.S. nor its many Caribbean neighbors can change that geography or simply put that history behind them. What they can, and should, do is take into account the policy relevance of the kind of global changes that the general editors of this series note in the General Preface: transformations that have brought about an intensification in U.S.–Latin American relations. Yet, even as we place our analysis within the context of U.S.–Latin American, and even broader global international dynamics, we argue that there is no escaping the peculiarly Caribbean characteristics of the relations with the U.S., both in terms of its continuities and its changes.

1.2 Globalization and the Modification of Hegemony and Sovereignty

The tendency to see the decline of the state as an actor on the world scene has led to the notion that both U.S. hegemony and nation-state sovereignty are in open decline. "[T]he capacities of all nation-states," asserts a well-known Chilean intellectual and statesman, "have been diminished due to the process of globalization, forcing them to share power with supranational, transnational, and subnational entities."[14] This, he says, goes beyond the argument that the U.S. "hegemonic presumption" had ended. It is now a matter of an end to U.S. hegemony itself, to the point of allowing Latin America to adopt a "benign neglect" stance *vis-à-vis* the U.S.[15]

We do not share this view of the decline of U.S. hegemony, in the Caribbean or anywhere else. We believe quite the opposite: that there has indeed been what Donald Kagan sees as the reassertion of the traditional U.S. ideology of hegemony. He predicts that this will last a long time.[16] Robert O. Keohane, who in 1984 published his highly influential *After Hegemony; Cooperation and Discord in the World Political Economy*, posited the decline of hegemony generally and the rise of international institutions and the normative rules they set. More recently a whole group of prominent intellectuals has argued that since 1989, the world system has been marked by the U.S.' holding of the greatest degree of single-power hegemony since at least the 1860s, and probably before, and that it should behave accordingly. Because the U.S. is unchallenged economically, politically, and militarily, they argue, "we need to accept responsibility for America's unique role in preserving and extending an international order friendly to our security, our prosperity, and our principles."[17] What makes the U.S. carry its hegemony more lightly is the fact the most of the world now shares a value system, a set of rules of the game supported by institutional arrangements by which even the powerful must abide. According to Joseph S. Nye, these arrangements allow the U.S. to exercise another of the powers in which it has near-hegemonic status, "soft power." By this, Nye means not to have to use coercive but rather persuasive instruments in securing adherence to its policies.[18] It is this fact that allows Donald Kagan, the cochair of The New American Century Project, to speak of "American leadership, not domination," on his own admission, however, always keeping in mind the "reality" of a "preponderant" military capability.[19]

In few areas of the world, as already noted, are U.S. hegemonic capabilities more unencumbered. At the same time, in few other areas does U.S. soft power appear to work as smoothly. The vast majority of the elites in the region share with the U.S. the values and the willingness to use the multiple international institutions that today provide the architecture of international relations. All the preceding observations allow us to speak of a "modified" hegemonic system governing U.S.–Caribbean relations. Were we to define hegemony purely in terms of the relative powers (especially economic and military) of the participants in any given relationship, then the idea that a modified hegemonic relationship exists in the Caribbean would be meaningless. However, we are interested not only in the capacity to establish and maintain the rules that will govern any particular systems of relations by threats or direct coercion but also in the degree of willingness and readiness to utilize that capacity. When our study of the region indicates, as we believe it will, that there has been a significant change in the U.S. willingness to act as the *hegemon* we have come to know historically in the region, then we find it useful to speak of a modified hegemonic system. It is more soft power and less Marine Corps power. Again, it would be reckless indeed to abandon totally the concept of hegemony; one has to retain a fundamental understanding of the ultimate consequences of the hegemonic capacities of the U.S. and, by extension, many of its corporations that operate in the region.

Similarly, to the extent that globalization means, first, greater interdependence and interconnectedness and, then, greater reliance on international and transnational institutions, traditional notions of sovereignty have to be revised. The focus cannot be exclusively state-centric or merely on elites in the public sector. To be sure, modifications in the definitions of state sovereignty are occurring. Beyond that, however, both nationally and internationally, private groups are operating across borders and without much state supervision in an increasing number of vital areas. New terms such as "sovereignty-free" actors and "global commons" all express the relaxation or relativization of rigid, state-centric forms of sovereignty.[20]

None of this, however, should lead anyone to believe that the sentiments and attitudes that provide the underpinnings of sovereignty—national identity and cultural–political nationalism—are dead. Quite the contrary.

One could cite the case of American patriotism. "Comparative public opinion data reveal," says Seymour Martin Lipset, "that Americans are more patriotic" (proud to be Americans and more willing to fight if their country goes to war) than citizens of the 30 or so other countries polled by Gallup. This is part of what he terms "American exceptionalism."[21]

Theoretically, the only productive approach to understanding international relations is to assume that all national elites behave in accordance with what can be called "strategic nationalism," i.e., they always attempt to maximize the benefits to their country from any exchange and use the concepts of sovereignty and nationalism to make their case. The elites of even the smallest state take the choices and actions of others into account, but they behave with as much self-interest as national capabilities, circumstances, and the power of their opponents or competitors permit.

Having said that, however, the issue of the degree or margin of sovereignty and independence in small-state decision-making should be approached as an empirical question to be answered through the analysis of specific historical and contemporary cases, and not argued *a priori* by linear, deterministic, or ideologically driven paradigms.

The premise of this study is that in multinational archipelagic regions such as the Caribbean, the study of international relations has to include a mix of case studies and analysis of regionwide trends. In both cases the focus should be on the actual behavior of goal-seeking and self-interested actors rather than on their rhetoric. This means, of course, that the analysis is invariably *post facto* for two reasons:

1. There are general trends, such as the forces of globalization that affect the region as a whole. This is only part of the descriptive task because of the second reason.
2. From a strictly methodological point of view, there is no actual unit of analysis called "the Caribbean," no matter how defined. Different elites make strategic calculations based on quite different domestic and international structural constraints and preferences. There is no such thing as a regional response to the general trends impacting the region. Understanding requires studies of national elite responses to these trends for theoretical and empirical reasons. Theoretically, one has to agree with E.H. Carr that although the historian "thrives on generalizations," one has to be careful with "over-generalizations." Carr is in agreement with Marx's caution that "Events strikingly similar, but occurring in different historical milieu, lead to completely dissimilar results." Marx, says Carr, was especially suspicious of conclusions based on "feelings of familiarity," which led to false analogies.[22] The empirical point flows directly

from this, specifically, the importance of the "local" even in the midst of globalization and Americanization. "The same processes that destroy autonomy," says one of a growing number of sceptics about global homogenization, "are now creating new sorts of communities, new kinds of locality and identity."[23]

How the combination of regional analysis with case studies works to show trends in U.S.–Caribbean relations can be illustrated by three case studies of U.S. policy formulation: the Platt Amendment in Cuba (1901), the attempt to do something similar in Panama in 1978, and the more recent negotiations with Caribbean states over the right of hot pursuit. One case predates the Cold War, one unfolded during the Cold War, and the third was a post–Cold War negotiation.

The speedy victories of the U.S. in both the Caribbean and the Pacific made the U.S. a two-ocean power, but especially a Caribbean Sea power. Just a little more than a decade later, the opening of the Panama Canal gave the U.S. a definition of national security that had both a geostrategic center of gravity and an appropriate doctrine (Mahan's) to accompany it. In each of the cases of Cuba and Panama in the early 20th century, the U.S. acted as the undisputed *hegemon* of the region. The Platt Amendment and the Treaty of Paris were the results of that hegemonic power. By the third quarter of the 20th century, however, we notice a significant change in form in the U.S. pursuit of its vital national interests. Here we focus on President Jimmy Carter's 1978 negotiations with the Panamanian leader General Omar Torrijos over the transfer of the canal to the Panamanians. The Carter administration went all out to conclude a treaty that had formally been on the table for some 15 years and which ex-Ambassador to Panama William J. Jorden calls "the most controversial treaty in 60 years."[24]

Carter was helped by the fact that Panamanian military strongman Torrijos trusted him, and this helped control Panamanian nationalist opposition to what appeared to be an eternity of debates in the U.S. Senate, complete with repeated insults and offenses to Torrijos and Panamanians.[25] Keep in mind that President Carter signed the Panama Canal Treaties on September 7, 1977. Between that date and the final ratification by the U.S. Senate in April 18, 1978, the debate in the U.S. was a bitter one. Panamanian anger was at a boil.

The very crucial thing about the U.S. opposition to the treaty was that it had as context remnants of old-fashioned jingoism, very reminiscent of the imperialism of the early 20th century, and Cold War anticommunism. Few conveyed these sentiments more fervently than Ronald Reagan, past governor of California and already campaigning for the presidency. He knew that his views coincided with those of his Republican Party: the 1975

GOP platform called for retention of U.S. "sovereignty" over the canal. Polls were showing widespread support of this position.

Groups such as the Veterans of Foreign Wars were unanimous in their opposition to the treaties. They had been convinced by Cold War rhetoric such as that of Governor Reagan. Because there is "clear evidence" that Fidel Castro (and behind him, the former USSR) coveted much greater influence over Panama, Reagan saw it as evident that "the new basic treaty's provision relinquishing the rights of sovereignty represents a fatal flaw."[26]

The American Conservative Union surveyed Senate mail on the issue and of the 66 Senate offices responding, 93.46% of the mail was against the treaties, with only 6.6% in favor.[27] Favoring the treaties was a group that in many ways reflected the forces we would later identify as those of a globalized world: big business, which was interested in Latin American and world goodwill to expand markets; major mass media in the U.S., Europe, and Latin America; organized labor with ties to Canal Zone unions; the Joint Chiefs of Staff, who saw the declining military value of the canal; and the Majority and Minority leaders in the Senate. Along with these organizations there was a circle of figures of world standing who remained in contact with each other: John Wayne, Graham Greene, Gabriel Garcia Marquez, Julio Cortázar, and a wide assortment of European and Latin American social democrats. They could not compete, however, with the public constituency rallied by the opponents of the treaties.[28]

The treaties were voted in two parts in the U.S. Senate. The first part, the Panama Canal Neutrality Treaty, carried the necessary two-thirds majority, i.e., 68, yes, and 32, no. The final vote on the treaty was carried by the same margin.

In many ways, one has to accept President Carter's elation with this victory at face value. "These treaties," he said, "can mark the beginning of a new era in our relations not only with Panama but with all the rest of the world, the small nations of the world, on the basis of mutual respect and partnership."[29] History records that it was a Pyrrhic victory for Carter, but a victory nevertheless. The key question is: since no force was used to retain the canal, had the U.S. abandoned its hegemonic designs on Panama and the Caribbean region, which had always been its first line of defense? A quick review of the evolution of U.S. perceptions of its hegemony in this part of the world helps answer the question.

Although much emphasis has been placed on Theodore Roosevelt's 1904 "corollary" to the Monroe Doctrine as the beginning of U.S. hegemonic behavior, its origins were earlier than that. The real watershed was 1885: it was when the British were forced by President Grover Cleveland to back down from imposing a grossly unfavorable border delineation on Venezuela and negotiate instead. One can recall Secretary of State Richard Olney bragging that the U.S. was "practically sovereign in this continent and its fiat is law upon the subjects to which it confines its interposition." One should also recall that there was a second part of the famous (or notorious) Olney declaration of 1895. Asked why the U.S. was "practically sovereign" in this hemisphere, he answered: "It is because, in addition to all other grounds, its infinite resources combined with its isolated position render it master of the situation and practically invulnerable as against any or all other powers."

A more blatant declaration of hegemonic capacity, intent, and action could hardly be imagined. America had come of age as a global power and the Caribbean was the fundamental focus of that process.

And yet, it is quite evident that two of the reasons why the U.S. Senate gave President Carter his victory in the first place were more typical of hegemonic attitudes than of the idealism of the Carter initiatives. First, there is the fact that they voted 75 in favor and 23 against for what became the DeConcini Reservation (after junior Senator Dennis DeConcini of Arizona.) This reservation sounded unnervingly similar to the Platt Amendment imposed on the Cubans in 1901 and permitted the U.S. "the use of military force in Panama, to reopen the Canal or restore the operations of the Canal, as the case may be."

Carter accepted this reservation knowing he needed it to get the treaty approved in the first place; Torrijos accepted it for exactly the same reasons. Pragmatism and a heavy dose of realism were evident even among those who favored the treaty and opposed DeConcini's efforts to scuttle it. No one seemed to have any illusions about enforcing U.S. hegemony as a last resort. Note Senator Birch Bayh's (D-Indiana) explanation of his vote:

> We have not been bashful [in Guatemala 1954 and the Dominican Republic 1965] And frankly we have not looked for a whole lot of treaties and international precedents to rely on. And I suggest . . . that once this treaty is ratified, or is not ratified, we are going to take whatever steps are necessary, adjacent to that Canal, in order to protect it.[30]

How different in intentions and perceptions of ultimate capabilities is this from what Secretary of State Elihu Root told the U.S. military governor of Cuba Leonard Wood in 1901 on the issue of the Platt Amendment: "It gives to the U.S. no right which she does not already possess and which she would not exercise."[31] No surprise, then, that contemporary advocates of a more "robust" U.S. foreign policy can speak of a long history of an American ideology directed toward making the U.S. the world's greatest power.[32]

The concept of a modified hegemonic system does not, therefore, make either theoretical or empirical assumptions that intrinsic capabilities and ultimate intentions have changed fundamentally. The history of the

Caribbean has taught us that when U.S. elites perceive that there exists an imminent danger to national interests, they will act, in concert with others if possible and unilaterally if necessary. Bayh mentioned 1954 and 1965; had he had a crystal ball he would have mentioned Grenada (1983), Panama (1990), and Haiti (1994).

How both hegemony and sovereignty have been modified in the post–Cold War era is evident in the nature of the sometimes difficult process of negotiating a "model" agreement that would allow the U.S. the right of hot pursuit into territorial waters and air space. The purpose was the interdiction of drug-running vessels that took advantage of the sovereignty of territorial waters of individual states. The first state to sign the model agreement with no modifications was Trinidad and Tobago.[33] The Trinidad government stood on its sovereign right to negotiate as it felt best. The drug trade, it argued, was a greater menace to its sovereignty than this agreement.[34] Eight other Caribbean Community (CARICOM) states signed the model agreement.

In Jamaica and Barbados this was regarded as Trinidad and Tobago "giving away" its legal sovereign rights guaranteed under the 1982 Law of the Sea Convention. The region's academics were even harsher in their condemnation of U.S. "hegemonic" designs. A New York-based columnist for the *Jamaica Gleaner* called the proposed agreement "tantamount to being recolonized, insulted, denigrated . . . some of the most scandalous and downright nefarious acts of diplomatic torture conceivable."[35] The Jamaican government argued that the U.S. was imposing an agreement that was unacceptably open-ended. They insisted on Jamaican authorities having the final say on "all boarding, seizures, detentions and enforcement" in their territorial waters and airspace, and on no shooting at vessels flying the Jamaican flag. Additionally, they insisted on reciprocity: either party would have to "make a special request to the other party for *ad hoc* permission" to engage in hot pursuit.

In Jamaica, the prime minister did not limit his arguments to the convention of international law; he acted on the emotional, nationalist content of sovereignty. His assertion "We will not grovel!" brought the entire parliament to its feet in a sustained standing ovation.[36] The U.S. was forced to negotiate separately with Jamaica and Barbados. The words "*hegemon* tamed" were heard by this author at a major university forum,[37] and scholars celebrated the stance that led to an agreement "based on the fundamental principles of reciprocity and respect for sovereignty and the rule of law."[38] (No doubt a correct interpretation, but only one half of the story.) The other half was the U.S.' willingness to negotiate with Jamaica and Barbados despite calls from some hardliners or "neorealists" to act unilaterally. Arguing that the small states were probably "unviable" and certainly incapable of fending off the advances of organized international drug mafias, former Assistant Secretary of State (under President Reagan) Elliot Abrams called for direct U.S. action.[39] In fact, he suggested that "a new form of commonwealth status" with the U.S. might be in everyone's interest. Abrams was arguing as the *hegemon* of old, convinced of the geopolitical merits and full capability for a U.S. unilateral action. Reflecting the new reality, the U.S. administration acted with discretion, conscious as it was that the "war on drugs" involved more than just hot pursuit. It also involved negotiating extradition treaties (done in 1992), mutual legal assistance on drug, tax, and money laundering issues (done in 1995). In a complex, post–Cold War world, cooperation trumped coercion as a diplomatic tool. It might be too much to expect nationalistic posturing to recede completely, but it is incumbent on us to explore U.S.–Caribbean relations at all levels. To be sure, Jamaica showed that it understood the new reality when it made ample use of that new dimension of global diplomacy, the private lobbying firm that operates behind the scenes. The law firm of Holland and Knight had "lobbied hard" to stop the decertification of Jamaica in 1996 for noncooperation in the war on drugs,[40] and the same firm assisted significantly in reaching the modified Shiprider Agreement. The fact is that both Jamaica and Barbados made concessions on any absolute interpretation of sovereignty and acknowledged that the U.S. hardly acted as a conventional *hegemon*.

Our analysis deals with explicit forms of negotiation, the nature of the power exerted by the U.S., and the responses of the Caribbean states that are part of the negotiations. We understand that the exercise of power runs on a continuum from emulation, persuasion, and co-optation to threats and, ultimately, outright force. What is evident in the comparison between Cuba in 1901 and Panama in 1978 is the move from coercion towards the emulation and persuasion pole of the power continuum. The expectation is that in a modified hegemonic system, there will be more Carters, prepared to negotiate at considerable length because the international system encourages and rewards that and because the objects of those negotiations— the people and nations of the Caribbean—expect no less. This was evident in the Shiprider negotiations.

Finally, no one dealing with the international relations of the Caribbean can beg the question of what Antonio Gramsci called "ideological hegemony": the U.S.' cultural dominance. The Americanization of the region is too evident. In that Americanization, cities such as Miami play an increasingly important role for good and for bad, as we shall see. As Peter M. Haas has explained, networks of knowledge-based experts, advancing new ideas and information, can lead to new patterns of behavior and be an important determinant of international policy coordination. He calls these networks "epistemic communities." To the extent that the control of knowledge and information is an important dimension of power, that power resides more and more in the U.S.[41]

Here again, however, our study of the region, and the Puerto Rican case specifically, has made it quite clear that Gramsci's concept is inadequate for a full appreciation of two powerful forces that often overlap and are beyond total U.S. hegemonic control: nationalism, especially cultural nationalism, and ethnicity. The Puerto Rican case, but also that of the French Departments d'Outre Mer (DOM) in the region, show very clearly that although cultural nationalism is neither a necessary and sufficient precursor of statehood, it does express the national identity of a people. This, in turn, has created a paradoxical situation. The very dominance of the means of communication by the U.S. acts to make cultural nationalism a transnational phenomenon, as intensely nationalistic ethnic diasporas in the U.S. and island natives are in constant interaction. This sharing in the symbols and meanings of that nationalism augments its intensity.

For all these reasons, U.S.–Caribbean relations in the post–Cold War era are best described as a modified hegemonial system: cooperation is preferred over coercion even as the capability to use the latter remains intact.

CHAPTER **2**

The Caribbean during and at the End of the Cold War (1970s to 1980s)

2.1 Historical Antecedents of the Cold War

The nature of the change in the world and hemispheric politics was reflected in the agenda and conclusions of the Tenth International Conference of American States held in Caracas in March, 1954. That conference ended with a "Declaration of Solidarity for the Preservation of the Political Integrity of the American States against the Intervention of International Communism." Clearly, the post–World War II U.S. confrontation with the Soviet Union and the anticommunism it engendered were the mainspring of these new developments. The Great Powers had emerged from the war with an undeclared, but quite evident, acceptance of spheres of influence that had a nearly global reach. However, there were also important Caribbean and Latin American ideologies and movements that had their roots in the period before 1954. It was in 1954, though, that the U.S. decided that the international communist movement, no matter from where it came, represented a direct threat to U.S. security.

Perhaps the most important case of this post–World War II era began in Costa Rica in 1947 when the incumbent president, Teodoro Picado, attempted to annul the election results of that year. With strong support from the influential communist party, and in a strange alliance with the hierarchy of the Roman Catholic church and elements of the landowning aristocracy, Picado used a small army against an uprising led by José

Figueres. The resulting civil war of 1948 took on Caribbean-wide importance when the close cooperation of democratically elected leaders helped put together a small fighting force called *La Legión del Caribe*. This alliance of Figueres with presidents Juan José Arevalo of Guatemala and Carlos Prío Socarrás of Cuba, and exiled leaders such as Juan Bosh of the Dominican Republic and Rómulo Betancourt of Venezuela was later called the "Democratic Left" of Latin American politics.[1] Most of the politicians would subsequently join the resurgent European social democratic Socialist International movement. Their main targets were the traditional dictators, especially Rafael Leonidas Trujillo in the Dominican Republic and Anastasio Somoza in Nicaragua. To them, intervention was justified only when fighting dictators. This was their definition of the threat to peace in the hemisphere. The U.S. had a different definition and so the Democratic left did not consider the U.S. an ally in this antidictatorial struggle. The U.S., under the strong leadership of Secretary of State John Foster Dulles, regarded stopping communism as the fundamental task of U.S. foreign policy in the area and, if dictators such as Trujillo and Somoza were ready to help in that endeavor, so much the better. Anticommunism, in whatever form, was good enough for Dulles. Yet, despite the differences in goals, the important point was that both groups were interested in stopping the communist forces: the U.S. for global reasons and the Democratic left for local reasons.

The Figueres victory in Costa Rica in 1948 and the formation of an alliance of social democrats throughout the Caribbean were the first major signs that even before 1954 there were important new players in the international relations scene in the Caribbean. The second major event, indicating that a U.S. Cold War theme would fall on receptive ears because anticommunism had already entered into local Caribbean politics, took place in British Guiana (later, Guyana). There, a Marxist party, the People's Progressive Party (PPP), won the 1953 elections, but it soon experienced a split between the Leninist wing led by Cheddi Jagan and a group led by the more pragmatic Forbes Burnham. Although this split responded as much to ideology as it did to the Indian and black divisions of the local society, it was also part of a much wider, Pan-Caribbean battle which the Cold War would encourage and aggravate[2] and which carried overtones of what would later be called transnational processes.

In the early 1950s, a major struggle was taking place—not between states or governments directly, but through surrogates (later called NGOs, or non-governmental organizations). The Moscow-dominated World Federation of Trade Unions (WFTU) was pitted against the West-dominated International Confederation of Trade Unions (ICTU). In the Western Hemisphere, the anticommunist attack was led by both the U.S.

and Great Britain. The American Federation of Labor (AFL)-supported Inter-American Regional Workers' Organization (IARWO) worked hand-in-hand with the British Trade Union Congress (TUC). In 1952 and 1953, the ICTU and the IARWO scored major victories throughout the still-colonial West Indies. In Jamaica, Norman Manley's party, the People's National Party (PNP), expelled the major Left-wing leaders of the Trade Union Congress. Manley's trade union, the National Workers' Union (NWU), joined its rival, the Bustamante Industrial Trade Union (BITU), in becoming members of the ICTU. In Barbados, Grantley Adams, first president of the WFTU-related Caribbean Labour Congress, called for disbandment of that congress, saying it was dominated by a Caribbean-wide clique of communists. In Trinidad, the few Marxist trade unionists were isolated even further from the evolving political arena. In Guyana, Burnham's British Guiana Labour Union joined the ICTU in 1952, thus formally associating itself with such "moderate" West Indian politicians as Manley, Bustamante, and Adams—all subjects of virulent attacks as "bourgeois labor unionists" in Cheddi Jagan's paper.[3]

The battle did not remain at the local level, however. Following major labor disturbances and conflicts in Guyana between the PPP and the British governor in 1953, British troops landed, suspended the constitution, and threw the PPP out of office. This was the overt intervention; the covert intervention, later amply documented, was being sponsored by the U.S. Most Guyanese did not realize that what was unfolding was the first major anticommunist offensive by the U.S. in the Caribbean—an offensive in which the U.S. had substantial local support. In British Guiana, Forbes Burnham broke with Cheddi Jagan on the grounds that their party was "not a communist party nor is the party affiliated to any communist organization outside or inside the country."[4] Anticommunism was not just an American stance; it was a popular attitude in much of the Caribbean. A similar congruence of U.S. global and hemispheric interests, and the same of local groups occurred only a year later in Guatemala—an event that can be said to have ushered in a new era of U.S. unilateralism. Since the machinery for collective security proved to be of little use to the U.S. in this new era, old-fashioned hegemonic actions took their place.

After the fall of the long-lived Ubico dictatorship (1931 to 1944), Guatemala entered a period of truly progressive-minded government. Unfortunately, as Robert Alexander explains about the 1944 revolutionaries, they were sincere but naive about the workings of international power politics. They came to power in the pre–Cold War days when everything seemed to be "sweetness and light" between the democrats of the great Western powers, and the communists inside and outside the Soviet Union.

"The Guatemalan revolutionary leaders," says Alexander, "never got over this wartime honeymoon."[5] That the honeymoon between the two world powers had indeed ended, the reformist government of Col. Jacobo Arbenz soon discovered. Heavily infiltrated by members of Guatemala's resurgent communist movement, Arbenz's regime began to take a revolutionary reformist internal policy and an openly pro-Soviet international stance. On March 1954, the American and Latin American delegates at the Caracas conference of the Organization of American States (OAS) adopted an anti-communist position. The fact that its central target was the Arbenz regime in Guatemala was hardly dissimulated. Events followed naturally, not so much from that act but from the U.S. decision that such a regime could not exist any more than Jagan's could.

In contrast to its prompt and effective action in the ten cases before 1954, the OAS suddenly developed leaden feet. Hegemony, not collective security, is what operated as a working principle. One key to the reason for this might be found in the statement made in 1963 by Senator Thurston Morton, who recalled the following conversation he had with President Dwight D. Eisenhower, illustrating the "tone" of the new Cold War era:

> When the plans were laid to overthrow the communist government of Guatemala . . . the President said, "Are you sure this is going to succeed?" He was reassured it would, and said: "I'm prepared to take any steps that are necessary to see that it succeeds. For if it succeeds it's the people of Guatemala throwing off the yoke of Communism. If it fails, the Flag of the United States has failed."[6]

The factor of prestige or "face" is evident in the U.S. attitude; it tends to be an important motivation of Great Power action in their spheres of influence but hardly one that would find support in the OAS charter. That support had to come from another source. This explains the sudden revival of the Monroe Doctrine.

One day after Arbenz resigned, Dulles went on radio and television to inform the American public that "this intrusion of Soviet despotism in Guatemala was, of course, a direct challenge to our Monroe Doctrine, *the first and most fundamental of our foreign policies . . .* For 131 years that policy has well served the peace and security of the hemisphere. It serves us well today."[7] Paradoxically, yet fatefully, it was precisely because the Monroe Doctrine had been used so successfully in the Caribbean and in Guatemala, in 1954 in particular, that it failed so miserably in Cuba only 5 years later. The Cuban government must have taken a cue from a State Department press release dated July, 1960 which stated that the principles of the Monroe Doctrine were "as valid today as they were in 1823 . . . Specifically, the

Organization of American States Charter and the Rio Treaty provide the means for common action to protect the hemisphere against the interventionist and aggressive designs of international communism."[8]

The events leading to the formulation and then reiteration of a U.S. hegemonist position had all occurred in and around the Caribbean. There was a continuity in U.S. responses from the entry into the Spanish–American war and the intervention in Panama in 1903 through the multiple interventions in Mexico, Nicaragua, Haiti, the Dominican Republic, and Cuba. What varied was the definition of the perceived threat and the language used to confront that threat. The U.S. now had to pay at least lip service to the conventions on sovereignty and nonintervention so painstakingly armored by the governments of the hemisphere over the previous decades. By the 1960s there was no hemispherewide support for the American perception and definition of threat, much less agreement with the justifications given for unilateral U.S. action. As we shall see in the cases of the Dominican Republic (1965) and Grenada (1989), the Monroe Doctrine could serve as "legal" cover to an intervention, but it could not prevent the events which made such an intervention eventually "necessary" in U.S. eyes. And, of course, hemispheric hesitation and even opposition were not enough to stop the intervention in the first place. An exception to this one-sided definition was the hemispheric response to the so-called Cuban Missile Crisis of October 1962.

A phenomenal drama was played out on the Caribbean Sea as satellite and U-2 spy plane photographs showed missile installations in Cuba, leading to a U.S. naval forces "quarantine" of that island. In this particular case, the collective security mechanisms of the OAS charter were called into play and the U.S. received complete hemispheric support for its actions. In terms of the opposition to the presence of Soviet missiles in Cuba, ideology, legality, and political will were in harmony at the hemispheric level. It was a rare occurrence.

Much more typical of U.S.–Caribbean relations were the relations with the Dominican Republic as they unfolded in 1965. The marines were already on the beach of that island when on April 29 the administration of Lyndon B. Johnson called for an emergency meeting of the OAS Organ of Consultation. The action was clearly unilateral, even though there were significant local and regional actors who applauded and supported it. To the extent that unilateral action was the core of what would be known as the Johnson Doctrine, it was not new. Not new, also, was the fact that U.S. actions had strong local support within broad sectors of the Dominican Republic. The only novelty was that the concept of linkages was given a Cold War slant: the perception was that the menace emanated from Cuba and transcended the boundaries of the Dominican Republic, threatening to spread to the rest of the region. The U.S. had had a geopolitical interest in the Dominican Republic since the middle of the 19ᵗʰ century. By the time President Woodrow Wilson decided to intervene in 1916, the politics of that country were in disarray. With the Panama Canal already in full operation, U.S. Marines already in Haiti, and strong suspicions of German interests in gaining a foothold somewhere in the Caribbean, the U.S. needed to give few reasons for its imperial act. This did not, of course, stop the moralizing which invariably accompanies such acts.

Samuel Flagg Bemis is one who believes that there was material and moral benefit from stopping Dominicans from exercising their "sovereign right to suicide."[9] He was content to conclude that "after this timely tutelage, the Dominican Republic has been 'running on its own' very successfully." Unfortunately, it was the peace of a cemetery—a cemetery run with an iron hand by the man the U.S. put in power, Rafael Leonidas Trujillo. Dominican scholar Bernardo Vega has traced the ins and outs of U.S. policy formulation. So, it was not, nor has it ever been, a single-minded operation. The network of officers of the U.S. Marine Corps that trained Trujillo's new *gendarmerie* also successfully lobbied for him with many a U.S. administration.[10] They were so influential in the administrations of Hoover, and especially Franklin Delano Roosevelt, that they completely neutralized the anti-Trujillo sentiments of such important diplomats as Under-Secretary of State Sumner Welles. Again, geopolitical and ideological perceptions, not economics, were at the core of this division. This, says Vega, created a two-track policy towards Trujillo—that of the state department and that of the military. The latter invariably won, at least until the early 1960s when their friendship with Trujillo was perceived not only as an embarrassment but also as a hindrance to the anticommunist strategy of the moment. At that point, and in keeping with past practice, the CIA was put in charge of policy towards the Dominican Republic. This included the 1961 assassination of Trujillo. Arthur Schlesinger, Jr., a close advisor to President John F. Kennedy, was less than straightforward when he wrote that the assassination of Trujillo "took Washington by surprise."[11] In fact, U.S. agencies such as the CIA had had in-depth discussions with the Executive branch on the wisdom of joining those whom they knew were plotting such an assassination. The CIA would later describe its involvement as a "success."[12]

Indeed, Schlesinger relates how President Kennedy summarized U.S. strategic options in a most realistic albeit colorful fashion:

> *There are three possibilities, in descending order of preference: a decent democratic regime, a continuation of the Trujillo regime or a Castro regime. We ought to aim at the first, but we really cannot renounce the second until we are sure that we can avoid the third.*[13]

The key point is that Washington's contingency plans had been laid out very succinctly by the National Security Council on May 5, 1961, and approved by Kennedy on May 16, 1961:

> "Agreed that the Task Force on Cuba would prepare promptly both emergency and long-range plans for anti-Communist intervention in the event of crises in Haiti on the Dominican Republic (sic)"[14]

Predictably, the U.S. could respond to events, even unleash some trends, but it could not determine ultimate macrosociological processes. After the assassination of Trujillo, the U.S. became directly involved in attempting to bring the various "noncommunist" factions together. By mid-1961 this strategy of jawboning and cajoling was heading nowhere, and the Trujillo family was planning a comeback. The U.S. response to this latter possibility followed a time-honored tradition. It is described parsimoniously, but pithily, by John Bartlow Martin, one of the U.S. negotiators at the time and later U.S. Ambassador: "On November 19 we sent the fleet to the horizon."[15]

The show of force did stymie the Trujillo family plot but did nothing to settle the boiling Dominican political cauldron. To new geopolitical threats, old remedies seemed to be the order of the day during the Cold War years. This was proven in 1965 when fears of communist penetration and influence in a Dominican Republic torn by political confusion led to a U.S. intervention with a force of over 25,000 U.S. servicemen. The Organ of Consultation of the OAS was informed after the invasion had started and the Monroe Doctrine was invoked. The U.S. was not taking any chances in its sphere of influence.[16]

What has been called the "Johnson Doctrine" would dominate over the rest of the Cold War years. It was a combination of three elements: a determination never to relive the shame of the Bay of Pigs, a perception that Cuba was actively training and organizing Left-wing revolutionary groups from around the hemisphere, and a resolution to meet this communist challenge with overwhelming force.

As determined as the U.S. was to resort to force, it would be a gross misrepresentation of this period to argue that this was the only strategy used during this period of the Cold War. In fact, the years of the Kennedy presidency were characterized by a series of political efforts which, in many ways, anticipated U.S. strategies in the post–Cold War era. Kennedy's advisor, Theodore C. Sorensen, tells this nonmilitary side of the story. To him, the attempt was to create "a peaceful revolution."[17]

Aside from such actions as creating the Peace Corps, Kennedy's major thrust was the Alliance for Progress whose goal was democracy through economic reform. Geopolitics was very much in the fore. It was, in the words of one of its drafters, "the best means of isolating the Castro virus."[18] Nevertheless, it was one of the first major U.S. efforts that was designed and executed with substantial Latin American and Caribbean input. On this score, it was the role of Puerto Rico which brought this about. "The Puerto Rican experiment," Schlesinger says, "was an important source of the ideas behind the Alliance."[19] Puerto Ricans exerted influence in three ways. First, by highlighting the success of Luis Muñoz Marín's "Operation Bootstrap" in bringing about social reform, economic development, and political democracy. There were few at the time who denied the great changes wrought in what Rexford Tugwell had called a "stricken land." Second, some of the foremost architects of Operation Bootstrap became the main administrators and promoters of the Alliance for Progress. The key people among them were Arturo Morales Carrión and Teodoro Moscoso. Because they were Latin in culture, they managed to deepen the links with a whole network of Latin American social democrats, some (like Romulo Betancourt of Venezuela and José Figueres of Costa Rica) who were in power, and others who were still in exile (such as Juan Bosch of the Dominican Republic.)

Despite these hemispherewide contacts and support, despite the "minimum of 20 billion dollars" in public funds promised, and despite the acknowledged popularity of Kennedy in Latin America, the Alliance soon ran into an avalanche of problems—from economic downturns to the return of political authoritarianism. In addition, major U.S. sectors, including many in the State Department, were impatient. After all, Castro's Cuba was still there and, with Soviet assistance, appeared stronger than ever. By the end of the 1960s, the enthusiasm for reform promised by the Alliance had waned, an erosion spelled out by Arturo Morales Carrion. The Alliance, he noted, "had not been wedded to Latin American nationalism, the single most powerful psychological force now operating in Latin America." Morales Carrion could have been echoing the words of Eisenhower, who in 1957 reflected on the role of nationalism in the world. "It is my personal conviction," he wrote Senator Hubert Humphrey, "that almost any one of the new-born states of the world would far rather embrace communism or any other form of dictatorship than to acknowledge the political domination of another government even though that brought to each citizen a far higher standard of living."[20] Can even the hegemon and its military preponderance overcome this paradoxical situation?

This was the world into which the small states of the Caribbean were moving as independent players.

Already, by the 1960s, every government in the Caribbean—whether independent or not—faced two crucial questions related to viability and sustainability. First, could the economies of these small nations (especially the parliamentary democratic ones) handle the social tensions engendered by high rates of unemployment, declining agricultural production, urbanization, the mobilization of demands by both unionized and nonunionized labor, and, crucially, the expectations of highly educated but unemployed youth? Second, and directly related to this question of economic viability, was a political question: could the political institutions inherited from the colonial period handle the kinds of ideological changes being demanded by an increasingly radicalized youth? To them it was not enough to reform the institutions; they were demanding a complete shift in the social class and racial composition of the state and the economy.

Writing in the late 1960s, Eric Williams was not in a sanguine mood. In fact, he held a very bleak view of the Caribbean region. He claimed to see everywhere the contrast between rising unemployment and rising per capita incomes. Relatively small pockets of wealth were engendering dangerous levels of rising expectations—expectations that were not being addressed, much less met, anywhere in the region. Most dramatically affected, he noted, were the young, the social sector from which the greatest threat to the existing system would come. Aside from these economic and demographic problems, there was, said Williams, a problem of context: the region had "no serious indigenous intellectual life" within which to debate these issues. The Caribbean, he concluded, fit author V.S. Naipaul's "harsh but true" description of West Indians as being "mimic men," i.e., imitators of all things foreign.[21]

One of the "foreign" doctrines Williams feared was Black Power. "As the Black Power movement makes headway in the U.S. in its fight for black dignity," he argued, "there are the obvious repercussions in the Caribbean." To Williams, this issue of race conflict expressed itself in different forms, but everywhere in the Caribbean of the late 1960s and early 1970s the signs of racial trouble were ominous:

> Jamaica is seething with racial tension, black vs. brown and white. The labour unrest in Antigua and the labour riots in Curaçao were both responses to Black Power propaganda. The large Indian population of Guyana, Suriname, and Trinidad and Tobago adds another dimension to the racial disharmony.... In this bleak picture, the only bright spot is the apparent success of Castro's Cuba with the full integration of the black population into his society.[22]

Despite this bow to Cuba, Williams was not about to recommend the Cuban path. "The real tragedy of Cuba," he wrote, "is that she has resorted to the totalitarian framework...."[23] He had earlier adamantly rejected the "Castroist organization of the economy" as an authoritarian and ineffi- cient system which had "turned its back on the Caribbean" to integrate itself into the socialist bloc.[24] According to Williams in the 1960s and beyond, the Caribbean could not escape the Cold War which he defined as the confrontation between the dominant ideologies and points of view that faced the world: capitalism and socialism.

This link between race and revolution held true for much, but certainly not all, of the Caribbean. Race, for instance, played an insignificant role in the Cuban Revolution of 1959, though it surely played an important part in the Wars of Independence and in the "revolution" of 1933 to 1934. Similarly, although race was a major part of the Dominican Republic's sense of identity, the country's identity was based on its unique relationship with its neighbor Haiti, its occupations, and its conflicts. Race has not been demonstrated to have been a factor in the 1965 uprising in the Dominican Republic. In Puerto Rico, even as incisive a critic of Caribbean race relations as Gordon K. Lewis had to admit that while race discrimination existed, it had a "Latin" form and certainly was not important in the island's politics. Where race, or at least skin tone, has historically played a vital role is on the island of Haiti. And yet, as James Leyburn noted quite early on, the element of caste divisions was so much stronger than the element of class as to make Haiti a *sui generis* case. Where race did play a fundamental part in the political processes and social movements, peaceful and violent, was in the English-speaking Caribbean and, to a lesser—but still important—degree, in the Dutch island of Curaçao.

External forces encouraged the growth of stronger and, at times, bitter racial feeling, as in the racial policies of South Africa, the assumption of power by a white minority in Rhodesia, Britain's immigration policy, the support given by many people in Britain to Powellism, and the discrimination and injustices to which black people were subject in the U.S. West Indians also found an increase of racial prejudice in Canada, which was long a haven and refuge for their students and for those seeking advancement. The militant Black Power movement in the U.S., led among others by Trinidad-born Stokeley Carmichael (Kwame Touré), encouraged a more articulate and positive assertion of blackness, of black dignity, and of the right of black people everywhere to equality before the law and to equal opportunities of employment. The American movement was the protest of a minority group, whereas in the Caribbean it was a claim by the majority group to economic as well as political power. The Black Power militants of the U.S. were convinced that it was only self-contempt and discrimination that shut off blacks from a share of the good things in American life that they saw white Americans enjoying. The West Indians had black power through universal adult suffrage; almost all who symbolized political authority, whether governors-general or prime ministers, were black. However, what about "national control of our national resources?" They began to ask whether political independence did not mean financial independence and also a shift away from the essentially authoritarian attitudes of a colonial administration.

Events would prove Williams only partly right: the political processes of the 1970s through the 1990s were certainly traumatic, but the institutions inherited from the colonial past proved to be equal to the task, their resiliency a testimony to the ability of ex-colonial populations to make democracy work in ways the colonial masters had not thought possible.

2.2   Regional Geopolitics and Local Perceptions of Threat

Many of the factors which made politics in the Caribbean in the postindependence era increasingly conflictive were as much domestic as they were exogenous. West Indian leaders would probably have disagreed among themselves on the particular weight that should have been attached to each foreign influence, but they would have agreed that in the postindependence period, Cold War geopolitics (and the ideological divide that drove it) was an influential factor in many of the area's political processes. First, there had been a decisive shift from a Eurocentric orientation in most things (education, defense, culture, recreation, and commerce) to a U.S.-centered one. With this shift came, of course, all the perceptions and definitions of the U.S., and its vital interests, both at home and within its sphere of influence. The latter took on special significance when it came to the role of Cuba in the region. It is obvious that even though the U.S.' conflict with Cuba preceded the entry into independence of all the new Caribbean states, it slowly but surely became an integral part of their concerns during the postindependence era.[25] Many Caribbean states wished to establish their independence from Washington by establishing relations with Cuba. This was done jointly in 1972 by Jamaica, Trinidad and Tobago, Barbados, and Guyana. But even as they were all asserting their newly minted sovereignty, one of them, at least, was voicing its concerns over Cuba's foreign policy, as well as rejecting its political and developmental model. To Trinidad's Eric Williams, "the real tragedy" of Cuba was its adoption of communist totalitarianism. This was not a path the newly independent islands wished to emulate.[26] Trinidad's minister of external affairs was decided in his condemnation of "those states which indiscriminately seek by force" to impose a pattern of government and of society on peoples outside their borders. He was referring, he said, to the activities of Cuba. Facing the Cuban delegation at the 22nd Regular Session of the United Nations General Assembly,[27] the Minister warned that "unwarranted intervention in the affairs of other states cannot justify intervention in your own. Exporting revolution, be it remembered, is a two-edged sword." The Caribbean's fear of foreign intervention was real during the Cold War.

Second, the entry of Cuba as a regional geopolitical player was reason enough for the entry of other players, especially the so-called middle powers, Venezuela and Brazil, and the transnational actors representing ideological interests (Marxist-Leninists, Christian Democrats, Social Democrats, trade union federations) as well as transnational corporations.[28] It is important to note, however, that the traditional and historical openness of the era continued so that very often the presence of these actors was more invited than imposed. This certainly included the Cubans whose presence was often used as leverage on the international community, particularly the United States, but also Western Europe, all of whom provided levels of financial assistance which were not insignificant to these economically strapped islands. The suspicions which Cuba aroused in the late 1960s changed in the mid-1970s, into open fear of that nation's capabilities.[29]

By the end of the decade, a series of events made the actions of Cuba a matter of direct concern to the U.S. certainly, but also to the post-independence leadership of the West Indies. In fact, three different Cuban involvements in the Caribbean brought that island center stage while at the same time revealing the fact that the region had entered a new phase in its international relations.

First was the 1975 airlift, through Barbados first and Guyana later, of a division of Cuban troops for Angola. Eric Williams of Trinidad was particularly put out by the discovery of what old Cuba-hand, Herbert L. Matthews, called "this sensational development in hemispheric history."[30] To Matthews, Angola was as much a part of Moscow's designs as it was of Cuba's. It is this perception of a wider Cold War related threat that led to the first discussions on mutual security assistance between Trinidad and Barbados.

It was in the context of the dramatic Cuban actions in Angola that West Indian apprehensions escalated in the months after a *coup d'etat* toppled the government of Eric Gairy in Grenada in 1979. While the movement against the increasingly eccentric and incompetent Gairy had wide support in Grenada and in the region, it was actually led by a small group of middle class radicals called The New Jewel Movement (NJM), although the fighting was actually done by a few longshoremen.[31] Their leader was a charismatic young lawyer, Maurice Bishop, whose Marxist ideology was not revealed to the Grenadians until after the *coup d'etat*, but whose wide appeal and popularity were undisputed. Such was the unpopularity of Gairy in the other West Indian islands that the initial shock at this first violent overthrow of an independent West Indian government changed to a posture of cautious hope on the part of many.

The West Indian government leaders, however, with the exception of Forbes Burnham of Guyana who was a strong supporter of the revolutionaries from the very inception, were not as sanguine. They eventually adopted a stance of silent vigilance and studied neutrality *vis-a-vis* the Grenada People's Revolutionary Government (PNG). There was no neutrality on Cuba's part nor on the part of the United States. They quite rapidly made Grenada part of their ongoing conflict in the region. Cuba almost immediately had the only resident ambassador on the island, who soon presided over a growing Cuban presence. It seemed to replicate the situation in Guyana, where the Cuban mission took up nearly half a city block and where Cuba's multiple involvements had long been the talk of Georgetown. Some 15 Cuban doctors arrived; so did fishing trawlers and instructors. On November 18, 1979 Prime Minister Maurice Bishop told a rally that he expected 250 Cubans to start building a new international airport.

Eventually there would be 700 Cuban workers. There would also be a full-scale Soviet embassy staffed by a diplomat whose previous post was Ambassador to Argentina, the Soviets' most important trading partner in Latin America. As Yuri Pavlov, a veteran of the Soviet foreign service, would explain later, the Cubans had persuaded the Soviets that Maurice Bishop and the NJM could lead Grenada to "some sort of socialism." "There were no indications of any serious differences between Moscow and Havana in Grenada." Moscow granted the NJM the status of "fraternal party." All this meant that relations between Grenada, Cuba and the Soviet Union were "party-to-party" relations. The same as had been extended to Michael Manley's People's National Party (PNP).[32]

The irony of these Cuban-Soviet actions in the Caribbean was that they were occurring just as the Jimmy Carter Administration in the U.S. was shifting into a less aggressive and confrontational posture towards Cuba and the Caribbean radical movements. In the past few years, the United States had returned the Chaguaramas Base to Trinidad, concluded a major treaty with Panamá on the return of the Canal, and generally taken a more conciliatory attitude toward Cuba. These changes, plus an emphasis on a much lower military profile in the area, characterized a style of diplomacy toward the Caribbean which attempted to dispel entrenched memories of past hegemonic behavior.

Radical and dramatic shifts in the foreign policy of a major nation are rare occurrences. Not only do vital interests not change that readily, but the weight of the past continues to influence contemporary attitudes and predispositions. So it is with the thinking of certain official and unofficial circles of the American foreign policy community about the Caribbean. In these circles the "psychological" dimension of strategic thinking on the Caribbean remains.

The problem was that it was not just Cuban and Soviet actions in Grenada that eventually pushed American policy back towards the more explicit military end. In 1979 the presence of Cubans in Angola and Cuban and Soviet weapons and assistance to the Sandinistas in Nicaragua and the FMLN in El Salvador, became associated with presence of a Soviet combat motorized brigade in Cuba. Given the nature of U.S. competition, Carter's moderation became untenable. Even his Democratic party allies such as Senators Frank Church and Henry Jackson began calling for the with-drawal of the Soviet troops. Republican presidential candidate Ronald Reagan joined the chorus of alarm, turning Cuba and all its involvements once again into an issue of domestic politics. In few places of the globe was it easier for domestic politics to force a shift back to traditional hegemonic postures. But, shifts were occurring in the Caribbean also.

By the early 1980s, West Indian leaders appeared to have few doubts about Cuban military capabilities and every incident involving the Cubans contributed to the perception of a threat, even those which were not so intended. A defensive attitude began to develop very rapidly. By the early 1980s, for instance, the nations of the Eastern Caribbean were ready to do something positive about their security. What developed was a set of ideas increasingly called the "Adams Doctrine," after Barbados Prime Minister Tom Adams. This doctrine was premised on the belief that threats to their small democracies would not come from external forces directly but from the critically timed assistance these external forces might give to the small groups at home who would subvert democracy. The need, then, was for a small but mobile force which counted speed as its most effective asset.

The Adams doctrine was as much a product of the thinking of the Ronald Reagan administration in the U.S. as it was of Tom Adams' own geopolitical views and of events which unfolded in the area during the late 1970s. It is important to know, therefore, that the first use of the Adams doctrine was not in Grenada, October 1983, but in Union Island in the St. Vincent Grenadines (97 miles due east of Barbados), early December 1979. An invasion of alleged Rastafarians from the Grenadian island of Carriacou led to a St. Vincent request for assistance. Elements of the Barbadian de-fense forces intervened to help put down the movement. This was the first intervention in the name of collective security in the young history of Eastern Caribbean sovereignty. It was this incident, and the suspicion that the rev-olutionary government in Grenada was training others for similar acts, that led eventually to the signing of a formal collective security under-standing in September 1982. The "Memorandum of Understanding" re-garding security and military cooperation was signed by Barbados and all the independent states of the Organization of Eastern Caribbean States (OECS), except Grenada. It is one of those ironies of history that it should have been the fear of the ultimate intentions of one of their own which led these islands to shape their first collective security agreement. The Western Hemisphere's collective security treaties, from the Act of Chapultepec (Mexico, 1945) to the Pact of Rio de Janeiro (1947) and finally the charter of the Organization of American States (Bogotá, 1948), had been directed at outside forces, the Axis powers and later Soviet communism. The independent West Indian islands had created what they thought was additional protection to what these treaties already granted.

And yet, aside from the case of Grenada, how much of all this perceived Cuban involvement or subversion was real and just how much receptivity was there for socialist-type change? Clearly in the 1970s there was at least a surface unity among the area's new and Cuba-leaning Marxist-Leninist groups. This could be seen, for instance, at the public launching of Jamaica's Communist party, Trevor Munroe's Workers Party of Jamaica (WPJ), formerly the Worker's Liberation League. In attendance were delegates from the Communist parties of the USSR, Britain, Canada, the United States, and Cuba; in attendance from the English-speaking Caribbean were representatives of Guyana's People's Progressive Party and the Working Peoples Alliance, the Barbados Movement for National Liberation, Grenada's New Jewel Movement, Saint Vincent's Liberation Movement, and the Saint Lucia's Workers' Revolutionary Movement.

To see Cuban machinations behind this unity, however, is to ignore two things: the political weakness of these movements, and the long-standing ties between Caribbean radical groups—ties that predate the Cuban Revolution and that, more often than not, are the result of specific and independent decisions of each island. Take as an illustration the 1966 parliamentary elections in Trinidad. Table 2.1 shows the dismal performance of the Socialist Workers and Farmers Party, a party full of stellar figures from the English-speaking intellectual Left circles.

Two decades after universal suffrage, this was very clear proof of the fundamental weakness of the radical Left movement in Trinidad. Politics had already become a racial matter in which ideology played a minimal

Table 2.1 Percentage of Votes in the Parliamentary Elections in Trinidad, 1966

WFP Candidate (Socialist)		Candidate of the People's National Movement (PNM) (Afro-Trinidadian)	Candidate of the Democratic Labor Party (DLP) (Indo-Trinidadian)
Lennox Pierre	.355	54.6	40.9
Eugene Joseph	.891	88.9	4.5
C.L.R. James	2.8	53.8	40.8
George Weekes	4.9	28.06	51.2
Basdeo Panday	3.5	15.0	65.8
Stephen Maharaj	5.5	39.2	53.9
John Kelshall	1.2	49.9	46.2

Source: Report of the Parliamentary General Elections, 1966 (Trinidad, 1967).

role. After two successive PNM governments, the number of declared Marxist–Leninists had been reduced to a negligible figure. In 1965 an official enquiry calculated the number at 15.[33]

The standing of other communist parties in the region was not much better, as Table 2.2 shows. The only place where a Marxist party came into

Table 2.2 Eastern Caribbean Elections in the 1980s

Country	Party and Date Founded	Total Population	Estimated Communist Party Membership	Last Election % of Vote
Antigua	ACLM	0.064	—	1980/1.2%
Dominican Republic	Dominican Communist Party (1944) PSP	7.1	750 500	1986/0.28%
Grenada	Maurice Bishop Patriotic Movement	0.09	—	1984/5.0%
Guadeloupe	Communist Party of Guadeloupe	0.341	3,000	1988/52.4% for Local Assembly
Guyana	People's Progressive Party (1950)	0.765	300 (leadership cadres)	1985/16.8% *
Haiti	Communists Unified Party of Haitian (Puch) (1968)	6.5	350	Boycotted
Jamaica	Workers' Party of Jamaica (WPJ) (1978)	2.5	100	1989 Did not contest 1986 0.2%
Martinique	Martinique Communist Party (1957)	0.331	1,000	1988 4.4% for Local Assembly

Source: Richard F. Staar (ed.), *1989 and 1990 Yearbook on International Communist Affairs.* Stanford: Hoover Institution Press, 1989 and 1990; Douglas Midgett, *Eastern Caribbean Elections, 1950–1982.* Iowa City: The University of Iowa, n.d.

* Probably a rigged election.

power through elections was Guyana, and there race, rather than ideology, has always been the decisive factor.

The pro-Cuban *coup d'etats* in Grenada and Suriname involved the overthrow of unpopular regimes by small groups of lightly armed men. Like the rest of the Caribbean, these were "open" systems where the only protection was the degree of legitimacy of the regime, a legitimacy the leaders in Grenada and Suriname appeared to have lost. Both cases show that Cuba's role tended to be most effective in situations where regime legitimacy was eroded and where a process of antagonism had the makings of a broad-based social movement against the regime.

Be that as it may, and while it would be a mistake to underrate the significance attached by Caribbean observers to the political and ideological role defined by the Cubans, and to the capacity (indeed, audacity) of their intelligence and diplomatic corps, it is hard to tell to what extent the regional definition of the threat was a carryover of the U.S. national definition. Even, or perhaps especially, in spheres of influence, behavior tends to be strategically geared to deriving the maximum advantages from the dominant force in the sphere. The ministate was becoming an adept player of the geopolitical game, sensing Washington's not-too-subtle swings in foreign policy moods. The fact was that during the 1970s and 1980s, in island after island, radical, pro-Cuban parties were going down to overwhelming defeat in campaigns in which their Cuban and Grenadian connections had been made an issue. Because pro-Cuban governments such as Grenada, Suriname, and Guyana were also authoritarian ones, the Cuban issue became much more than a purely foreign policy matter; by the late 1970s it was central to the discussion of the type of society desired and the role that elections would play in making that decision. Popular political sentiment was clearly on the conservative side: retain the parliamentary system, regardless of the type of economic system that was proposed within it. Elections were perceived as opportunities for change when such change was mandated by failure, especially economic failure. Nowhere in the Caribbean was this more evident than in Jamaica during Michael Manley's second of two terms (1976 to 1980).

Faced with increasing economic problems due to a decline in the price of bauxite, the migration of significant numbers of native technicians, and a general sense of economic malaise, the Cuban connection became a handicap to the otherwise popular Manley. The Cuban mission in Kingston during the Manley years (1972 to 1980) had become an impressive complex, complete with radio-transmitting antennas similar to those of their U.S. and British counterparts. The Cuban ambassador—not infrequently the center of political controversy—presided over an ever-increasing network of Cuban activities in health, education, construction, agriculture, tourism, sports, and—some maintained—politics. In international affairs, the Manley government occasionally spoke of "party-to-party" relationships with Cuba, and their joint declarations had a strident and even revolutionary tone. In 1975, while addressing Cuban workers at Alamar near Havana, Manley sounded both determinist and voluntaristic notes. "We believe that the forces of change, the process of revolution are irreversible in history, but we believe that the process can be hastened . . ." He described the U.S. as "morally isolated."[34] His speeches from the stump invariably sounded more radical than the more pondered thoughts put to paper. In 1974, for instance, he noted that he favored pluralist democracy because "the democratic method is more likely to afford an opportunity for equality than any totalitarian system yet devised."[35]

It is only fair to note that minus the geopolitical or East–West competition which was already engaged in the region, Manley's efforts to restructure the society through a mixed-economy model was not all that radical. In fact, it was in keeping with the trend in a wide spectrum of the political elites of these nations to move toward a state-directed populism through an economically active state, an assigned role for the private sector, and an active, nonaligned Third World foreign policy. The evidence now seems to be that this was, in fact, as much as the existing West Indian political cultures were willing to bear. The development of socialism, with all the sacrifices that necessarily entails, appeared in the late 1970s and early 1980s as a very remote possibility.

In 1974, Carl Stone concluded that "in Jamaica there is neither a will to achieve the socialist alternative nor the necessary political supports to sustain it even if such a will existed." It was clear, at least by 1978, that the majority of Jamaicans were in no mood for radical Left experiments in "scientific socialism," as the data in Table 2.2 indicate. Even among the urban working class, the most radical in Stone's sample, only 19% favored government expropriation of land and only 12% saw the private sector as exploiters (though 48% saw it as selfish). Hardly surprising, therefore, that fully 63% of the urban working class disliked the leader of the communist party, Trevor Munroe, and that 65% disliked D. K. Duncan, the visible radical in Manley's circle. That this radicalism was very much an urban phenomenon is illustrated by Stone's finding that fully 42% of the small farmers could not even identify the radical leaders.

Why, then, the so obvious playing of the Cuban card? Two answers appear plausible: it was a response to domestic political exigencies or to external factors. Why, as Michael Kaufman notes, the accelerating Left-wing course just as the popularity and influence of the Left had been eroded? Kaufman himself answers: an effort, ultimately futile, to keep the radical Left in the PNP.[36] The external factor was the suspicion that the U.S., through the

CIA, was actively attempting to destabilize the regime. The evidence has remained weak. To Anthony Payne, "the circumstantial evidence that [CIA] agents were active in Jamaica in 1976 is strong—too strong, finally, to be ignored."[37] Payne's data appears to be drawn mostly from Michael Manley's own presentation of a "circumstantial case."[38]

Whatever the nature of the evidence, there can be no disputing the historical analogies to other well-documented instances of CIA involvement. Manley showed real interest in the cases of Guatemala, Cuba, and, especially, Chile. The perception of a hostile U.S. government was founded on real historical, but weak, contemporary facts. In the final analysis, however, Manley's decision to play to Cuba and to the Left, and to antagonize the U.S. was a mistake.[39] Certainly, after his massive electoral defeat in 1979, Manley dropped the radical rhetoric and the talk of CIA destabilization, and returned to his traditional social democratic political base.[40]

The myth of the modern, revolutionary nature of Caribbean societies stems from a misunderstanding of the nature of many of the movements that brought revolutionary elites to power. Even in modern-conservative societies (as Lenin theorized and demonstrated), a determined elite can bring about a designed outcome. This is so because after the initial mobilization, the movement tends to enter into a qualitatively new phase. This phase has dynamics of its own, dynamics that tend to represent a combination of the unpredictability and complexity of all mass action, and the more predictable—or at least understandable—actions of revolutionary cadres and elites. The latter can turn the movement in a revolutionary direction even in modern—conservative societies; they are less capable, however, of initially generating a revolutionary mobilization in such societies.

This was evident in Grenada and Suriname. It was also evident in the Dominican Republic in 1965.

In his study of the Dominican revolution of 1965, José A. Moreno found that the common thread running through all rebel groups was not the installation of socialism but the desire to eradicate corruption. The struggle was for "moral regeneration."[41] It was, he says, not unlike Cuba in the 1950s.

Three years after the 1965 rebellion, Andre Corten and Andres Corten found that fully 72.1% of their urban sample favored foreign investments with only minor forms of controls, whereas mere 15% opposed them. Similarly, 62.1% believed that Puerto Rican development was good or excellent, 0.9% believed that it had been bad and 19.6% thought it was "fictitious" or a "mirage." The authors concluded their study by noting that in the Dominican Republic, it was difficult for a radical intelligentsia to play a "vanguard role."

This explains why the Suriname Revolution (1980) and the Grenadian Revolution (1979), like the Nicaraguan Revolution, had to coexist with strong private sectors, established churches, and other aroused, but hardly revolutionary, sectors. These regimes were confronted with the complexity of the modern–conservative society, which explains as much about the failure of revolution as does the implacable opposition of local democrats and, certainly, of Washington.

The general conclusion is that the parliamentary system appeared to work for these small states. If there had been a dramatic political failure during those Cold War years, it was that of the Caribbean Left. As Brian Meeks has noted, given the speed with which erstwhile dominant Left positions and models lost credibility by the end of the 1980s, it is perhaps even more appropriate to talk of a "paradigm collapse."[42]

Three interacting and mutually reinforcing factors explain that collapse. First and foremost was the Caribbean peoples' resistence to socialist revolution, or its obverse, the defense of political pluralism, which ultimately defeated the socialists. Second was Cuba's misguided policies. Without understanding this conservative political culture, Cuba overplayed its hand.

In its zeal to support and assist ideologically like-minded leaders and revolutionary groups in the area, Cuba had underestimated the basic conservatism of the region. This conservatism, including a tenacious sense of independence and respect for nonintervention of the new nations of the region, came into play in the face of Cuban diplomatic audacity. Despite the fact that the same spirit of independence was also evident in their relations with the U.S.—often in a more fretful, even petulant, style—events in Grenada pushed West Indian solidarity beyond the pale. It is at such moments that the asymmetry of power in the Caribbean reveals itself in the most dramatic form, i.e., the hegemonic capabilities of the U.S. and the fact that the major sectors of the Caribbean society often welcome that use of force. This certainly was the case in Grenada.

This point leads to the third, fundamental, but often overlooked factor in U.S.–Caribbean relations: the essentially cordial relationships that exist between the two peoples. To be sure, the historical immigration to the U.S. has something to do with it. But there is a much more pervasive "diffuse reciprocity" which involves admiration for the principles of U.S. society. As Left-leaning Barbadian novelist George Lamming lamented in 1981: "It is very difficult to get the local population of the Caribbean to think critically of the U.S."[43]

Most of the nations of the Caribbean entered the post–Cold War era with their democratic institutions intact, and with societies and elites well disposed to the U.S. None of this, of course, meant that they had solved the basic social and economic ills which tend to keep their societies mobilized. Be that as it may, most of these societies would face the challenges of the post–Cold War era as democracies—something contemporary economic theory now concedes is an advantage in the development process.

It bears repeating that even during the Carter years when U.S. policy was being seriously modified, there was never an abandonment of willingness to exercise U.S. power. Circumstances, or perceptions, made it necessary. "The Carter Administration," says Robert Pastor, "started with an interest in promoting economic development . . . but eventually returned to a concern for national security."[44]

Even during periods of expansive reflection, hegemony might be modified but not abandoned.

CHAPTER 3

The End of the Cold War and the Changing Hegemonic Relationship

3.1 Paradigm Changes in the Dominican Republic and Trinidad and Tobago

Victory occasionally brings out the best in the victor. One of the ways in which this sentiment is demonstrated is by a retrospective candidness, an "owning up" to some dark deeds of the past. This is exactly what occurred in 1990 when the journal *The Nation* arranged a meeting between Guyana's Cheddi Jagan and the former Kennedy advisor Arthur Schlesinger, Jr. It was 30 years after the U.S. schemed, not once but twice, to oust the democratically elected Jagan that Schlesinger acknowledged what was hardly a secret anymore but what must have been music to Jagan's ears, considering his exposure to so many Cold War schemes:

> There was a great feeling after the Bay of Pigs, where the impression arose that Eisenhower had prepared an expedition to get rid of Castro, that Kennedy had lacked the resolution to follow it through. It was just politically going to look very bad if the dominoes began to fall in South America . . . The fear was that Congress might use aid to British Guiana as a means of attacking the whole aid bill then before it . . . Then of course what really happened was the CIA got involved, got the bit between its teeth and the covert action people thought it was a chance to show their stuff . . . I think a great injustice was done to Cheddi Jagan.[1]

If certain sectors of U.S. society were ready to "forgive and forget" the actions of the Left, the same was occurring in the Caribbean except in the reverse ideological direction. Former radicals such as Michael Manley in Jamaica, Cheddi Jagan in Guyana, and Basdeo Panday in Trinidad were speaking a more moderate and "realistic" language. Pragmatism rather than ideological fixity seemed to be the order of the times. The same was true in academic and intellectual circles. Former Marxist and "dependency" theorists were reworking their ideological framework.

The key issue still remained: did the removal of Cold War exigencies and therefore strategies, viz., containment and linkage fundamentally modify the circumstances of U.S.–Caribbean relations? The answer is that the end of the Cold War brought very little change in fundamental U.S. attitudes and policies towards the Caribbean. Cuba remained a thorn in the side of every new U.S. administration, and the Grenadian denouement had preceded the fall of the Berlin Wall by 6 years. Additionally, Washington was all too aware that the basic conservatism of the region was the primary bulwark against radical social change. Apologies such as that of Schlesinger were well intentioned but, in the final analysis, irrelevant to the ongoing and undergirding fundamentals of U.S.–Caribbean relations. Economics was one of these fundamentals, and the reflexion and policy reconsiderations in the economic area had preceded the end of the Cold War by many years.

From a geostrategic standpoint, one notes that some of the 31 "essential" U.S. foreign trade routes run through the Caribbean—the busiest routes all border Cuba, following the Windward Passage (between Cuba and Haiti) and the Straits of Florida (between Florida and Cuba). Obviously, these routes are also crucial to the Latin American and Caribbean countries that have the U.S. as their main market. These trade routes took on even greater importance as the area's monocultural economies began to diversify.

It was the Dominican dictator Rafael Leonidas Trujillo who brought an end to the foreign ownership of the island's plantation system. By the end of World War II, Trujillo had articulated and implemented a new nationalist economic model. Development became inner looking and state directed. Agricultural diversification was sustained by the profits of the nationalized sugar industry. This sugar industry also financed a limited import substitution industrialization program. All this did not take place under the direction of a new industrial and agro-industrial bourgeoisie, but rather under the near total control of the dictator himself. Much of what he nationalized, he personalized. This explains why at Trujillo's death in 1961, the state had already been converted into the principal national capitalist owner. It controlled 80% of sugar production, 70% of the industries engaged in import substitution, and 100% of energy generation, as well as enormous tracts of land.

Notwithstanding its essentially agrarian base, this statist enterprise gave rise to new social and political actors: an urban, middle-class bureaucracy which provided the "retainers" for both the political and economic systems. It is crucial to understand that Trujillo had completely marginalized the traditional oligarchy from these statist initiatives and in that way excluded them from the political spoils. This oligarchy (i.e., those who did not go into exile) went about its own business, waiting for a possible return to power, economically and politically.

With the defeat of Trujillo and his apparatus, the oligarchy exerted its influence by pushing for the downsizing of the state for both political and economic reasons. The oligarchy needed to emasculate the Trujillo-built state as an economic competitor. This explains why this oligarchy had little difficulty articulating a new arrangement with the one surviving member of the Trujillo apparatus, Joaquín Balaguer. In exchange for ceding political and military control and space, the oligarchy was allowed to pursue its private economic interests without competition from the state. Interestingly enough, this oligarchical push to trim the state had some unexpected consequences. First, it encouraged civil society to reenter the political arena through the revival of political parties and the competition for state control. Second, and crucially, it contributed to the separation between the military and the civilian political structures.

All these changes were amply demonstrated in the heatedly contested, 1982 elections and the military was unable to put a crimp in the competition. As Jonathan Hartlyn has explained, 1982 was the year when the Dominican political system finally shifted from the centralized authoritarian model to a new openness in political negotiations and pacting. Here, it is crucial to note that the new emphasis on human rights and transparent elections of the Jimmy Carter regime in the U.S. had greatly contributed to making this democratic opening possible.[4]

It is important to highlight the fact that none of this was a result of the end of the Cold War. The reconfiguration of the domestic political, social, and economic structures is a process that began with the fall of the Trujillo dictatorship. The loss of total state control, the rise of middle- and working-class activism, the redirection of economic activity towards exports, the acceleration of migration to the U.S., and the growth of a transnational culture were all processes of the 1970s and 1980s.

These came to a head during the Partido Revolucionario Dominicano (PRD) regime of Salvador Jorge Blanco (1982 to 1986). It was Jorge Blanco who articulated and executed the first "structural adjustment" program, stimulated the expansion of the tourist sector, and encouraged the new entrepreneurial class that was pushing for the creation of Free Trade Zones as a means of competing with other export-driven Caribbean economies. Jorge Blanco also began the redirecting of Dominican foreign policy, giving it a much more overtly pro-American orientation. Rosario Espinal and Jonathan Hartlyn have described very well his attempts to articulate a new foreign policy, which was defined by Jorge Blanco himself somewhat contradictorily as "aggressive, prudent, and moderated." Basically, the Dominican Republic was searching to step up and maintain a position of recognition and regard in the international political debate. The dilemma was how to project a social democratic Third World vision, while maintaining and consolidating good bilateral relations with the U.S. "This dilemma," say Espinal and Hartlyn, "was not exclusive to the Dominican Republic, it was also evident in other governments of the region that experimented transition towards democracy in the eighties; it was so in the cases of Perú, Ecuador, and Argentina."[5]

Despite its commendable initiatives, the Jorge Blanco period was also one of travails. It should be noted that these were also evident in other Latin American countries squeezed by the debt crisis of what has become known as the "lost decade" of the 1980s: the deterioration in the standard of living of the population, the accumulation of allegations of corruption in the development and privatization processes, and steady erosion of the credibility of the governing party. In mid-1984, all these pressures led to an explosion of popular discontent and anger in the urban areas. It was the first of many urban "mobilizations."

Although the fact that the PRD regime of Jorge Blanco survived these upheavals speaks well for the "taming" of the military and the consolidation of democratic institutions, they did lead to the defeat of the PRD in the 1986 elections. As had occurred in Trinidad and in other places, a program of belt tightening on the part of the state and liberalization of the economy had exacted a heavy cost on its architects. In 1986, the old caudillo Joaquín Balaguer was elected to power for the fourth time. He promised and delivered a return to economic protectionism and a more paternalistic state. Predictably perhaps, the results of this conservative interregnum, 1986 to 1990, was nothing short of a disaster.

The fundamental problem was structural: as the Dominican economy had already entered into a stage of manufacturing for export as well as an agricultural diversification forced by the U.S. cut of the sugar quota, it was no longer possible for the old statist and protectionist system to go unchallenged. The response of the president and his bureaucratic elite was to establish a full patrimonial system granting extensive clientelistic prependums to old and new economic elites alike. The result was corruption and inefficiency at all levels of the government. This attempt to marry a traditional "caudillistic" political style with the new neoliberal thrust of the economy was an absolute failure. His attempts to turn back the political clock were also unsuccessful. The elections of 1994 were hardly transparent, and the resulting "victory" of Balaguer and his Partido Reformista Social Cristiano (PRSC) did not receive the *visto bueno* of the international election monitors (such as the Carter Center), which were by now an integral part of elections in much of the Caribbean. Again, the culture of negotiation and pacting showed its durability, maturity, and utility when Balaguer agreed to shorten his term by 2 years, calling elections for 1996.

Despite this concession to democratic practice, however, and in a stunning example of Machiavellian opportunism, the old caudillo pacted one of the most unlikely political alliances imaginable: even as his own PRSC had its own candidate, Balaguer supported the presidency of Leonel Fernández Reyna of the erstwhile socialist Partido de la Liberación Dominicana (PLD).

In a process strikingly similar to what happened in Trinidad and Tobago, once radical Fernández, his PLD party still organized on the basis of the Marxist–Leninist system of cadres, denied in his statecraft and actions everything asserted in his previous philosophy and party programs. It could arguably not have been otherwise: the restructuring of the economy had crystallized the influence of the new economic elites; the nontraditional sectors of the economy—fundamentally tourism, economic production and free trade zones—were by far the key motors of the new Dominican economy and society as we shall see later on. The insertion of the Dominican economy into the world economy and, fundamentally, the U.S. economy was a reality. What Fernández did was to carry Jorge Blanco's foreign policy a few steps further. He redesigned the nation's foreign policy to provide a newly energized paradigm which could serve to promote the existing economic realities that he had inherited. Marxism and anti-Americanism were abandoned as English-speaking Fernández toured the U.S.

Fernández' plans were crisply articulated in his October 3, 1996, speech at the opening of the 51st session of the United Nations. Recognizing the end of the Cold War and the bipolarity it had engendered, Fernández outlined a foreign policy that could help his country meet the challenges of the "globalized" world.[6]

He pointed out five initiatives his government would take, all reflecting his outward, innovative approach to international affairs:

1. A new effort at cooperation at the regional, Caribbean, and Central American level.
2. The active pursuit of access to U.S. markets for Dominican and Caribbean Basin products. The goal was to seek "parity" with the NAFTA agreement.
3. Adherence to the rules set by the World Trade Organization (WTO), an expression of Dominican willingness to play by the new rules of the global game.
4. Relief from the burdens of the Dominican foreign debt.
5. Diversification investments and financial assistance by making full use of all the international arrangements available to his nation.

President Fernández would rearticulate these key points at the Meeting of Presidents in Miami on December 10, 1996. In a wide-ranging address, Fernández attempted to tie the various strands of domestic and foreign problems into one agenda of "development in a global age." Issues as diverse as foreign debt, national security (viz., drug trafficking and illegal migration), relations with the European Union and its Lôme partners and Asia, and remittances from the Dominican diaspora in the U.S. were all tied into a new scheme of national priorities for development.

Underlining the importance of their relations with the U.S., Fernández nominated one of his country's outstanding economists, Bernardo Vega, as ambassador to Washington. Wasting little time, Vega was soon promoting Fernández' new foreign policy and economic agenda. The ambassador advocated that there should be no delinking between Washington's need for Caribbean cooperation on issues such as the drug trade, criminal gangs, and migration and the Caribbean's need for investments and access to the U.S. market.[7] All these were parts of the new foreign policy which inserted the Dominican Republic into the global arena, generally, and the U.S., specifically. Ambassador Vega would later write a long memoir of his tour in Washington to "put in writing," he said, the success of the Fernández foreign policy vis-à-vis the U.S. and the broad consensus in the Dominican Republic to have it continued no matter which party was in power.[8] He was not totally sanguine, however, about U.S. relations with his country and the Caribbean, generally.

In a blunt 1998 speech to the Center for Strategic and International Studies in Washington, D.C., Ambassador Vega predicted that the many intractable issues in the U.S.–Caribbean agenda would lead to a "Second Cold War"—longer than the first.[9] Whatever the plausibility of this hypothesis, Ambassador Vega fully understood that U.S.–Dominican relations had been fundamentally modified by the end of the "real" Cold War.[10] The "paradigm" change involved both manifest and unintended consequences. For instance, subsidies and protection for U.S.-grown sugar led to drastic cuts in the Dominican sugar quota. This led to a diversification of agricultural production as well as markets. Western Europe became an important client. On the other hand, the growth of the textile industry encouraged by Washington's Caribbean Basin Initiative (CBI) further tied the country's economy into that of the U.S. Above and beyond all these issues, however, was migration to the U.S. and the large sum of remittances they sent home. With 10% of the Dominican population living in the U.S. and with remittances passing the $1 billion mark, it is hardly surprising that in 1998 President Fernández encouraged Dominicans resident in the U.S. to become U.S. citizens. Between 1992 and 1997, some 10,500 Dominicans a year were doing so.[11] Whatever the vagaries of U.S.–Dominican relations in the post–Cold War era, they were certainly qualitatively different from those existing before that era. Dominican isolation was a matter of the past.

Trinidad and Tobago is another case where a self-imposed statist model was ever-more rapidly substituted by deregulation. The key political question in the early 1960s in Trinidad was hardly ever whether there should be an activist state. State involvement and central planning were taken for granted. It was inconceivable that the nationalist state, led by a black nationalist, Eric Williams, should be perceived to be doing less for economic redistribution than the colonial one had done. The question was who should be the primary beneficiaries of such a state, given the climate of opinion, both local and, at the time, in the Third World. Equally inconceivable was to expect that the newly empowered party, the People's National Movement (PNM), and the newly independent state would not favor those who voted it into power and were its primary constituents, the Afro-Trinidadians. This preference was made all the more urgent precisely because this sector was perceived to be the most economically dispossessed sector on the island.[12]

Again, if the integration of the Afro-Trinidadian sector was to be accomplished, this would have, of necessity, to be through state action, and state action meant central planning. There is no disputing that much of the state planning was oriented toward the creation of a people's sector geared essentially to improving the lot of Afro-Trinidadians.

As has often been the case in the Caribbean—indeed, in the Third World—state efforts to create a self-sustaining "people's sector" were not successful. The ruling PNM's elite rhetoric about a people's sector had not been matched by its actions and certainly not in terms of the expectations it had created among the Afro-Trinidadian urban and educated youth. By 1970, both domestic and international forces conspired to resolve the incongruity between the ideology as articulated by the elite for political purposes and the less than equally enthusiastic actions concerning state control of the economy. These were radical times in the Caribbean and something had to give. From every corner of the Caribbean came the call to "socialize" the economy, and from the American Black Power movement (with Trinidad-born Stokeley Carmichael as one of its leaders) came the call for black ownership and control of the socialized economy. It all fell on receptive ears. After months of agitation and mobilization, a mass urban movement proclaiming "power to the people" nearly toppled the Williams regime. The regime's response was to bring its actions closer to the rhetoric of a people's sector.

Right after the rebellion ended, the PNM published the Chaguaramas Declaration, which clearly reflected the new political mood and climate of opinion concerning the role of the state. The publication conveyed this sentiment through two positions in particular: the vow to speed up national control of the commanding heights of the economy with special reference to oil and sugar, and the initiation of an immediate program of ownership and participation in banks and insurance companies.[13]

Accompanying this new posture was increased hostility toward the local private sector. The indigenous private sector was thought to have little initiative because the firms that existed were believed to be "generally tightly held and do not have the experience, vision, and income support needed to take the long view required to introducing fundamental change in the economy." The alternative was clear: "Indeed, the only body in a developing country endowed with characteristics comparable to those of the large corporation in the developed societies is the Government."[14]

Whatever the empirical truth of this comparison, the fact is that the government was leaving nothing to chance and certainly nothing to open competition. This economic nationalism was to be bolstered by two measures:

> "Certain areas of our economy are reserved exclusively for national effort. Government will take a leading part, including the use of direct participation, to expedite national control and ownership."[15]

No new 100% foreign-owned enterprises were to be permitted; the existing foreign enterprises were expected to hire nationals and begin to actively transfer "skills, knowledge, and expertise" to them. Two measures in particular had great political salience and would also stymie foreign investments. The "alienation" of land was prohibited. This responded to both the historical sense in many former plantation societies that the land should belong to the people as well as an objection to the tourist industry where there was presumption of resentment over blacks serving whites.

It is not surprising either, given the history of the hiring practices of banks and the political motivation of the macroeconomic changes, that one of the first areas on which the government focused was banking. The historical practice of hiring expatriates or local whites made the banks very specific targets of the Black Power movement, so that, as Leslie H. Scotland has noted, after the revolt the government logically "focused on the commercial banking sector."[16] Soon after the end of unrest, the government acquired the Bank of London and Montreal, created the National Commercial Bank, and began construction of the Worker's Bank. Hiring was nearly exclusively from the now politically dominant Afro-Trinidadian ethnic group. The Black Power movement of 1970 intensified the already tense relations with the private sector dominated by whites, Indians and Chinese, and their professional associations, compelling the Afro-Trinidadian political elites to accelerate the nationalization of major businesses and agricultural enterprises. For more than five decades, all major trends encouraged a significant expansion of the public sector. The nationalization of the petroleum industry, leading to the establishment of Petrotrin, the indisputable crown jewel of the economy, represented the culmination of this nationalization process. It continues to be in state hands.

That there were few, if any, domestic voices opposing this accelerated statism was reflected in the fact that the climate of opinion created by the intellectuals was hospitable to these actions. There was no such proclivity toward statism in Washington. And, yet, neither was there any evident pressure to reverse the process. The explanation of Washington's stance lay in the interaction of several conjunctural processes. First, and as distinct from the case of Michael Manley's nationalization of the bauxite industry in Jamaica, all nationalizations were duly compensated. The process was invariably accompanied by language concerning the creation of a domestic capitalist class rather than anti-Americanism or "Third Worldism." But above and beyond the domestic situation, there were the changes in Washington's public diplomacy towards the Caribbean.

It was Representative Dante Fascell of South Florida who in April 1973 enunciated the most complete outline of a desirable U.S.–Caribbean policy. Making a distinction between a U.S. "policy of self-preservation" and a "true" Caribbean policy, Fascell's proposals were premised on the beliefs that "While military considerations remain important to U.S. policy, they are not likely to become of overriding concern," and that given the dangers inherent in a relationship involving such disparities of power, "the United States should play a supporting and not a preponderant role in regional organizations."[17]

The Fascell approach, although new in its specific focus on the Caribbean, was in fact part of a wider public sentiment favoring change in inter-American relations in general in the early and mid-1970s. That the time was opportune for considering changes in the U.S.–Latin American or U.S.–Caribbean relations was apparent to the drafters of the Linowitz Report.[18] They were encouraged, wrote Sol Linowitz, by signs of growing recognition in Washington, D.C., and other capitals of the need for change. Even though not addressing itself to the Caribbean specifically, the report reflected the changing general mood in certain influential circles that would have an impact on thinking about the Caribbean. Very significantly, the report recognized that extensive bilateral concessional assistance from the U.S. to Latin America is largely a thing of the past, and that the U.S. should cooperate with other Latin American nations and multilateral development institutions in providing assistance. Three fundamental premises lay behind this multilateralism: (1) the need to respect diversity in ideology and economic or social organization, (2) the independent role of Latin American or Caribbean nations in international affairs, and (3) the global significance of the principal issues of U.S.–Latin American or U.S.–Caribbean relations.

The emphasis on multilateralism made its mark. Three years later, President Carter addressed the Permanent Council of the Organization of American States (OAS), outlining a "new approach" to "Latin America and the Caribbean." That approach, according to Carter, would be based on three elements: (1) a high regard for the "individuality and sovereignty" of each Latin American and Caribbean nation; (2) a respect for human rights ("You will find this country eager to stand beside those nations which respect human rights and promise democratic values"); and (3) a desire to press forward on the great issues that affect the relations between the developed and developing nations ("Your economic problems are also global in character and cannot be dealt with solely in regional terms").[19]

The new diplomacy was carried forth by some able and experienced U.S. diplomats. An early and influential adviser was Phillip C. Habib, whose first diplomatic posting had been to Trinidad, where he developed a good relationship with Prime Minister Eric Williams. Equally impressive was Andrew Young's trip, reported as follows by *The New York Times*: "'There really had been a change,' Mr. Young has been saying throughout the tour, and the responsiveness of the Caribbean leaders . . . has seemed at times to be more than the visitors expected."[20] "During the trip, hosts and guests sometimes seemed to be bursting with eagerness to cement the new relationships with praise."[21]

Clearly, the surprising paradigm change that took place on the island in the early 1980s responded to domestic factors, not any hegemonic pressures from Washington. Even as the local intellectuals were still advocating statism, the PNM, the same political party which had initiated the era of economic nationalism, was now ready to shift paradigms in a dramatic way. In the invariably policy-setting budget speeches of 1984, 1985, and 1986, PNM Prime Minister and Minister of Finance George Chambers called for what he had not called for in his campaign, that is, changes in the array of legislation that adversely affected foreign investment. Internally, it was evident that what became known as government "giveaways" were at an end. Prime Minister George Chambers conveyed the message in typically colorful Trinidadian language in his 1982 budget speech that "the fête is over and the country must go back to work."[22]

There have been no broad studies—certainly none for public discussion— that have analyzed the failure of one phase of government policy as it might relate to the transition to another. There also is no evidence of significant public discussion of alternative economic strategies. But a transition has occurred, and something had to have brought it about.

To radicals, the shift was imposed from outside. It was the "typical" hegemonic pressure, exercised through the International Monetary Fund (IMF), which forced the shift to neoliberalism. It is a fact that the 1983 negotiations between the Trinidad and Tobago government and the IMF for a "Draft Development Plan" for 1983 to 1986 went smoothly. Not insignificantly, the Trinidad and Tobago government team in those negotiations was led by a distinguished Trinidad economist, William Demas, past governor of the island's central bank, and in 1983, president of the Caribbean Development Bank. There certainly were other compelling factors which contributed to the change. First, the Black Power movement no longer carried any political weight. It had disappeared in the U.S. and in the Caribbean. Second, the windfall of OPEC-driven oil prices and profits was gone. Turning to the IMF was an act of necessity. Finally, by the early 1980s, political leaders everywhere in the Caribbean had witnessed the failure of the socialist or at least radical statist model in Jamaica, Suriname, Guyana, and Cuba. The tragic end of the Grenada revolution merely crystallized the sense that a change in economic policy was unavoidable.

Although the government did not broadcast its policy changes, and there were no society-wide debates on economic policy, the political opposition did pick up on the new trends and made its thoughts widely known. Led by radical-leaning trade unionist Basdeo Panday and former Deputy Prime Minister A.N.R. Robinson, the opposition began to lambaste the "sell-out" mentality of the PNM.[23] It was in many ways this radical anti-IMF rhetoric, plus the formation of a multiracial alliance, that led to the 1986 defeat of the PNM by Robinson and his National Alliance for Reconstruction (NAR) party. This was the first significant truly multiracial political alliance in the island's history.

Despite Robinson's rhetoric during the campaign, immediately upon taking office he adopted the 1983 IMF-designed restructuring guidelines. He began by changing the nature of central planning, arguing that instead of the top–down approach of the past decades, an attempt would be made to increase consultation and inputs from wider sectors of the society. Soon, the more radical Indian wing of the government was expelled and returned to a vociferous attack on the NAR's neoliberalism and on Robinson's "sellout" to the local capitalists. In the midst of the attacks, considerable trade union agitation, and clamors to do something about the high rate of unemployment, the government pushed its neoliberal program even more resolutely. In August 1988, it released the most comprehensive restructuring program ever put up for discussion, the Draft Medium Term Programme, 1989–1991. This program was amplified further in the 1988 Budget Speech.

Noting that the whole world, "even communist countries," was acknowledging "the realities of today's world," Robinson promised a flexible and receptive approach to foreign investments and initiatives by the native private sector. At the core of the program was a call to restructure the local economy in such a way as to make the island attractive to all forms of foreign capital, whether as direct investments, portfolio capital, or monies from multilateral lending institutions. To achieve this, the government proposed doing the following:

1. Reducing government expenditures and, therefore, state deficits by (a) downsizing state bureaucracies, (b) privatizing money-losing state enterprises, (c) encouraging exports as a means of earning hard currency rather than using hard currency through export substitution, and (d) reducing the scope and depth of the social net
2. Adopting a new, supportive attitude toward existing elites in the national private sector, regardless of their ethnicity
3. Accepting the theoretical formulations of international and multilateral agencies such as the World Bank and the IMF regarding competition and the role of foreign investment capital
4. Although not disregarding continued asymmetries, rejecting the paradigm of a basic North–South divide and accepting the idea that even the smallest state is part of an interrelated global economy

A more complete formulation of what would soon be called the Washington Consensus could hardly be imagined. In 1990, the Alien Landholding Act, in many ways the symbol of the economic nationalism of the 1950 to 1980 period, was abandoned in favor of the Foreign Investment Act.

By 1990, the "structural adjustment" measures began to squeeze the middle and working classes. Selwyn Ryan quotes studies by local academics Ralph Henry and Dennis Pantin showing that between 1982 and 1990, the increase in unemployment was 66,000 while an additional 100,000 had dropped below the poverty level. Between 1986 and 1990, the private sector had retrenched over 8,000, while the public sector laid off 3,529. Additionally, the remaining public sector employees took a 10% salary cut and suspension of their cost of living allowance (COLA). As Ryan noted, "Comparisons were being made with 1970 and 1981 when public servants also took to the streets to protest."[24] The call was for government to abandon the "IMF-imposed" structural adjustment program.

In the midst of widespread discontent and public protest, the NAR government stood firm on the reforms and was even planning an early election. On July 27, 1990, a militant sect of Black Muslims (Muslimeen led by Abu Bakr) attempted a power grab, taking the prime minister and many from his cabinet and Parliament as hostages. The uprising was defeated but not before widespread looting and arson had laid much of the capital city of Port-of-Spain to waste. As in 1970, the 1990 events were led by elements of the urban, Afro-Trinidadian population. Not surprisingly, Blacks perceived themselves to be the main losers of the NAR liberalization program just as they had seen themselves as losers under the previous PNM governments. In Ryan and Barclay's colorful imagery, Afro-Trinidadians were the "sardines" in the island's business world.[25]

Whether as trade union leader, intellectual leader of the Indian community, or leader of the opposition in Parliament, Basdeo Panday had always been an outspoken opponent of economic liberalization. In fact, he often sounded as if his foremost enemy was the local business sector. During the 1991 elections, his most vehement attacks were directed at the local white business community, whom he invariably referred to as a "French Creole parasitic oligarchy."[26] A review of his speeches from the year he was elected up to 1995 does not reveal a single instance of a sympathetic analysis of the neoliberal reforms in place since 1983. Whatever his ideological frame of mind has been since 1995, Panday took power just as the program of divestment of government holding was accelerating, and he has done nothing to slow down this process, much less reverse it.[27]

The most recently available data on the level of foreign investments, and the sectors to which they have been directed, make the speed and dimensions of Trinidad's insertion into the global economy quite evident (see Table 3.1).

Measured on a per capita basis, Trinidad in the 1990s was second only to Canada as a U.S. investment partner in the Western Hemisphere. The investments and the liberalization program that made this possible were palpable evidence that the elites were making macroeconomic decisions that conformed with their political interests and dovetailed nicely with the rules of economic conduct recommended by both Washington and the multinational lending agencies such as the IMF and the World Bank.

Table 3.1 U.S. Direct Investments in Trinidad, 1996–1999

	Totals (US$ in Millions)	Petrochemicals (%)	Oil and Gas (%)
1996	89	55	34
1997	1,228	51	44
1998 (estimated)	1,378	44	42
1999 (estimated)	840	32	50

Source: U.S. Embassy, Trinidad and Tobago, July 18, 1998.

What did not evolve as rapidly, however, was the political rhetoric supporting and explaining this liberalization of economic policy. Clearly, given the history of the political use (rhetorical and actual) of statism for ethnic mobilization, and in the absence of any public promotion of the advantages of privatization, divesting what is commonly regarded as the nation's main patrimony, the energy sector, will not be easy going. According to a study conducted for the Economic Commission for Latin America and the Caribbean (ECLAC), the private sector on the island appears quite solidly behind the new macroeconomic program; it worries, however, that the lack of public discussion and disclosures of the privatization process will harm its chances of total success. According to ECLAC, the business elites believe that it is the political elites' fear of organized labor that explains this lack of information and proselytizing.[28] Be this as it may, the divestment program continues uninterrupted and, at the turn of the millennium, was knocking on the door of the last bastion of state control, the energy sector. As has been the case in the Dominican Republic, the Trinidad and Tobago private sector was finally given the green light to assert itself. This has been done with verve as we shall see in the following section.

3.2 Haiti: The U.S.' First Post–Cold War Intervention

It is a truism that no nation is an "island." It is also true that even in the American sphere of influence and area of "hegemonic" control, local political systems operate according to the perceived needs of their elites and the moral codes and biases of the political culture, in general. This has been demonstrated in the Caribbean in cases as dissimilar as those of the Dominican Republic and Trinidad and Tobago.

One of those countries that has always presented the U.S. with difficult choices is Haiti. Its independence in 1804 followed that of the American colonies and was, at least indirectly, a response to the same call for human freedom. However, there were enormous differences. In the U.S. the movement towards independence coexisted quite harmoniously with slavery. In Haiti, the struggle for independence was coterminous with the struggle for liberation from slavery. It was the latter that delayed U.S. recognition of the Haitian state until the U.S. had itself liberated its slaves. It is this fundamental, even heroic, fact that appears to have crystallized the Haitian's national identity.

According to David Nicholls, the foremost foreign scholar on that country, Haiti's independence, achieved after a bitter and bloody struggle, was based upon a conception of race. This identity included very importantly, and hardly surprisingly, an anti-White, antiforeigner attitude which all sectors of the society shared.[29]

Despite this solid, historically grounded sense of national identity, Nicholls tells us that there has always been a contradictory attitude. When conflicts over power take place, groups that define their local interests in class and color terms have no objection to calling on outside intervention for their cause. None of these interventions, however, ever did much to change the nature of the island's political culture.

The U.S. was never far removed from these trends, but it was not until 1915 that the U.S., suspecting that the German kaiser had an interest in Haiti, acted as the *hegemon* that it had become; it occupied the island. The triggering cause was the total breakdown of law and order after a massacre of political prisoners in the presidential palace, but the real reason was geopolitical. Once there, that other side of American behavior abroad, republican humanitarianism, also came into play. Unfortunately, it did more bad than good, because it was a humanitarianism fraught with the rotten stuff of Jim Crow racism. By the time the marines exited in 1934, they had pacified the country by killing between 2,500 and 3,500 Haitian "guerrillas" but left a bitter legacy. Today, that intervention remains a ready target for Haitians who would pin every ill—from militarism to dictatorship—on the Americans.[30]

It is true that the American occupation and its creation of a "professional" military force bequeathed a fact of extraordinary significance for the future of Haitian politics: it eliminated the peasant guerrilla. In a barren country such as Haiti, guerrillas have been no match for an organized military force that enjoys aerial observation and surveillance capabilities. Thus occurred the genesis of the fundamental principle of Haitian politics: whoever can control the army in the city controls uncontested state power. Only splits in the army, not degrees of popular support, bring down governments in Haiti.

This is the reason why President John F. Kennedy's mighty efforts to bring down the dictator François ("Papa Doc") Duvalier were futile. Only a military intervention could have achieved that. The frustration of U.S. administrators with François (Papa Doc) Duvalier's Haiti was described by former Secretary of State Dean Rusk in 1978 in unequivocal language:

> " . . . We made all sorts of efforts to bring about changes in Haiti. We used persuasion, aid, pressure, and almost all techniques short of landing the outside forces, but President Duvalier was extraordinarily resistant."[31]

Unwilling to use outright military force and given the fact that the Duvalier regime was neither an ally of Fidel Castro nor in any other way a threat to U.S. security, coexisting with it was very much the preferred policy option during the Cold War years.

With the collapse of the Duvalier dynasty in 1986, the U.S. tried in many ways to influence the course of events on the island. The U.S. thought it had succeeded in bringing democracy to Haiti when in 1990 the Haitian people elected Jean Bertrand Aristide in a decisive fashion. The overthrow of Aristide a year later led to the efforts of the U.S. to, in the words of President Bill Clinton in his 1994 State of the Union Address, "press for the restoration of true democracy" in Haiti. Clinton would learn what Presidents Kennedy, Jimmy Carter, and George H.W. Bush had: this was a goal not so easily achieved. The reasons were a mix of traditional and new constraints on U.S. action, domestic and international, of the post–Cold War scenario. Among the traditional elements was the continuity of a fundamental operating principle of Haitian politics: it is a deadly game in which there are no second prizes; winning is everything. Call it holistic intransigence. This certainly explained the overthrow of Aristide and also partly explained Aristide's unwillingness to compromise with those who overthrew him, even as the U.S. pressured him to do so.

Also predictable was the international community's opposition to any form of military action. Arguments about human rights were no match for an opposition based on historical memories of U.S. hegemonic behavior in the hemisphere, especially in this case where the U.S. had occupied Haiti from 1915 to 1934. The first to object to military action—publicly, that is—was Aristide himself. Although it certainly was a matter of legal interpretation, the Aristide people had been arguing that two articles of the 1987 Haitian Constitution specifically prohibited supporting a foreign military intervention. First, Article 21 defines "crimes of high treason" to include bearing arms in a foreign army against the Republic or serving the interests of a foreign nation against those of the Republic. The second is Article 263/1, which specifies that no military or armed force other than the army of Haiti can exist on national territory. How would the "surgical strike" he called for[32]—with or without the support of the legitimate government—modify these provisions? However, even if Aristide had openly called for a military intervention, the military option still had to address other controversial aspects and opposition in the U.S. and in the international community.

Even though, as Tom Farer, a former member of the Inter-American Court of Human Rights, maintained Haiti was arguably the most telling case of a country that was recognized to need outside assistance—both to reinstate its democratic mandate and then to defend it—there was no consensus on how this should be done.[33] One need only read the opinions of the late Michael Manley, former prime minister of Jamaica and one of the most prominent Caribbean diplomatic troubleshooters. According to Manley, any forceful intervention to reinstate Aristide "would destroy everything of symbolic importance for Haitian democracy."[34] Manley's recommendation was that Aristide undertake another round of negotiations with every sector in Haiti. Haitians, needless to say, had heard this before. Their trust in the international community's commitments was not then, or perhaps ever, profound, and for good reasons.

The international community's response to the criminal sabotage of the 1987 elections had been pusillanimous. In that same vein, the U.S. Senate's resolution of December 7, 1987, noted that it "deplores" the failure of Haitian government to bring about democratic elections and supported the U.S. government's decision to embargo the Haitian government. The OAS also "deplored" the acts of violence and disorder and expressed its "solidarity" with the Haitian people. In the same breath, however, the OAS telegraphed its irresolution to the enemies of democracy in Haiti by stating that it reaffirmed the principle that "states have the fundamental duty to abstain from intervening, directly or indirectly, for any reason whatever, in the internal or external affairs of any other state in accordance with Article 18 of the Charter."

To many Haitians, the response to the 1987 crisis laid the foundation for the response to the 1991 crisis: statements of regret but reassertions of the principles of state sovereignty as an absolute prohibitor of effective international action. Heraldo Muñoz, Chile's ambassador to the OAS, made his country's position on forceful intervention quite clear—and public—when he noted that even a request from President Aristide, though "it might be well founded on moral–political grounds," would be "on shaky juridical terrain given the fact that existing law clearly does not allow the use of force, unilaterally or collectively, on behalf of democracy."[35]

Although of more recent vintage, the context within which the U.S. administration had to formulate policy was a carryover from the Vietnam years. As distinct from having U.S. foreign policy include the use of military force under the exclusive authority of the executive, any action now had to follow a process of consultation between branches of government with proper regard for public sentiment about foreign involvements, generally, and military interventions, specifically. Any decision to intervene had to go through considerable prior scrutiny and discussion. In 1993, the context did not seem propitious for such a move. There was a strong public perception that another intervention going on at the time in Somalia was in danger of recreating the Vietnam morass; the question of "It is easy to go in, but how do you get out?" could not be readily answered by either military or civilian authorities. The fear of "creeping involvement" weighed heavily in curtailing any U.S. predisposition to use its overwhelming force to achieve policy goals in the region, generally, and in Haiti, specifically. Rather than swift unilateral action, as in Grenada or even Panama, to return an elected leader to power and put an end to abominable violations of human rights, during the 1991 to 1993 period the U.S. pursued negotiations in what turned out to be a tortuous search for consensus at home and abroad. The U.S. first attempted action through the OAS, then through the UN, and finally even through negotiation with the military usurpers in Haiti themselves. After the latter signed an agreement to allow the return of the exiled president, they refused to honor their word and forced a deeply embarrassing withdrawal of the ship bringing U.S. and Canadian personnel for an agreed-upon training mission. Was this any way for the only remaining superpower to behave? Could the Haitian mouse face down the American lion? Duvalier certainly did in 1963. Were the Haitian generals following this example?

These were questions both the U.S. and the foreign press were asking. The question of honor or "face" in international relations was starkly and poignantly posed. And, yet, if the U.S. was not to act as in 1915 or at the height of the Cold War, what was to be done? The complexities of U.S. policy formulation in the post–Cold War era were evident.

However, if Aristide showed little, if any, determination to resolve his problem himself, and the Latin Americans continued to be opposed to military intervention, how was democracy to be restored? President Clinton was certainly undecided or at least cautious and for evident reasons. First, even if one were to base policy recommendations on an apparently sound understanding of Haiti, such an understanding is only one part of any foreign policy decision. The other parts are subject to international dynamics and, crucially, U.S. domestic political considerations. An American administration committed to a domestic agenda and already once "burnt" by Somalia was obviously twice shy about committing troops anywhere else. Second, as had often occurred in the past, there tended to be a special dynamic created by the interaction of Haitian and U.S. policy elites. This domestic consideration often led to unpredictable combinations and variations of many original policies. This dynamic was evident in the recommendation of the members of the U.S. Congressional Black Caucus (CBC). Their October 27, 1993, resolution calling on the U.S. government to do "everything in its power to promote democracy and economic development within this hemisphere" was clearly a sign of their frustration with the policies of the U.S. administration, which in 1993 appeared dead in the water. The CBC went one step further and called for providing Aristide and his government with a "protective military force." The basic problem of this suggestion was that it did not address the fundamental step prior to "protection": getting the Haitian usurpers out of power. In other words, how to create the basis for a transition in power that could then lead to consolidation?

The divisions in the U.S. were quite evident in the radically divergent editorial positions of major newspapers. *The New York Times* editorialized on October 29, 1993, to "Tighten the Sanctions on Haiti" and more dramatically on December 25, 1993, wrote "For Haiti: Sanctions That Bite." Leaving aside the apparent inconsistency that *The New York Times* (October 8, 1993) simultaneously demanded that the U.S. "get out" of Somalia and opposed the embargo on Cuba,[36] there was a glaring absence of any mention in the *Times* that this was a proven approach. *The New York Times* had often argued that, in the Cuban case, the embargo had certainly failed the tests of consistency, cogency, and practicality. On what grounds could it be recommended in the Haitian case?

There obviously had to have been many strong, positive arguments in favor of sanctions for this option to have emerged as the preferred policy of the U.S. and, to a certain extent, the international community. Indeed, it is precisely this international consensus on Haiti, though not on Cuba, which was the option's strongest suit. There were, of course, other features that recommended it, not the least of which is that it best balances the tension between international and domestic considerations. Sanctions in the form applied to Haiti, i.e., embargoes on weapons and oil and the freezing of assets in the U.S., allowed the U.S. administration and the international community to buy time (not invade) without appearing to be indifferent by doing nothing. Similarly, exempting humanitarian assistance from the embargo avoided the impression of callousness. Finally, it drew heavily from, and provided sustenance to, what one can only call—in the case of Haiti as well as Cuba—"chronological optimism": the thought that the sanctions will eventually work. Evidently, such optimism can only be based on the assumption that some conjuncture of circumstances, not the embargo per se, will cause the policy to work. If that conjuncture does not occur (as it has not in 40 years in Cuba and did not in 3 years in Haiti), the policy does not achieve its purpose. Indeed, it did not, just as it had not against Duvalier from 1963 to 1964.

A different opinion was held by the *Washington Post* (December 22, 1993) in an editorial entitled "The Haitian Deadlock," which expressed a widely-held post–Cold War impatience with "imperial impositions." The *Post* stated starkly that for 2 years President Aristide had demonstrated a troubling, because it was limited, view of his own role. It was up to him, said the editorial, "to devise a strategy to bring about his own return" and meanwhile the U.S. should disengage further. The *Post*'s position was that the embargo of the island was only augmenting the suffering of the masses while doing little to dislodge the usurpers, and it was futile for Aristide to wait for an imposition through "the colonial solution," i.e., the use of foreign troops to take him home. Although the *Post* had correctly raised the issue of Aristide's evident lack of resolve, the paper overestimated what any exiled Haitian leader could or had done from exile, through negotiations, or any other strategy.

The reality was that the Haitian opposition in the 1990s had failed to dislodge the military usurpers for many of the same reasons that the opposition, decades ago, failed to dislodge Papa Doc Duvalier. The parallels are striking. Haitian social scientist Leslie F. Manigat, who served for a brief period in 1988 as president, had itemized the opposition to Duvalier in the 1960s and 1970s as follows:[37]

> Internal divisions and betrayals, "even in the face of systematic terror."
>
> A profound "anxiety to assume power through foreign support," which led them to ignore the organization and synchronization of the internal movement.
>
> The "overestimation of the effectiveness of aid cut off and underestimation of the Haitian people's capacity for suffering."
>
> A lack of a proper appreciation of the international and especially Latin American opposition to intervention. Duvalier knew very well that "with all its military power, the U.S. could be reduced to a 'paper tiger.'"

Slowly but surely, the nonmilitary options appeared to be canceling themselves out. Much of the U.S. public was being persuaded by the argument that attempts at forcing compliance on Haiti (as on Cuba), through embargoes and general isolation, were causing serious damage to these societies.[38] The strategy had worked as punishment but had not brought about the desired policy goals. Not only could embargoes be broken, but there was—and is—also the calculation concerning the all-important public opinion, namely, that the public in democracies, such as that in the U.S., has a short attention span. Given the predominance of domestic concerns, there is little patience for any one foreign policy problem. Haiti was becoming a foreign and domestic nuisance. And here, history appeared to be repeating itself. The urge to be rid of "the problem," combined with a clear sense that it was militarily "doable" at low cost, began to gain support. Among the early evidence of this were two editorials in *The Miami Herald*: "Time for the Marines" on December 22, 1993, and "Solution for Haiti: Force" on January 15, 1994. It is quite evident that Florida was being adversely affected by the Haitian situation. First, politically, there was public resentment at the continued arrival in Miami of Haitian "boat people." As long as Haiti was under a dictatorship these people had, at least theoretically, a claim to refugee status. Second, Florida was being impacted economically. The embargo had put a stop to commercial flow. While relatively small in overall terms, it was significant for Miami.

It is quite revealing of the kind of momentum that builds in pluralist democracies, such as the U.S. around a foreign policy decision, once something akin to the "law of necessity" kicks in. With all other options and patience exhausted, two major arguments began to emerge, both linked to the supposed post–Cold War consensus on boosting democracy and stopping "crimes against humanity." First, there was the moral argument.

An "optimum" type of world peace can only be secured by a world order that emphasizes the value of human dignity in international relations. This means putting people first and carries with it a presumed right to defend those systems where a regime of human rights has demonstrably been implemented or attempted through democratic institutions and behavior.[39] In Haiti, such a regime has been sought since at least 1986, and one such regime came into office (though clearly not into power) albeit only briefly, with the election of President Aristide in 1990. Second, there was the "nation building" argument. Fundamental to nation building would be the renewal of the flow of international development funds, which under the Aristide administration had reached a promised $500 million over 2 years. By restoring the democratically elected government and providing it protection, the country's development program could proceed without interruption, and development funds would reach their intended targets rather than be squandered by corrupt administrators.

In keeping with its "new" resolution not to act unilaterally (as it had done in Grenada and, certainly Panama), the U.S. sought international support for a military action. The UN Security Council and the OAS had already approved the application of severe sanctions against Haiti. The UN Security Council, not the OAS, finally voted to approve military action.

It should be understood that, whereas the OAS' vote to impose sanctions on Haiti was argued on the grounds of the 1991 Santiago Declaration pledging OAS support to restore democracy in the hemisphere, the UN Security Council's resolution was based on the premise that the situation in Haiti represented a threat to regional peace. The UN has no authority to act to restore democracy anywhere; it could only act if there was evidence that the consequences of authoritarian action threatened regional peace. Note Tom Farer's argument:

> . . . There is a plausible basis for claiming that the overthrow of a democratic government threatens regional peace and security. To be sure, the threat may not become concrete for some time. But even in the short term, it can compel neighboring democracies to shift a slice of government revenue into nonproductive military expenditures, with consequent aggravation of social tensions. Moreover, as the United States can attest from its experience with the claims of Haitians to refugee status, the overthrow of an elected government and the effort to rule without electoral legitimacy can send people spilling across national frontiers in search of safety and hope. This process, however, can sometimes impair their neighbors' "security," in the wider sense that term has acquired over the past several decades.[40]

Once restored, President Aristide would write that this had been done by "the international community"—plain nationalistic face-saving. Aristide was restored to power by the only nation that had the capacity and, ultimately, the political will to send in 24,000 troops. The fact that other nations then sent "peacekeepers" only confirmed that in the post–Cold War era, hegemonic capabilities were not inconsistent with new international conventions regarding peacekeeping and regional security. The U.S. did none of this, as has been noted, without considerable international consultation and support. From that point of view one can speak of a "modified" hegemonic inclination.

Equally true was the evidence modification of conventional concepts of sovereignty. Those who adhere to a traditional, state-centric concept of sovereignty have to consider how this can coexist with two fundamental Haitian realities. First, for all practical purposes, Haiti has already lost sovereign control over critical parts of its economy and society to foreign agencies.[41] According to the UN Development Program, Haiti ranks 137th among the 173 nations of the world in terms of health, education, and purchasing power. More than 450 NGOs perform most of the duties in public health, education, and the daily feeding of nearly one million children. Second, any serious effort to reform that society will undoubtedly involve an even greater and more direct foreign presence, and thus an even greater retreat from sovereign control, at least for the medium term.

In the final analysis, and above and beyond the legal arguments regarding sovereignty and intervention, there are the social, economic, and political realities that govern the behavior of whole societies. What 6 years of U.S. military intervention in the 1990s proved, however, was that in terms of the Haitian domestic situation, the results were not significantly different from what was accomplished in the 19 years of the first U.S. occupation, i.e., very little change. Whether during the Cold War or post–Cold War era, foreign military occupation, even by the most powerful nation, is no guarantee of positive change. Three years after the restoration of "democracy," authoritarianism appears once more to be the order of the day in Haiti.

CHAPTER 4

Globalization and the Challenges to Intraregional Integration

4.1 Size and Vulnerability: Dilemmas of Tourism, Transportation, and Agriculture

It was not simply the U.S.' preoccupation with the Cold War that provided the Caribbean with opportunities for extraregional economic integration and preferential trade arrangements; it was also the existing colonial relationships. Understanding the perpetuation of many of these relationships is vital to understanding many aspects of U.S.–Caribbean relations in the post–Cold War era.

What the Cold War did engender was a heightened awareness that as these islands decolonized and their metropolitan former masters moved towards new forms of economic integration, they could not just be cut loose to fend for themselves. The particular postcolonial economic arrangements depended on the particular political decisions made—both in the metropolis and in the former colony—to ensure proper "postcolonial" development.

These extraregional arrangements were deepened during the Cold War precisely because the Caribbean had become an important battleground during those years. It was an effort to keep these islands on the "right" side of the Iron Curtain.

The problem for the post–Cold War years was that each of the various metropolitan governments decolonized and also fought the Cold War battles in their own particular way. To reiterate the methodological point made in Chapter 1, there was no such thing as a "Caribbean" decolonization process or a "Caribbean" Cold War strategy. Both the development of extraregional arrangements as well as the particular postures adopted during the Cold War have to be studied in terms of the different metropolis–territory associations. This is the only way to understand the slow and (yes, why not say it) frustrating history of attempts at regional integration.

The post–World War II breakup of great empires, driven by a call for self-determination, created some 90 new states within a few decades. A large number of these states had small populations. UNITAR has fixed an upper limit of one million people as the definition of a "small state." There are some 44 "small" independent states, many with populations below one million. Many of these "mini states" are in the Caribbean as Table 1.1 shows.

Although it is true that establishing degrees of vulnerability between "small," "mini," or "micro" states can be a difficult exercise, it is now widely accepted that independent states with populations under one million are especially vulnerable. "There is clear evidence," says an important study, "that severely restricted human resources can be a crucial constraint on a country's overall capacity to function effectively as an independent member of the international community."[1] Thus, the vulnerability is not strictly military. Let it be understood, however, that there has been no unanimity on this point; in fact, there was a time when there was considerably less agreement on the relationship between state size and vulnerability or viability. Ideological proclivities of the Cold War period tended to determine where scholars stood on this issue. Whereas some felt it necessary to make size, and specifically "smallness," an integral part of any calculation of economic viability,[2] others questioned the utility of size as an analytical tool. Some argued from economic theory.[3] Most, however, were driven by ideological considerations.[4] To Lloyd Best, size was a "manipulatible variable," one that served established elites and their economic allies in the metropolis. Similarly, others argued that "resource insufficiency" was a myth useful to colonial, political, and economic elites. Size, said another, "is the bugbear of the Caribbean." The focus should be on social class divisions, not national size. This focus on national social structures led to a narrow framing of the question of state viability. Note the emphasis by a highly influential academic: The fundamental question for small states, he argued, should be, "What form and level of productive (economic) system is the material base of society capable of bearing?"[5]

There were, of course, many voices that warned against this dismissal of the relationship between size and viability in a global context. "Any West Indian politician," noted Errol Barrow, then premier of the not-yet-independent Barbados in 1963, "who thinks he can go it alone in the face of world economic competition, stiff tariff barriers, and special subsidies . . . is either blind or insane."[6]

By the mid to late 1980s, however, a series of political fiascoes in the newly independent states led to a sea change in the attitude toward size and both viability and vulnerability. First came the attempted coups in Curaçao and Trinidad and Tobago, then the fall of the socialist experiment in Grenada in 1983. This was followed by the failure of the military regime in Suriname and the backtracking of Aruba from its intent to seek full independence.

In the Netherlands Antilles, the issue of the vulnerability of size does not seem to faze certain leaders. In Dutch Sint Maarten (population 42,600) there is a definite move towards an Aruba-like separation from the Netherlands Antilles. On the island of Curaçao (population 145,000), the elections of May 2003 led to a coalition government of five parties with a prime minister who started off on a strident nationalist note. She would not, for instance, speak Dutch with anyone other than the premier of the Netherlands or receive a delegation from the Dutch parliament. It was, as a major newspaper put it, "a Babylonian state of affairs."[7] Although polls indicate the majority of the Dutch want Curaçao to go independent, certain Dutch legislators insist on friendly attempts, fearing being called "arrogant and neocolonialist."[8] It appears that the smaller the society, i.e., the "weaker" in geopolitical terms, the greater the propensity of the metropolis to accommodate what can only be called small state bravado. Be that as it may, there is sufficient vulnerability in the independent countries in the region to lead to repeated questions over the years about their long-term viability. In 1985 the Commonwealth Secretariat put aside the academic debates of the 1970s over the size of the states, and declared that the "smallest" and "weakest" states were "inherently vulnerable" to a series of threats. It said:

> We believe it to be indisputable that the smallest and the weakest within the international community, those with the least political clout, military strength or economic resilience, are among the ones who are likely to suffer most. . . .[9]

The secretariat stated that the issue of vulnerability had two dimensions. One was ideological and geopolitical in nature: threats from outside forces to national security, including, importantly, international organized criminal groups. We now know that the threat from ideology-based groups has been considerably reduced by the end of the Cold War, and the threat of organized crime has become one of the critical threats in the contemporary Caribbean. Another kind of threat mentioned by the Commonwealth Secretariat that has increased following the end of the Cold War is posed by the vulnerability to a series of challenges of an economic kind. This explains the particular consideration given to these states in the 2001 Doha

Round, to which we will return. No amount of diplomatic and negotiating skills, however, can fully compensate for the reality of being small states. As the hemisphere discussed the possible implementation of a Free Trade Area of the Americas (FTAA) by 2005, the small Caribbean states were marginal players at best. The total population of the Caribbean Community Secretariat (CARICOM) nations (including the seven million Haitians) is only 1.74% of the hemispheric total, while its GDP is a mere 0.23% of the FTAA's estimated $13 trillion economy.

In terms of the role of the U.S., it is evident that forceful U.S. actions during the Cold War contributed mightily to ending the geopolitical threats. Paradoxically, U.S. action or inaction in the post–Cold War period appears to be increasing the threats to internal vulnerabilities. This is especially true in terms of economic challenges, or more accurately, dilemmas posed to Caribbean decision makers.

Because a dilemma is by definition a set of options none of which is optimal, any choice involves trade-offs and opportunity–cost calculations. This has clearly been the case in terms of development strategies in agriculture and in tourism. U.S. policy has been disastrous for the former but the best hope for the latter.

4.1.1 The Agricultural Challenge

The greatest agricultural challenge by far is represented by the enormous subsidies enjoyed by U.S., Japanese, and European agriculture. *The New York Times* put it bluntly when it editorialized that poor and developing nations have long—and rightly—complained that whereas the richest countries want open markets for their manufactured goods, "they rig the game when it comes to agricultural products."[10] *The Financial Times* of London calls this situation "hypocrisy."[11] We hesitate to go into details since this is being written on the eve of a major World Trade Organization (WTO) meeting on the issue in Cancun, Mexico, in September 2003. Even then, it is expected that some vital details will be negotiated after Cancun.

It should be clearly understood that all this negotiating will be between the major industrial countries and the so-called G-22 led by Brazil, India, China, and South Africa, which can hardly be called small countries. It has been noted that in 2002 the 30 industrial nations of the Organization for Economic Cooperation and Development (OECD) spent $311 billion on farm subsidies, more than the combined GDP of all the countries of sub-Sahara Africa and six times their combined foreign aid programs.

There are two dilemmas confronting the small independent countries of the Caribbean. They claim that the WTO rules are intrinsically unfair, and vow to be "strong and united" against any attempt to eliminate tariffs at the September 2003 meeting at Cancun.[12] They, of course, depend heavily on import tariffs for their government revenues and have not yet begun the fiscal restructuring necessary were there to be a drastic reduction in these tariffs. The percentage of total revenues from tariffs run from a high of 40% for the Bahamas, St. Vincent, and Dominica to 25% for most of the others. The second area that would be affected by WTO reforms is the various preferential trade agreements they enjoy. Not surprisingly, the small countries of the Caribbean are demanding a special, i.e., a more gradual, schedule for tariff elimination. This has yet to be agreed upon, not so much by the U.S., but by the larger South American and Central American nations.[13]

There is nothing simple about the "banana war" for the simple reason that it is not so much a war as it is a complex number of battles. A review of these battles tells us a great deal about the pre–Cold War and post–Cold War years.

Paul Sutton has noted that the banana supply to Europe was "fragmented and owed little to economic rationality." It did, however, owe a great deal to past imperial preferences and present vested interests.[14] Under the Lômé Agreement IV, which continued the privileged arrangements the Europeans gave their African, Caribbean, and Pacific colonies (ACP states) upon decolonization, these ex-colonies are allowed to export bananas free of licenses and tariffs, but the Latin American producers (so-called "dollar bananas") have both quotas and a 20% common external tariff to contend with. Without these barriers, the Latin American bananas, which cost half as much to produce and are perceived to be of superior quality, would eliminate the competition. France subsidizes the bananas from its overseas department (DOMs, Martinique and Guadeloupe); Spain, the bananas from the Canary Islands; and Great Britain, those from former colonies in the Caribbean, Jamaica, St. Lucia, Dominica, St. Vincent, Grenada, and Belize. Of these, it is the small Windward Islands that are at greatest risk. An estimated 50% of their work force and 50% of their foreign exchange earnings are based on this trade. Because there is no substitute for the crop in sight, the consequences of true free trade would be, in the words of two Caribbean analysts, "disastrous." That disaster would have "a socially unmanageable fallout, including an explosive political situation.[15]

"Bananas," says Vaughan Lewis, the ex-prime minister of St. Lucia, "are to us what cars are to Detroit."[16] The first aspect of the controversy that has to be understood is that the opposing parties are fervently engaged and convinced that they have right on their side. If there could be "no compromise" with communism during the Cold War, neither can there be any in the banana war. "Experience has shown," said the European Union's Commissioner for Agriculture Franz Fischler, "that the word 'compromise' is not a word one associates with discussions on the banana regime."[17]

What, then, was the issue? In simplest terms it was a battle for market share in Europe and equal terms of access to those markets. It is what U.S. Trade Representative Mickey Kantor called, in 1994, a battle against a trade regime that was "trade distorting, discriminatory, and lacking in transparency."[18] Indeed, in terms of the U.S. definition of an ideal free trade regime, it is that. It is quite understandable, therefore, that these islands deeply resent the fact that the U.S. government should have chosen the banana issue as the first case brought before the WTO for adjudication. "There was no reason for them to go to the WTO," said Jamaica's ambassador to the U.S. " . . . It was a breach of faith with the Caribbean."[19] In terms of the real regime of protectionism for agricultural products of U.S. and other OECD countries, it is quite conventional.

It might have been a breach of faith with the Caribbean, but the U.S. action was applauded by those Latin American states (Ecuador, Honduras, Guatemala, and Mexico) which were joined as plaintiffs by Germany, which has the only "free market" of bananas in Europe and, of course, by Chiquita Brands. The latter had mobilized an extraordinary coalition of Democratic and Republican senators and members of the House to pressure the White House into action. Caribbean leaders singled out Chiquita Brands as the main influence behind U.S. actions.

Under the leadership of Carl Lindner and his family, the company diversified and bananas were marketed by Chiquita Brands International, Inc. It is by far the largest grower, shipper, and marketer of bananas in the world. It is undoubtedly Mr. Lindner who has been the field marshal of the major battle over bananas. As David E. Sanger of *The New York Times* put it, "Lots of industries complain about their treatment abroad, but Mr. Lindner, a big contributor to Democrats and Republicans alike, has been more skilled than most in getting the political establishment to take up his cause—no easy task when barely a single American job is at stake."[20]

In what clearly is a true reflection of the changed environment in Washington for the small Caribbean states, they could marshal little, if any, support. A strategy paper of the CARICOM recommended, among many others, building a coalition with those Latin American countries that had accepted the concessions made by the U.S. and refused to be a party to the WTO suit: Venezuela, Colombia, Costa Rica, and Nicaragua.[21]

These countries had received preferential quotas from the U.S. (the so-called Framework Agreement) in exchange for not challenging the existing regime with the ACP countries. Although this divided the Latin American ranks, that was clearly not where the crucial battles had to be fought, and the Caribbean strategists knew it. They recommended that they "continue to build support in the United States against the action of the Government of the United States . . ."[22]

To be sure, they did receive some support from leaders in the black community. Randall Robinson of Trans-Africa Forum, leader of the successful U.S. boycott against apartheid in South Africa in the 1980s, remarked to the *Cincinnati Enquirer* that it was "a clear issue of [Chiquita] buying trade favors.... The President ought to be ashamed of himself." He twice dumped bananas in front of the White House, and he did get the Reverend Jesse Jackson and actor Bill Cosby to write letters of protest to President Bill Clinton.[23]

The problem is that standing up for Windward Island bananas is not equivalent to standing up against communism or apartheid. No bananas are grown commercially in the U.S. There is no labor union issue and the fact that the American consumer pays considerably less per pound of Chiquita (or Dole or Del Monte) bananas than the British do for theirs is reason enough to ignore the issue.

It is not just that Chiquita's parent company, American Financial Group, was the fourth largest giver of soft money to both American political parties in 1997; it is also that the "free trade" argument, no matter how selective and hypercritical, fits into the present climate of opinion.

At the heart of the dispute, which began in 1993, was a shift in the EU regime for the importation of ACP bananas. The key U.S. Latin American banana producers claimed that this new set of protocols took away almost half of the market share of U.S. firms and gave it to EU firms. The WTO ruled in favor of the U.S., claiming that U.S. firms had been harmed to the tune of $191.4 million per year, and this unleashed a minor trade war for the equivalent amount on EU goods.

On April 11, 2001, the U.S. and the EU announced an understanding on this bitter dispute. There would be a phased implementation of the following steps:

1. By July 1, 2001, the EU would adopt a new system of banana licenses based on historic past trade reference periods.
2. By January 1, 2002, the EU would shift an additional 100,000 tons of bananas into a tariff quota (with U.S. firms gaining a substantial share).
3. By January 1, 2006, the EU would introduce a tariff-only regime for banana imports.[24]

The 9-year dispute was ended through an agreement between the U.S. and Brussels. No matter how much the "Joint U.S.–EU Release" in April 2001 spoke of protecting "the vulnerable" ACP producers, that protection had a definite time period—another 5 years of privileges. Coming on the heels of this losing war on bananas was another challenge: sugar production. In mid-2003, Brazil, Thailand, and Australia, all major cane sugar producers,

Table 4.1 World Exports of Raw Sugar

Production Areas	1984–1985	1989–1990	1994–1995	1999–2000	2002–2003
North America	82	70	—	83	80
Caribbean	8,372	7,845	3,208	3,978	2,975
Central America	740	935	1,345	1,747	1,798
South America	4,350	1,738	2,644	8,500	11,003
Western Europe	33	—	—	2	2
Eastern Europe	288	—	8	46	20
Africa	2,172	2,103	1,575	2,409	2,725
Asia and Oceania	5,894	5,668	8,676	7,027	7,056
Middle East	470	—	—	—	—
Total	**22,401**	**18,459**	**17,456**	**23,792**	**25,659**

Source: United States Department of Agriculture (USDA), Foreign Agricultural Service (FAS).

challenged the EU sugar regime. This regime has linked the prices paid to sugar-producing ACP countries to the subsidized price it offers to its beet sugar producers. A cut in this subsidization necessarily meant a cut in the price extended to the ACP. Beyond the politics of subsidies and economic compensation, there was the stark reality that the Caribbean, including the former sugar bowl of the world, Cuba, was no longer a world player. Table 4.1 shows the dramatic decline in that region's export of raw sugar.

Once again, the Caribbean was forced into an untenable position: CARICOM requested that the three countries delink their challenge to EU subsidies from the protocol extended to the ACP countries. Perhaps sensing the futility of the whole affair, the EU offered CARICOM $150,000 to cover its legal fees in the WTO dispute which in 2004 ruled against all sugar subsidies.[25]

The writing had been on the wall for over a decade. Now the islands had to seek other sources of income and employment. Tourism would be a logical place to look.[26]

The tourist industry in the Caribbean had always been for the select few of the "jet set," Bermuda, Barbados, Bahamas for the English.[27] It was not until after World War II, with the beginning of a broader middle and working class tourism in the U.S., that the Caribbean was discovered. Few industries demonstrate the depth and breadth of Caribbean ties with the U.S. as does tourism. An analysis of that industry reveals the promise, but also the vulnerabilities of that link. With Miami Beach being the first experiment in mass tourism, it was the State of Florida's prohibition of casino gambling that pushed a considerable number of those tourists to head further south to Havana. The latter was an "open" city accessible by Pan American seaplanes as well as a ferry out of Key West, FL. The romance of Havana was enhanced by the presence there of figures like Ernest Hemingway and George Raft.

When the Cuban Revolution moved against the industry in 1959, gambling and entertainment were taken elsewhere in the Caribbean. The boom in Caribbean tourism is a post–Cuban Revolution phenomenon. But it was not a welcome trend everywhere in the Caribbean. To many leaders of the decolonization movement of the 1960s, tourism was hardly a priority. Consequently, their countries have had a rather late start.

The leadership of the new Caribbean states cut their political eye-teeth listening to horror stories of how U.S. tourism "perverted" Cuba, with all the negative associations of gambling casinos run by figures from U.S., organized crime, prostitution, and hordes of uncouth, white U.S. tourists lording it over native servants. Cuba, so went the myth, had been converted into a nation of bartenders, busboys, and pimps. It is not at all surprising, thus, that a heavily partisan and ideological literature soon emerged, attacking virtually any offshore activity. Foreign capital was especially frowned upon.[28]

It was Gordon Lewis who put the criticism of the tourist industry in starkest terms when he claimed that "no country could for long escape the moral consequence of a flourishing tourist program." He seemed to speak for a whole generation of radical thinkers when he asserted that those moral consequences had been seen in the "cultural pauperization of Havana."[29]

Whatever the ideological predilections of the early leadership, there was no stopping the growth of an industry that had two fundamental dynamic sources: (1) the rising income and leisure time of the American population, and (2) the lackluster performance and prospects of the—until then—major employer, agriculture. Each and every Caribbean island was presented with a Hobson's choice: develop tourism or be left at the station. Each island tells its own story of its tourist industry, its promises, and its vulnerabilities. There are, however, certain regionwide trends that can be generalized into a categorical statement: Caribbean export–agriculture is on its last legs, and tourism is a major alternative. In Jamaica, for instance, sugar exports went from 330,000 tons in 1968 to 110,000 tons in 1985. Tourist arrivals during that period went from 90,000 to 600,000.[30]

In 1998 the insular Caribbean received 11.9 million tourists. If Cancun and Cozumel in Mexico (both members of the Caribbean Tourist Organization) are included, the figure is 15.3 million. The main destination was the Dominican Republic (2.3 million), followed by Cuba (1.4 million) and Puerto Rico (1.2 million). At the present rate of growth of 4.6% per year, it was expected that the region would receive 28.4 million visitors in 2010.[31]

The growth in tourist arrivals was explosive until the U.S. went into recession in 1974. When the U.S. economy recovered and Americans began to travel again, Jamaica was largely bypassed. Between 1975 and 1977, arrivals fell by 33%. This was the period of intense and violent political and ideological confrontations on the island. Growth did not renew until the end of those battles in 1980 with the defeat of Michael Manley's experiment in socialism. By 1985 tourism was Jamaica's largest earner of gross foreign exchange, followed by mining and other merchandise exports. With 90% of the rooms Jamaican-owned, by the early 1990s tourism was the sector with the most linkages to other sectors such as agriculture (including manufacturing), construction, and services.[32]

Seventy percent of the tourists came from the U.S., and throughout the 1990s, this kept Jamaica among the top five Caribbean destinations. Its rate of growth, however, had been reduced to 1.9% per year. Jamaicans were candid about the reasons:[33]

1. The negative impact of media publicity about violence and mass demonstrations
2. Harassment, including violence against tourists
3. Weak road and port infrastructural investments
4. Maturity of the Jamaican product and the inability to compete with other lower priced destinations offering a more attractive product

The term "maturity" in this industry indicates that a particular destination is not offering a more diversified tourism product compared to other areas, especially for American tourists. Maturity seemed to characterize much of the region's offerings, forcing it to play "catch-up" to competitors such as the cruise industry.[34] A clear example of how this has worked in the Caribbean is offered by the case of the Dominican Republic, perhaps the latest to come to the trade.

As late as 1985, the Dominican Republic had a mere 5,000 rooms, virtually all located in the capital city. By 2001, the country had 50,000 rooms. The expansion has especially been explosive on the northeast coast, the Punta Cana–Bavaro Beach stretch. Two developments will illustrate the changing nature of the product. First, the Punta Cana Resort and Club with 20,000 rooms, is a low-density resort (no more than four stories per building and 15 rooms per acre) that appeals to ecotourists and nature lovers. It has its own airport, a championship golf course designed by P.B. Dye, and a 100-slip marina. American arrivals have gone from 4,600 in 1996 to 206,000 in 2001, despite the major dip after September 2001.

Not surprisingly, new developments are in the works; the $3 billion, 30,000-acre Cap Cana resort that sports three Jack Nicklaus golf courses, and Jamaican Butch Stewart's Sandals resort, served by his Air Jamaica.[35] It is worth noting that one of the special features of developments such as

Punta Cana–Bavaro Beach is its isolation from major cities and the capital city in particular. In an industry notoriously prickly about any and all forms of disturbance, from riots and blackouts to harassment by the "homeless," geographical isolation goes one-up on the walled "all-inclusive" that Jamaicans pioneered.

However, the very small size of most islands makes it virtually impossible for such an escape from urban contact. It is this sensitivity to a range of factors that best illustrates the vulnerability of the industry. Two types of vulnerability and their causes are evident. First, there is the unexpected event whose fallout none of the islands can either anticipate or, indeed, prepare for. Given the overwhelming presence of the U.S. in this area, it is fundamentally the events in the U.S. that make the islands vulnerable. The periodic economic recessions are one such event. Another type of event, mercifully rare, is represented by the terrorist attack of September 11, 2001, in New York City and Washington, D.C.

The other type of vulnerability is domestic: a negative image, reports of social disturbances, violence, and theft. In July 2002, several cruise lines decided to stop sailing to St. Croix, U.S. Virgin Islands, expressing concern over local crime.[36] This is particularly bad news because the competition for the cruise business is the hottest competition in the region. Although cruise ships have long plied the seas, the advent of the modern age of mass cruising is relatively new. According to two industry experts, ever since the maiden voyage of the cruise ship Sunward from Miami, FL, in December 1966, the cruise has become no longer just a fancy way to get to an exotic destination; it is an exotic experience all in its own.[37]

Three factors in particular explain the explosive growth of cruise line tourism in the Caribbean:

1. Favorable images emanating from a number of nonadvertising sources: typical was the TV series "Love Boat." These images made cruising appear grand, glamorous, and safe. There are no comparable images on U.S. TV about land-based tourist destinations.
2. A sense of having visited several foreign destinations within a short period of time.
3. The very favorable cost comparisons with land-based tourism. In their authoritative 1997 book, *Selling The Sea,* Dickinson and Vladimir price median cruise and land-based hotel costs at an even $204 per day.

Even George Ritzer, the widely read postmodernist critic of new forms of mass entertainment and consumption, has to admit that among the "cathedrals of consumption," the cruise ship " . . . offers the expanse of the sea and the beauty of tropical islands and also hotel-like facilities, a casino, a mall, a health spa, . . . etc., etc."[38] Not surprisingly, cruise liner passengers in the Caribbean grew from 3.6 million in 1990 to 6.14 million in 2000. Dickinson and Vladimir believe that it will grow at 8% per year.

Several consequences have flowed from this success. First, Miami has displaced New York as the cruise ship capital of the U.S., and indeed, the world. The three leading cruise lines—Carnival, Royal Caribbean, and Princess—are based in Miami, although all fly foreign flags. In other words, the cruise line industry is another of the offshore industries that we will later analyze. Second, the glamour and growth of this segment of the industry had begun to make most land-based settings seem dated, even stodgy.

Land-based tourism is especially dependent on air transportation. Regional carriers such as Air Jamaica, BWIA, and LIAT serve the islands at a considerable loss each year. This is done as a matter of regional solidarity. Enter American Airlines, connecting the islands to their main market, the U.S. By 1995 that airline had 70% of market share in the region, operating out of two hubs, Miami and San Juan, Puerto Rico. In April 1998, American Airlines decided to cut 12 of its daily major jet routes in the islands. They would be replaced with planes from its commuter airline, American Eagle. American Airlines was losing money on its Caribbean runs. Without constraints such as regional solidarity, American Airlines approached its restructuring as strictly business. As Larry Rohter of *The New York Times* put it, the airline was unapologetic: "The airline, currently enjoying near-record earnings, says that all of its routes must be profitable all of the time and rejects the idea that any civic obligation it may have takes precedence over its responsibility to stockholders."[39] The region, from Puerto Rico down through the chain of islands, was said to be in an "uproar."[40]

The potentially disastrous results to the islands' tourist industry was avoided when the various governments each agreed to pay American Airlines a US $1.5 million subsidy per year. The new realities of the changed rules of the economic game hit the island governments in the two places where it hurt most: their pocketbooks and their pride. "We have no choice, but to accede to American Airlines," lamented Grenada's Prime Minister, Keith Mitchell.[41]

The islands' battle with the cruise line industry over a tax to assist in harbor cleaning was not as perilous. Tourists arriving by these liners spend only one ninth of the amount spent by those arriving by air. Nevertheless, with one company, Carnival of Miami, taking the lion's share of the market and threatening to move its assets elsewhere, the sense of vulnerability of the region was obvious, although not despairing.

Although the actions of American Airlines or Carnival were the actions of private companies, the unwillingness of the U.S. government to exercise a moderating influence on them describes the changed nature of economic relations as well as the growing resentment against the U.S. Be that as it may, there is a positive side to this hardcore competition: local airlines have had to shape up, and by 2001, appeared to have been given yet another chance to move out of the red. A case in point is Air Jamaica, which was privatized and is becoming increasingly active. Using Montego Bay as its hub, it expanded its service to Los Angeles, Houston, and to several destinations in Europe. In recognition of the very large Jamaican community in Broward County, FL, Air Jamaica began four flights a day out of Fort Lauderdale-Hollywood International Airport.

With most of the tourist facilities in local, private hands, the tourist industry is shaping up. Yet it remains vulnerable to external shocks, be they acts of terrorism, financial downturns, the money problems of major U.S. airlines, and negative domestic conditions, particularly crime, which will be more fully analyzed in Chapter 6.

4.2 Integrating Globally: Caribbean Export Processing Zones and Multinationals

The Caribbean certainly has its share of "antiglobalists" and critics of anything that can fit under the rubric of "neoliberalism." However, as already described, the Caribbean also has a significant number of observers who are keenly aware of the relationship between size and vulnerability. They will note, for instance, that even after three decades of negotiations and treaties, intra-CARICOM trade still represents only 16% of total exports, and that 89% of these are fuels, lubricants, and chemicals exported by one member, the oil- and gas-rich Trinidad and Tobago. The imperative for looking "out" for globalization is clear.

In 1983 under President Ronald Reagan, the U.S. enacted the Caribbean Basin Economic Recovery Act (CBERA), better known as the Caribbean Basin Initiative (CBI). It was a clear case of attempting to stem the inroads being made by Cuba and other Marxist forces in the region. The success of this U.S. initiative to allow many products duty-free access to U.S. markets varies greatly among the 24 countries involved. Generally speaking, it was a positive element.

In the post–Cold War era, the concern in the islands was no longer the "red menace"; it was the NAFTA menace. The trade playing field was simply not level as Mexico enjoyed greater duty-free and quota-free advantages besides the advantages of lower wages and geographical proximity. The Caribbean lobbied hard to secure parity with the Mexicans. In 1989, the Caribbean spent $86.5 million on lobbying in Washington compared to $45 million by the whole of South America and $19.5 million spent by Mexico and Central America.[42]

When the Clinton administration announced on October 2, 2000, that it was signing the Caribbean Trade Partnership Act (also known as the NAFTA Parity Act), it meant the culmination of a long lobbying effort on the part of Caribbean countries. Most of the countries (Cuba, Suriname, and the French DOMs excluded) would now be able to export to the U.S. on terms equal to those operating under NAFTA.

A review of the history of U.S. trading policies with the Caribbean is revealing. The expectation was that with the new quota-free and duty-free benefits, the 24 beneficiary islands would attract new foreign direct investment (FDI). The main goal was gaining jobs. Events did not quite work out that way, however. Although there certainly were savings among American apparel and footwear importers, there was very little new investment in the islands. Production was increased in the existing plants. "They're saving money off the existing operations, but I don't see significant investment," a source told Manchester Trade Ltd. Two causes were cited:

1. Asian currency devaluation made investments there more attractive. It was cheaper to import from Asia and pay the duties than to shift production to the Caribbean.
2. The uncertainties regarding the extremely complex rules of eligibility were made even more complicated by the authority granted to U.S. Customs to implement these rules.

Whatever the U.S. geopolitical reasons for expanding market preferences to Caribbean countries in the early 1980s, that move benefited both the U.S. and the Caribbean. The point was, however, that it benefited the U.S. more. By 1996, after 10 years of the Caribbean Basin Initiative (CBI), the Caribbean was in aggregate the tenth largest export market for the U.S. and one of the few regions of the world where U.S. exporters maintained trade surpluses. In 1995 trade had increased 160% over the 10-year period to reach $15.3 billion with a surplus favorable to the U.S. of $2.6 billion.[43] U.S. exports to the region nearly tripled from $5,942 million to $15,306 million while Caribbean exports to the U.S. doubled from $6,687 million to $12,673 million.

The explanation for this U.S. surplus was evident: the full integration of the Caribbean into the U.S. economic sphere. It was estimated that between 60 and 70 cents of each dollar spent by the U.S. in the Caribbean Basin was being spent back in the U.S., while for Asia the figure was only 10 cents of each dollar.

Be that as it may, the CBI did provide the Caribbean with access to a market, as well as development assistance, that it would otherwise not have had. For some countries, that meant significant job creation; for most, however, the number of jobs created were rather small. Articles 806.3 and

807 of the CBI provided for tariff reduction on goods produced in the U.S. that were sent outside and then returned to the country in a processed form. What the tariff fixes in these cases is the added value of the raw goods exported and processed outside. Article 806.3 refers to metal transformation. Article 807 applies to products exported ready-for-assembly. As long as these do not lose their physical identity, the added value is recognized. It is in this latter case that textile imports enter the U.S. from the Caribbean Economic Processing Zones (EPZs).

Two dramatic shifts in the U.S.–Caribbean economic relationship followed the collapse of the Cold War competition. First, U.S. aid and development assistance virtually dried up. With the exception of Belize, Guatemala, and especially Nicaragua, U.S. assistance to CBI countries declined by 36.5% between 1984 and 1992. The message was that in the future it was to be trade, not aid. The problem was that for the Caribbean, the trade part was being dealt a second blow by NAFTA.

One of the areas in which the CBI had stimulated job creation in places like Jamaica and the Dominican Republic was in the garment industry. In pre-NAFTA years, the Caribbean held its own with Mexico. The story after NAFTA was quite different. Before NAFTA (1991 to 1993), Mexico and the CBI countries' exports to the U.S. grew by about 23% per year. After NAFTA, Mexican exports grew by 50.2% in 1994, against the CBI's 15.7%. By 1995, Mexico's exports had grown by 61%, CBI's by only 20%.[44]

With the privileges under Lômé destined to disappear (the banana regime was the harbinger) and NAFTA shifting more and more trade to Mexico, the Caribbean had to change policy directions. One thrust was to put a new emphasis on the operation of EPZs, which had been in existence since the 1970s but were given considerable impetus by the CBI in 1983 and the later CBI II in 1990, which established their presence permanently.

The goals of the EPZs were straightforward enough: diversify and expand the economic lease, increase employment, and increase the foreign exchange earnings. In fact, the EPZ turned out to have another major benefit: it was particularly suited to be the engine of development during a period of transition for two aspects of the macroeconomic environment, domestic and foreign.

In 1980 the total volume of the Dominican economically active population (EAP) was 2.1 million people, out of which almost 24% were unemployed. The domestic manufacturing industry employed 10% of the labor force, the central government employed 11%, and the EPZs only employed 1% of the EAP, representing only 12% of the labor force occupied in the manufacturing industry.[45]

The Dominican labor market had transformed a great deal 10 years later. The EAP had increased by a million people to reach three million.

Unemployment was high at 23%, but the employment structure had been reshaped. Industrial employment had decreased to half compared to 1980, now representing only 5% of the EAP. The central government employed 6% of the EAP, which meant a decrease of 4% compared to 1980. Only employment in the EPZs had increased, now at 4.4% of the EAP, representing 93% of the labor force employed in manufacturing activities.

The EPZs may be the best example of the new conditions imposed by the global market, illustrating the dimensions of its effects in the underdeveloped economies of the Caribbean. In fact, the EPZs are economic enclaves that allow execution of the politics of free trade and export promotion without the need for serious transformation in the fiscal structure and economic protectionism in the rest of the domestic economy. It was precisely this removal from the highly centralized and bureaucratized national economies that attracted investors. Even though the majority of the investors are of foreign origin, it has also attracted, at least in the Caribbean, an increasingly significant sector of local business investors.[46]

To the extent that an EPZ is designated by national legislation to be a specific geographical area governed by special customs and tax controls producing for export, the whole Caribbean has EPZs. Their impact on economic policy has everywhere gone beyond the assigned geographical zone. Among the CARICOM states, Antigua/Barbuda, Belize, Jamaica, St. Lucia, and Trinidad and Tobago have them. Outside CARICOM all the islands have EPZs.

As in so many other areas, the success and impact has varied from island to island and despite all the talk of regionalization, there is, as of 2002, no harmonization of legislative frameworks of the EPZs in the region.

In 2000 Jamaica had three EPZs with modest foreign exchange earnings: $15 million. Trinidad has had a more robust performance in warehousing, manufacturing, transshipping, and international trading. The Trinidad and Tobago EPZs employ over 3,000 people and have attracted much local investment.[47]

Not every EPZ is a manufacturing entity. In Antigua, for example, the EPZs are still limited to virtual casino and sports wagering, with mostly U.S. clients. They employ some 350 people but their future has to be considered uncertain, given the general antioffshoring mood in the U.S.

The Caribbean country that has clearly benefited the most from the EPZ strategy is the Dominican Republic. The reader will recall that an urban uprising in 1965 led to a full-scale U.S. intervention. This dramatic event hardly seemed to figure in U.S.–Dominican relations 10 years later. Nothing, up to the 1980s, would have predicted this dynamic growth. Dominican governments, from Rafael Trujillo through the five terms of Joaquin Balaguer, were statist to an extreme. Large government bureaucracies depended on import duties for their income and protected local, quasi-monopolistic economic sectors with tariffs and a complex array of nontariff barriers such as licensing and consular approvals. In the Dominican Republic, as elsewhere, the EPZ was the appropriate vehicle for avoiding these statist controls.

The EPZ strategy was begun by Law 299 of Incentive and Industrial Development.[48] Between 1969 and 1987, what were then called "industrial parks" reached three in number with 199 firms employing 66,000 workers. It was in 1988 that the renamed EPZs began to hit their stride. By 1995, there were 33 industrial parks spread throughout the country, with 469 firms employing 165,571 workers.

By 1992 the EPZs in the Dominican Republic were concentrated in textile production (61.3%), shoes (9.3%), jewelry (5.2%), and electric equipment production (4.5%), with the remaining 20% distributed in diverse categories such as the fabrication of cigars and leather manufacturing.

The main EPZ firms in the Dominican Republic are of American origin, as is, of course, their main market. By 1995 the South Korean firms contributed the greater investment volume, again targeting the U.S. market. That year, whereas the U.S. concentrated 38.1% of its foreign investment in the EPZs with a total volume of $938.5 million, South Korean firms' investment represented 50.3%, the European investment was 4.8%, and the Canadian investment accounted for the remaining 6.8%.[49] By 1999 there were 74 EPZs operating with a cumulative investment of $760 million, of which 80% was foreign (two thirds was U.S. capital).[50] Several factors explain the phenomenal growth in Dominican EPZs. First are the low wages, comparatively speaking. In 1975 the per-hour salary paid in the Dominican EPZs was $0.44, whereas in the U.S. it was $6.36. This meant that the American salary per hour was 14.4 times higher than the Dominican; i.e., the Dominican salary per hour represented only 6.9% of the American salary. In 1990 the Dominican salary per hour had only increased by 24%, representing $0.56 per hour. In turn, that same year the American salary increased by 77%. In this new context, the Dominican salary had moved farther away from the American salary; in 1990 the American salary was 25.3 times the Dominican salary. During the 1990s the Dominican salary improved but still maintained a significant distance compared to the American salary. Dominican salaries increased to $0.92 according to the Economic Commission for Latin America and the Caribbean[51] (ECLAC), to $0.56 in 1990, according to *The Economist,* and to $1.61 per hour in 1995. This represented a relative increase of 54.7%. However, according to ECLAC, in this same period the American salary increased from $6.56 to $9.62.[52]

The second key aspect in the development of the EPZs in the Dominican Republic has been the fiscal and legal benefits. Law 299 mentioned above granted practically a 100% exemption from income tax or utility taxes for a 10-year extendable grace period to firms that produced for the external market. This exemption was calculated to encourage the creation or growth of employment. Subsequently, Law 69 (1979), and Law 8-90 (1990), authorized access to local-market foreign exchange for manufacturers and exporters. In addition, the exchange regime imposed after the beginning of reforms or structural adjustments in the 1990s favored EPZs manufacturing exports and improved profitability. In particular, this was due to salary reductions followed by the devaluation of the Dominican currency. Not surprisingly, it was after those years that the main EPZ firms dedicated to textiles developed. To all these legal and fiscal benefits are added the infrastructure facilities, the geographic proximity to the U.S., and the lower cost of transportation.[53]

As we can see, the EPZs had, overall, a clear positive impact on direct employment creation, export increase, and foreign currency generation. The distribution of industrial parks throughout the country that hosted the EPZs has had a positive impact because there is a corresponding redistribution of employment in the geographic zones of the underprivileged. By 1995, according to the National Council of EPZs, out of a total of 469 firms, 25.4% were located near Santo Domingo, concentrating in that area 29.2% of total EPZ employment. Of the rest, 38.6% of the firms, with 36.5% of EPZ employment, were located in the northern part of the country. The same can be said for the southern part of the country, traditionally poor and backward, where 10.8% of the EPZ firms were concentrated, with 7% of total employment. In the eastern part of the country, traditionally a sugar production and livestock region, 25.5% of the EPZ firms generated 26.6% of the total employment. It was the northeast region that was least favored by the significant growth of EPZs; it had only 2% of the firms (10 in total) generating 1.5% of the total employment. By the year 2000, the EPZs employed 170,000 people compared to the 244,000 employed by the government in all its state agencies and autonomous corporations.

By 1994, the Dominican export structure had been totally reorganized. First, its volume had increased to $2,042.8 million, representing an increase of 44% compared to 1981. Second, the export of sugar had practically disappeared as a hard-currency earner, at only 4% of the total. Now the general export structure depended primarily on the EPZs, which contributed 69.3% of the total volume (with $450 million) of the foreign currency generation.

The EPZs have become, along with tourism, the main axis of the Dominican service-exporting economy and the focal point of the new service-export development model.

Quite obviously, the Dominican Republic had made great strides within the arrangements made by the U.S., and not surprisingly, its textile export trade is directed mainly to the U.S. with the greatest growth between 1980 to 1995, according to the Dominican Republic's Office of Foreign Affairs. The ten main Dominican export products, which in 1980 amounted to 44% of total exports, represented 73% by 1995. Of these, the garment production for men and children moved from 1.1% in 1980 to 17.4% in 1995. Likewise, lingerie and fabrics increased from 4.65% to 12.55%. By the year 2000, the Dominican Republic had become the fourth largest exporter of clothing to the U.S. after China, Hong Kong, and Mexico. At the same time, the island had become the sixth largest market for U.S. goods in the hemisphere. Only the much larger nations of Brazil, Venezuela, Argentina, and Colombia imported more U.S. merchandise.

Among the advantages the Dominican Republic had over its neighbor Haiti, political stability has to be ranked very high. In the early 1980s both halves of the Island of Hispañola exported the same amount of textiles. By 1998 the Dominican Republic was exporting 36 times more than Haiti.[54] This, however, was not the only advantage. Indeed, as Table 4.2 shows, were it not for the low score on the variable "Investor's Language Capability (English)," the Dominican Republic would score at a par with Barbados in terms of attractiveness for foreign investments. In terms of free trade zone incentives, only Jamaica equaled the Dominican Republic. By the end of the millennium, however, the NAFTA factor began affecting Dominican exports of textiles to the U.S. Whereas Dominican exports to the U.S. grew by only 1% in 1996, Mexican exports grew by 42% that year. The figures were similar for subsequent years.

It is not totally evident what the Caribbean Parity Act will do to level the playing field a bit, but clearly the years of the CBI and CBI II left a legacy. First, it compelled a reevaluation of the nation's infrastructure. If at one time the Dominican state was prone to building state housing, parks, monuments, museums, and showy highways, by the end of the millennium the emphasis was on roads toward new seaports, airports, and tourist locations and telecommunication facilities. The latter is especially critical if the country is to compete in the new age of informatics and services such as "800" call centers, business data processing, software processing, and, in general, information accessing for technological change.

In the Dominican case, it is clear that the business-sector component of the integrationist strategy is critically important. This is true because it is the business class that leads the integrationist action, based on the agreements established between the states, and also because it is they who have become the strategic agents most interested in this effort. The going has not been easy. In the Dominican Republic—as in the rest of the region—the greatest

Table 4.2 Comparative Attractiveness of Investment Locations

Caribbean and Competing Asian Investment Locations

Assessment Factors	Barbados	Antigua and Barbuda	Dominican Republic	Grenada	Jamaica	St. Kitts and Nevis	St. Vincent	Trinidad and Tobago	S.E. Asia	East Asia	Singapore
Market Access to U.S./EEC	1	1	1	1	1	1	1	1	3	3	2
Political Stability	1	1	2	3	3	1	1	3	2	2	1
Ambiance Security	1	1	2	1	3	1	1	3	2	3	1
Domestic Infrastructure (Utilities)	1	2	2	2	2	1	2	1	2	2	1
International Transport links	2	2	1	2	2	2	3	1	1	1	1
Investment Incentives	2	2	2	2	2	2	2	2	2	2	1
Freezone Incentives	3	3	1	3	1	3	3	3	1	1	1
Investors' Language Compatibility (English)	1	1	3	1	1	1	1	1	2	3	1
TOTAL SCORE	12	13	14	15	15	12	15	15	15	17	9

Note: 1—very good, 2—good, 3—not good; rankings based on professional judgments and perception of investor opinion.
Source: Mathew Stamp PLC; Extracted from *Comprehensive Review of CARICOM Investment Climate.*

resistance to integrationist efforts comes from the monopolistic faction of the business sector. Still-powerful remnants continue to exist from the period of import-substitution. The battle for viability of the export-oriented sector is invariably as political as it is economic. Part of what is forcing a retreat of the traditional protectionist forces is the emergence of a much more dynamic private sector in the region.

Although it is true that the vast majority of capital flows into the Caribbean have been, and still are, from outside the region, there has also been a significant growth in native Caribbean capital movements. The movement to locate operations across the region has been a spontaneous development within the area's private sectors. It suggests, says the CARICOM secretariat, the development of an increasing entrepreneurial capability on the part of investors emanating from the region.[55] In other words, they are true Caribbean transnational corporations. Again, there are significant differences between Caribbean countries—differences not readily explained by the differences in size.

The growth of the Barbados private sector and its cross-border expansions is arguably the most remarkable case in the region. Given its small population size (230,000) and its historical dependence centered on its sugar industry, Barbados' successes have been many. Of the companies listed on the Caribbean stock exchange, 8 of the 22 in Barbados had cross-border operations; 5 out of 45 in Jamaica, and 10 out of 28 in Trinidad and Tobago. Jamaica, which has 38 of the top 100 companies in the Caribbean, seems to be lagging in cross-border investments. Now ranked number one in cross-border operations, the Barbadian firm Goddard Enterprises has gone from its original meat and grocery store business (established in 1921) to operating in 15 countries. The secret of this family-owned and administered conglomerate has been to stick to what it knows best: supermarket operations and food catering. Its "flight kitchens" serve airlines throughout the Caribbean and Latin America. Its two ventures outside this niche have been in manufacturing insecticides and other household products in the U.K. and in shrimp processing for the U.S. market.

One should not overstate the vigor of this private-sector awakening, however. It is still a very small segment of the Caribbean's overall economic scene. Judging by the increase in the number of listings on the three stock exchanges in the region between 1990 and 2000, Jamaican listings went from 44 to 45, Trinidad and Tobago's from 30 to 28. Only Barbados showed significant growth in publicly traded companies—from 14 to 22.

The cross-border forays of these native multinationals are largely into CARICOM countries, sharing a language, a British legal system, and very often, personal acquaintances. Their major operations and profile are still fundamentally domestic. For instance, Trinidad's Ansa McAl's (9th largest) overseas profits (before taxation) were only 8.28% of its total in 1997 to 1998, and Royal Bank of Trinidad and Tobago (4th largest) has only 16% of its total staff outside its Trinidad and Tobago base. The comfort of the known is very strong.

If this is true of Trinidad, it is even more true of Jamaica where businesses have long depended on government protection and contracts, and where the experience with private development banking has not been a happy one. After a phenomenal growth spurt between 1980 and 1995 when total assets went from J$2.5 billion to J$192.6 billion, the entire sector collapsed after the mid-1990s. The government had to intervene in order to protect the 1.5 million depositors. By 1997, the Financial Sector Adjustment Company (FINSAC) owned or controlled all the domestic banks, except the smallest, and approximately 90% of the life insurance industry. According to one banker who lost his own investment bank during this period, part of the problem was that the private sector could not get clear and transparent information from the government about the general direction of the economy. "The concept of a favorable investment climate," wrote this banker, "is a very complex one, and the formulation of favorable policies, including legal incentive to invest, may not be sufficient to encourage investment."[56]

This banker represents one school of thought on the post–Cold War shift towards greater private sector participation in the Caribbean; it has not gone far enough to create a favorable investment climate outside the EPZs. The argument is that the whole economy ought to operate as if it were an EPZ and that neoliberal reforms cannot be limited to such geographically isolated enclaves. This is the criticism of those who favor free enterprise and capitalist competition. Not everyone does.

Certainly, as we have noted, the political climate everywhere in the Caribbean has given a new hearing to the free-enterprise school of thought. Even so, criticisms of the neoliberal model have not been stilled. There are two fundamental dimensions to this criticism. There is the by-now traditional critique of those who argue that global integration is premised on paying low wages, exploiting bad working conditions, and engaging in harmful environmental practices with impunity. Customary criticisms about the distorting effects on "penetrated" cultural systems continue to be heard.[57]

There is another critical approach that is less concerned with ideological, cultural, and political sensitivities and more with the longer-term consequences to the structure of these small economies. Central to this is the concern with the islands' phenomenal dependence on external funds to finance development projects and sustain economic growth. Trinidad economist and private sector consultant Mary King is none too sanguine about the future of entrepreneurship on her island, the richest of the

Table 4.3 FDI Stock as a Percentage of GDP in CARICOM

CARICOM Countries	1980	1985	1990	1995	1997
Antigua and Barbuda	20.9	46.5	73.8	88.5	94.5
Bahamas	22.3	12.7	10.7	14.2	26.0
Barbados	12.2	10.3	9.7	13.0	11.6
Belize	6.4	5.0	17.7	25.0	28.3
Dominica	—	5.7	38.8	84.6	102.8
Grenada	1.7	10.9	34.7	60.7	74.6
Guyana	—	—	—	—	—
Jamaica	18.7	22.7	16.3	29.9	33.1
St. Kitts	2.1	40.5	100.4	108.1	118.3
St. Lucia	70.1	90.7	78.9	91.7	106.4
St. Vincent	2.0	7.5	24.3	70.8	92.9
Suriname	—	—	—	—	—
Trinidad and Tobago	15.7	23.7	41.3	68.3	84.4
Latin America and the Caribbean	6.4	10.5	10.1	15.1	17.2
Developing countries	5.9	9.8	10.5	14.1	16.6

Source: UNCTAD, *World Investment Report,* 1999, reprinted in CARICOM Secretariat, Caribbean Trade and Investment Report, 2000; Kingston: Ian Randle Publishers, 2000, p. 215.

independent English-speaking islands. The dependence on foreign capital and technology and the current poor capital market, with little, if any, venture capital, contribute to the deformity of the economy and economic vulnerability. "This," she says, "is also a result of the low-risk culture of local investors who prefer to invest in the 'sure' things: banks, food production, diapers, and the like."[58] There is, she concludes, no confidence in indigenous abilities to innovate.

Table 4.3 shows just how important foreign direct investment is (as a proportion of GDP) in the CARICOM states. It certainly is much higher than it is in Latin America and other developing countries.

Such a high degree of dependence, say the critics, increases the vulnerability of these societies to the short- and medium-term ups-and-downs that characterize the global economy. In addition, it is foreign capital that is making the investment decisions, not the optimal context for local decisions of modernizing both the labor force and the production plant. As plausible as this critique is, the fundamental problem at the turn of the millennium is that a critique is not a development plan.

Although the Caribbean has produced some stellar critiques of neoliberal approaches, it has produced a scant few policy alternatives to neoliberalism— at least not ones with proven track records in the region or elsewhere. It is this reality that has the whole region, with the exception of Cuba, singing from the same neoliberal development hymnal.

It is interesting that Caribbean intellectuals seldom probe the public's attitude toward foreign economic participation. The available data suggest a much more favorable attitude than what is usually portrayed by those who equate sovereignty with economic nationalism. In 1986 Dominican pollster Bernardo Vega asked whether foreign investments should be encouraged. The poll results were 42% in favor, 16% against, and 42% had no opinion.[59] When given a specific sector such as tourism, 68% believed it to be beneficial and 21% harmful. In Jamaica, at the height of the Michael Manley rhetoric about socialist change, Carl Stone's polls were showing only a little support for communism and only lukewarm support for democratic socialism, as Table 4.4 shows.

Again, in the midst of the massive financial crisis of the late 1990s, a poll by *The Jamaican Observer* revealed the following answers to the question, "Should Jamaica seek outside help in this crisis?" The results: 71.4% said yes, seek outside help, 16.8% said no, the government can handle it, and 11.8% said they did not believe it makes any difference.[60]

There are reasons to believe, therefore, that when confronting the economic challenges of globalization, the people of these small Caribbean nations are not adverse to outside assistance. This is good to know as we probe the noneconomic threats that these nations face.

Before turning to issues such as crime, however, it is critical that note be taken of one of the very serious threats to a whole array of vital areas of Caribbean life: the tragic rise in HIV-AIDS infections. The Caribbean's adult prevalence rate is 1.96%, second only to sub-Sahara Africa's 8%. Fully 64% of the cases in the Caribbean are heterosexually transmitted. In

Table 4.4 Ideological Preferences, Jamaica, 1978—Poll Results (%)

Social Class	Support for Ideological Principles (February 6, 1978)			Views on Increasing Government Ownership (January 30, 1978)	
	Capitalism	Democratic Socialism	Communism	Support	Oppose
Kingston middle class	45	25	3	27	73
Kingston working class	20	38	14	48	52
Small farmers	4	33	2	21	79

Note: Percentages are of those with views on these ideologies.
Sources: Dr. Carl Stone Poll, *The Weekly Gleaner*, February 6, 1978, p. 1; and Dr. Carl Stone Poll, *The Weekly Gleaner*, January 30, 1978, p. 1.

stark human terms, it is estimated that 500,000 Caribbean people are infected with HIV, broken down as follows:[61]

CARICOM countries	136,000
Dominican Republic	141,000
Haiti	250,000
Cuba	2,500

This explains the welcome given to the U.S. government's commitment to a $15 billion Africa/Caribbean AIDS Program as well as to providing cheaper medications to combat this scourge.[62] Clearly, in a region with such large numbers of people on the move as tourists or immigrants, it behooves all involved to be proactive. It is the kind of case which demonstrates the point made in this book that the Caribbean is a region of ongoing complex interactions.

CHAPTER 5

Threats to Sovereignty

5.1 Small Players, Global Game: The Shifting Global Context of "Secrecy Havens"

5.1.1 Dimension of the Money Flow

The e-mail letter came from a bank, claiming to be a member of SWIFT, the Society for Worldwide Inter-Bank Financial Telecommunications. It, the bank explained, was an industry-owned cooperative supplying secure messaging services to over 7,000 financial institutions in 194 countries. Having established its *bona fides*, the bank promised to insure customers' financial interests through its ability to:

1. Receive transfers into your account in seconds
2. Send bank transfers anywhere in the world in seconds
3. Do these transactions in dollars, Euros, francs, and any other currency
4. Secure customers' international transactions

In other words, all banking would be done electronically and confidentially. No need to show your face or reveal your identity.

Now, this high-tech bank is not located in Switzerland, the Cayman Islands, or even the British Virgin Islands. It is located in Haiti, the most underdeveloped country in the Western Hemisphere. The key question is: Why would anyone put their money in Haiti when that island's own bourgeoisie is known for securing its money through capital flight? The ease, rapidity, and confidentiality of depositing and withdrawing monies—any type of monies—is the plausible answer.

Table 5.1 Tax Havens in the Caribbean

Anguilla	Dominica
Antigua	Grenada
Aruba	Montserrat
Bahamas	Netherlands Antilles
Barbados	Panama
Belize	Puerto Rico
Bermuda	St. Kitts/Nevis
British Virgin Islands	St. Lucia
Cayman Islands	St. Vincent/Grenadines
Costa Rica	Turks and Caicos

Source: A.P. Maingot, The Offshore Caribbean, in Anthony Payne and Paul Sutton (Eds.), *Modern Caribbean Politics.* (Baltimore: The Johns Hopkins University Press, 1993), pp. 259–276; Walter Diamond and Dorothy Diamond, *Tax Havens of the World* (New York: Matthew Bender Books, 1998).

To be sure, Haiti is not one of the 68 or so significant offshore centers (residence to some 4,000 offshore banks) which are estimated to hold somewhere in the vicinity of $5 trillion. Nor is Haiti known to be the residence of many of the some 100,000 international business corporations (IBCs) and trust companies owned just by U.S. entities and persons.[1] It is neither volume of transactions nor historical reputation which make the Haitian case remarkable. The significance lies in the ease with which any country can get into the international financial game with a high probability of securing a profit from at least part of the enormous sums that must be "parked" and "laundered" by the individuals who acquired them. This explains why, as Table 5.1 shows, virtually every island in the Caribbean (and elsewhere) has also gone into the offshore banking business.

This is, most definitely, not one business but rather a range of institutions and transactions which have been shifted offshore. There are those which absolutely depend on secrecy such as banking and finance companies, holding companies, international business companies (IBCs), and trusts.

Let us first deal with the clearly troublesome side of offshore. Hundreds of Websites as well as advertisements in travel magazines and newspapers make sure potential customers learn about their "fiscal paradises" or "secrecy havens." In just one issue of the highly respected *The Economist* (May 25, 2002) one finds seven major companies offering to open bank accounts and/or companies in some 45 offshore centers around the world. A review of their clients in Caribbean states (see Table 5.2) shows the following set of fees:

Table 5.2 Fees Charged Clients by Major Caribbean Offshore Centers

Country	Type of Company	License Fee US$	Incorporation Fee US$
Anguilla	IBC	230	750
Bahamas	IBC	350	750
Belize	IBC	100	500
Bermuda	Exempt	1,780	4,250
Cayman Islands	IBC	575	1,500
St. Vincent	IBC	100	795

There is usually a $125 fee for "postincorporation structuring." All insist on confidentiality and anonymity through numbered accounts, and on being tax free. A company in Switzerland states very assertively that "bank secrecy is not lifted for tax evasion." The only exceptions to bank secrecy are those acts which the Swiss Penal Code considers to be "serious crimes," viz., gun smuggling or drug trafficking. To those wanting to show business respectability, some offer "vintage" companies for immediate use: companies which have long been established but never used. Some offer "Belize Economic Citizenship" in their printed ads only to admit in their website that it has "recently" been suspended by the Belizean government. No matter, they can arrange economic citizenship in "other jurisdictions." All offer their faceless clients access to their monies through debit cards, ATM machines, and "secure" wire transfers.

It is hardly a mystery anymore where much of the money which sustains these secrecy havens comes from. Two dramatic cases raised the veil of secrecy, or as these banks call it, "confidentiality." The first was the investigation which unraveled Robert Vesco's $3 billion Ponzi scheme called Investors Overseas Services. Although a fugitive from U.S. law, Vesco was cordially received by one country after the other: Costa Rica, Bahamas, and finally Cuba. After the money he absconded with ran low, Vesco engaged in the drug trade and all other benefits which could be derived from corrupt governments in the Caribbean.

Even more important in revealing the dark side of offshore finances was the snaring of the largest rogue bank of modern times: the Bank of Credit and Commerce International (BCCI). In the face of indifference and lethargy on the part of U.S. supervisory agencies, it was the bulldog-like persistence and tenacity of Jack Blum of the U.S. Senate's Subcommittee on Terrorism, Narcotics, and International Operations who helped reveal BCCI's involvement in money laundering, arms trafficking, and corrupting regimes all over the world. It was this case which gave the critical push to Congress passing the Foreign Corrupt Practices Act.[2]

Asked whether the BCCI case was unique and unusual in the world of offshore banks, Blum was adamant that the difference was not of kind but of the size of the BCCI operation, including its control of three U.S. banks. "International organized crime and large-scale narcotics trafficking," says Blum, "depend on the banking services provided by the world of offshore banking and finance."[3] Blum was even more categorical in writing. "Today's offshore financial world is a 'Bermuda Triangle' for money launderers, financial fraud, and tax investigations."[4]

Within a decade, the flow of what is now called grey and black market money, seeking safe and anonymous financial havens, caught the attention of a select number of forensic investigators who had been given new weapons through three new laws introduced in 1970: the Racketeer Influenced and Corrupt Organization law (RICO); the Continuing Criminal Enterprise law (CCE), and the Bank Secrecy Act. What they all emphasized was that organized crime had cast a wide net to include legitimate businesses so that it had to be combated at all points of the enterprise.

It was not until 1986, however, that the U.S. Congress passed the Anti-Drug Abuse Act, which included a bill entitled the Money Laundering Control Act. Up to that point most prosecutions had been carried out under the fraud statutes of the Bank Secrecy Act. Ed Meese, President Ronald Reagan's Attorney General, had put the rationale for specific money laundering legislation as follows:

> *[Money laundering] is without question one of the biggest challenges facing law enforcement today. . . . Organized criminal groups, from drug trafficking rings to more traditional organized crime "families," could not operate as successfully as they now do without the means to launder money.*[5]

Calling it "the lifeblood of the drug syndicates and traditional organized crime," Meese believed that the new Act had finally given law enforcement agencies the tool they needed to attack money laundering. The link between the criminal drug trade flowing through the Caribbean and the presence of money laundering facilities there is in part explained by R. Thomas Naylor when he notes that "the ultimate objective of the criminal is to enjoy his gains, perhaps in a tropical haven, more likely within the same geographic milieu in which his criminal enterprise operates."[6]

The vast majority of the criminal cases identified in the criminal investigations of the Internal Revenue Service (IRS) in the late 1970s and early 1980s occurred in the Caribbean. Between 1978 and 1983 there were 464 such cases, of which 45% represented illegal transactions with legal income. Of the other 55%, illegal income was involved (161 cases of which dealt with the drug traffic). Of these, 29% involved the Cayman Islands, 28% involved Panama, 22% the Bahamas, and 22% the Netherlands Antilles. These four offshore sites alone accounted for 85% of the cases involving transactions with illegal income. The actual movement of large amounts of cash throughout the Caribbean made a mockery of official statistics on the nature of these economies, as well as giving the lie to their claim that they did not handle "dirty" money. On June 30, 1999, Anthony Maingot sent the following letter to *The New York Times* which was not published:

> On February 9, 1999, your paper reported that Gus Bevona, former president of local 32-B-32J of the Service Employees International Union, used a "bank" in the Cayman Islands to hold $123 million from a building contract you call "shrouded in mystery." Just a few days later, (2/14/99), you reported that there was "a mysterious" transfer of $1 million from something called the "World Aristocratic Academy" to the campaign of Yevgeny Nazdratenko for governor of the Primoreye region of Russia. The only known address for this "Academy" was a post office box in the Bahamas. From June 20 to 26, 1999, The New York Times ran three in-depth stories on Marin R. Frankel, who had absconded with hundreds of millions of dollars including the funds of the St. Francis of Assisi Foundation, located in the British Virgin Islands.

The crucial point is that with the disappearance of the Cold War and the U.S.'s declaration of a "War On Drugs," the indifference towards dirty money and its safe havens dissipated. By the end of the 1990s, even those international agencies which shied away from investigating offshore financial operations were actively investigating their noxious roles.[7]

The attention began to shift from outright criminally-derived monies to tax evasion and other schemes which would not be tolerated onshore.

In January 1997, the British Foreign Office, now under a Labour government, announced that it had given wider powers to the appointed governors in the Associated Territories of the Caribbean over legislation to counter money laundering.[8] Whatever domestic pressures accounted for the action, the fact is that the U.S. had threatened to sanction Britain and many of its dependencies in the Caribbean, considered havens for dirty money. The U.S., it was reported, had drawn up a "hit list" of people "at the highest levels of society and government."[9] Quite evidently, the many Brass Plate states in the world and in the Caribbean had been defined as threats to the U.S. national security. The reasons are not hard to find.

The top U.S. enforcement agency in the corporate world is the Securities and Exchange Commission (SEC). This makes its chairman, what *Fortune* magazine calls, the nation's "top earnings cop." In mid-1999 that top earnings cop declared war on what can only be called the "cooking" of the books, i.e., intentional misstatements in the financial reports of much of corporate America. "It's a basic cultural change we're asking for," he said, "nothing short of that."[10]

In 1999, *The London Observer* ran an in-depth series on the doings of Englishman Michael Ashcroft in Belize. At the time Ashcroft was treasurer of the British Conservative Party. It was his personal lawyer who drafted Belize's offshore legislation and his British Honduras International Corporation (BHIC) recalled the age of the banana republics. Ashcroft owned the following:

1. Belize's largest bank
2. 26% stake in the only telephone company
3. 20% stake in the only electrical company
4. 27% stake in the largest citrus company
5. 38% stake in Belize's only TV station
6. 90% ownership of the most important hotel
7. Joint ownership of the ship registry business with a firm in Panama

To Nick Cohen of *The Observer*, the election of Labour meant that Ashcroft no longer had the protection of the British government and could be exposed "for what he is."[11] As Cohen described Ashcroft, he was the creator of Belize's secretive banking sector, "a useful financial centre for rustbucket shipping tycoons and entrepreneurs in the booming nose candy futures market." According to Britain's International Transport Workers' Federation, the offshore registry which Ashcroft controlled was "the shabbiest, shoddiest, and most unscrupulous in the world."[12] According to *The Observer's* Cohen, the scandal of men like Ashcroft "is not that what they do is illegal, but that it isn't." Cohen should have specified that it is not illegal in the Brass Plate states. The point being that it is not only illegal in the countries whose laws and taxes they flout, but also increasingly perceived as a threat to their national security.

While this "war" of incomes was being waged, corporate America was having its way as far as taxes were concerned. Not only was Congress calling for further tax breaks for the corporations, the existing system provided enormous loopholes. According to the GAO, out of 2.3 million U.S. corporations, more than half paid no federal income taxes at all between 1989 and 1995.[13] The mechanism through which these corporations avoid paying taxes is described in the complaints of the chairman of the SEC. According to *The Wall Street Journal*,

> "They establish financial subsidies in tax havens. They indulge in tax shelters so complex government auditors can't always understand them. They shift profits to low-tax countries by manipulating prices when doing business with their own overseas branches."

While doing all this, they kept up a steady wailing about being overtaxed. Their armies of lobbyists made sure these complaints reached the right political ears. Meanwhile, the growth of overseas tax havens accelerated. It was a good deal for the tax-wise depositors and secrecy kept it a safe bet.

Only occasionally did authorities get to breach the wall of secrecy. On August 3, 1999, *The New York Times* reported what it called "an unprecedented insight" into banking in the Cayman Islands. This was achieved through the breaking of the encrypted code of a money laundering bank. Having penetrated the veil of secrecy, federal prosecutors felt that they had dealt the first serious setback to what one called, "one of the greatest allies of individuals committing crimes in this country." Originally established with the idea of handling European money, by the end of the 20th century 90% of Cayman Island customers were U.S. citizens. Interestingly enough, this particular bank first ran into trouble when it refused to pay a $250,000 bribe to a Cayman Island bank regulator. The bank was closed and planned to move to the Bahamas when its president was arrested by U.S. agents. He gave up the records of 700 "shelf" (a/k/a Brass Plate) companies as part of the plea bargain. "The Caymans," said an FBI special agent optimistically, "is no longer the safe haven that they were, because we have gotten our nose in the tent and seen how it works." The history of offshore banking in the Caribbean does not warrant that optimism. It is true that state supervision has pushed up the cost of laundering money from 6% to 8% in the 1980s and to 20% in the 1990s. The weight of investigations and the risks of outright ostracism from the world's banking system led many offshore havens to attempt to stay clear of drug monies. However, as some secrecy havens are forced to clean up their act, other countries pick up the discarded business.

In June 2000, the Paris-based Financial Action Task Force on Money Laundering included the following Caribbean nations among its list of 15 "non-cooperative countries and territories": Bahamas, Cayman Islands, Dominica, Panama, St. Kitts–Nevis, St. Vincent and the Grenadines. In 2001, the FATF removed the Bahamas, Cayman Island, and Panama from the list, but added Guatemala and Grenada. By April 2002, the following offshore havens in the Caribbean were still considered "non-cooperative": Dominica, Grenada, St. Kitts–Nevis, St. Vincent, and the Grenadines.

On July 8, 2002, following the lead of the OECD's Financial Action Task Force, the U.S. dropped St. Kitts–Nevis from its money laundering list.[14] Already the advertising for new secrecy havens have made their appearance, promoting themselves with a rhetorical question:

> *Disillusioned with the recent changes in confidentiality laws in the most "former" well established offshore jurisdictions like Jersey, Guernsey, Isle of Man, Switzerland, British Virgin Islands, the Bahamas, Cayman Islands, Bermuda?*[15]

With an estimated 50% of the over $30 trillion dollar world economy being banked offshore with the IMF calculating that some $1.5 trillion of that is laundered money, with 75% of Citibank's profits generated from offshore sources, with a "Who's Who" of U.S. corporations incorporated offshore, and with $85 billion moving through the major exchanges in a single day, there is ample business left for secrecy havens.[16]

Two events have changed the global context of offshore financial centers: (1) the September 11, 2001, acts of terrorism and (2) the financial and accounting scandals (and bankruptcies) of some of the U.S.'s major corporations. These two events have reopened an old debate between advocates of more state regulation of business and those favoring greater deregulation. Although the debate is mainly an American one, those states in the Caribbean which have chosen the "offshore" development path are squarely in the sights of both sides of the debate.

Although scholars such as Theda Skocpol have written lucidly on this debate in U.S. history,[17] the debate has taken on a new urgency. Ira Katznelson frames this policy debate in terms of what he calls "a new strategic game."[18] Indeed, as the description in the various Websites cited above indicate, when it comes to tax avoidance, these offshore centers are operating in a moral and legal grey area. It is this fact which encourages newcomers such as the Caribbean to the field of secrecy and tax havens. In order to sort out the arguments coming from the various parties to the game on the mainland and in the islands, one should conceptualize the game as involving two key "actors:" the "State" which is interested in increasing its receipts from taxes and "Capital" which is interested in exactly the opposite outcome. We can hypothesize the following arguments for or against offshore havens:

Actor No. 1—"Capital"

1. It is neither illegal nor, given the U.S. capitalist tradition, unusual or unpatriotic to minimize the tax burden.
2. There is an asymmetrical situation in the global economic scene which places U.S. corporations at a disadvantage in both competition and retention of profits.
3. Too drastic measures will not only kill innovation but will lead to even more nefarious schemes which will hurt not just the U.S. Treasury but civil society (the "public interest").

Actor No. 2—"State"

1. That industry contravenes directly and unapologetically two of the critical sovereign prerogatives of the state: regulation of the economy and assessment and collection of taxes.
2. "Free riding" (i.e., letting others carry their full burden but avoiding yours) is unfair and deleterious in two ways: (a) it deprives the state of revenues which pay for the infrastructure on which the

capitalist system sustains itself, and (b) it undermines public confidence and the legitimacy of the tax system.

The fact is that Caribbean secrecy havens have benefitted from the persuasiveness of "Capital's" arguments. They have taken these arguments as their own *raison d'etre*. A composite of the Websites mentioned on page 90 would have to highlight the words "financial independence," "personal freedom," and "avoiding state oppression." Note the statement of philosophy of the Omnicorp Financial Group in St. Vincent:

> "We believe that authorities and governments have made basic rights difficult [through] oppressive taxation, over-regulation, invasion of privacy . . ."

What the terrorist act of September 11 did was to strengthen the State's argument that while the practice of tax avoidance might have its "rational" side, it cannot be justified in an "age of terrorism" for two reasons: (1) It deprives that state of the additional resources needed to combat terrorism, (2) It serves the terrorist networks.

The enactment of the Patriot Act of 2001 and the new money laundering legislation, passed by a 412 to 1 vote in the House, reflects the public's mood. That Act enhances the government's ability to carry out the three "F"s: find, freeze, and forfeit by mandating, among other items:[19]

1. Facilitating and sharing of financial information through "a highly secure communications network"
2. Keeping a central register of all banks in the U.S. and abroad
3. A ban on all correspondent accounts with "shell" banks (banks that have no physical offices anywhere)
4. Extending the definition of money laundering to legally-acquired funds which end up in terrorist organizations (so-called reverse money laundering schemes)

The U.S. action was nearly immediately emulated by the 31-member, Paris-based Financial Action Task Force on Money Laundering (FATF). In late 2001, for the first time, the FATF focused on the role of money laundering in supporting terrorism fund-raising generally.

It should come as no surprise that one of the first types of transactions the Paris-based FATF looked at was credit card fraud. For years the U.S. Internal Revenue Service (IRS) has known that perhaps two million U.S. citizens hold credit cards issued by offshore banks. Lack of funds and authority prevented much investigation. Of the 1,500 cases in just the Cayman Islands, which the IRS felt needed investigating, only 10 were eventually looked at.[20] With the Patriot Act's far-reaching authority, Master-Card alone has handed over the records of 230,000 credit card accounts issued by offshore banks. Visa and American Express are said to be complying. After an investigation which began but went nowhere in September 2000, finally in May 2002, an FBI sting of the British Trade and Commerce Bank of Dominica (BTCBD) led to its pleading guilty to money laundering. BTCBD had accepted receipt of $250,000 through credit cards from a client in Grenada. Not surprisingly, both Dominica and Grenada are still listed by the FATF as Non-Cooperative Countries.

The State's case was also strengthened when the major Fortune 500 company Enron filed for bankruptcy in December 2001. Public disgust and indignation followed the revelation that while thousands of employees and investors were losing their life earnings, top Enron executives were receiving hundreds of millions of dollars in bonuses and had used "insider trading" advantages to sell their stock before the collapse.

What is evident in the Enron case is the role played by offshore centers, especially those in the Caribbean, to help that company do two things: (1) avoid taxes, and (2) disguise its rapid rise in debt, and, thus, insure its stock's continued standing in the market. While certainly not the key players in the whole affair, it is evident that by creating nearly 900 subsidiaries ("sham" or "shell" companies in the accepted parlance), Enron not only wiped out any U.S. income taxes but it, in fact, got tax refunds over 2 years. These are the Enron subsidiaries incorporated as of December 31, 2000:[21] Cayman Island, 692; Mauritius, 43; Bermuda, 8; Barbados, 8; Puerto Rico, 4; Hong Kong, 2; Panama, 2; Aruba, 1; British Virgin Island, 1; Guam, 1; Guernsey, 1; and Singapore, 1.

The way the standard scheme works is relatively simple:

Step 1— The U.S.-based company transfers the taxable profit to a newly created partnership with a foreign company registered in a tax haven.

Step 2— The foreign company returns the same amount to the U.S. company in a way no longer taxable as profit in the U.S.

Some of these Enron offshore arrangements have resulted in criminal prosecutions which, in the words of *The New York Times*, were more akin to those used in drug cases than in white collar ones.[22] The *Times* was referring to a scheme involving a total of 3,000 "off-the-books" partnerships which engaged in "circular trades," "financial swaps," and "structured financing"—all designed to cover real debts and profit top executives.[23] The criminal complaint paints a portrait of a group of financiers desperately working to deceive their employers to obtain huge profits for themselves. It is laced with details of secret meetings in the Cayman Islands, conspiratorial e-mail messages, and deceptive communications from both the bankers and Enron executives.

If these types of secret offshore arrangements appeared doomed by OECD and U.S. pressures, this was not the case with the "Bermuda strategy" of registering Foreign Sales Corporations (FSCs). This was a legal arrangement in the U.S., established by a tax treaty. The Bermuda case deserves scrutiny.

A traditional up-scale tourist destination and headquarters to most of the world's captive insurance and reinsurance companies, Bermuda's fortunes (and economic policies) began to change in the 1990s. Hong Kong's eventual reversion to China led to a massive flight of its corporations. Bermuda was a great beneficiary of this event. By 1997 nearly half the companies on the Hong Kong stock exchange established a legal presence in Bermuda.[24] By 1999, the *Times* could describe the island's booming insurance business and praise the absence of drug smuggling, money laundering, and other "fly-by-night schemes which have tarnished other so-called tax havens."[25] In 2001, Bermuda was the world's leading capital insurance center. It had 1,405 companies registered compared to 535 for the next largest, the Cayman Islands, and towering over two traditional centers, Vermont (with 527) and Guernsey (300).[26] Bermuda's real attraction, however, is that it made a categorical decision in favor of "capital," i.e., less regulation, promoting, and advertising its unencumbered *laissez-faire* regime of which low taxation was a major part.

To Caribbean leaders, the Bermuda type arrangement was one possible strategy to avoid the type of pressure coming from the OECD and its Financial Task Force "black lists." They were delighted when Secretary of the Treasury Paul O'Neill put out a statement in May 10, 2001 (this was, of course, before September 11) opposing the OECD-type sanctions. Later, O'Neill testified before the Senate's Permanent Committee on Investigations that the U.S. was breaking ranks with the OECD. "I do not think it appropriate," he testified, "for the United States or OECD to tell another sovereign nation what the structure of their tax system should be."[27] He was supported in this stance by conservatives in the U.S. Congress, think tanks such as the Heritage Foundation, the Center For Freedom and Prosperity, and *The Wall Street Journal*. As a result, which *The New York Times* reported, there was a stiffening in the position of many of the countries on the OECD "black list."[28] Caribbean elites are little different from those in the rest of the world: they are keenly attentive and responsive to any move in the U.S. which might affect their situations.

So now comes Stanley and a slew of other major companies planning to move to Bermuda. The CEO of Stanley provided the standard defenses: (1) it is legal (and has been since 1994), (2) it is necessary to keep the company competitive, and (3) it is good for stockholders, employees, and through higher earning overall, for the U.S. Treasury.[29]

It was *The New York Times,* however, which revealed one unmentioned but crucial aspect of this offshore arrangement: by incorporating in Bermuda and then establishing a legal residency in Barbados, not only did

Table 5.3 Associated Press Poll on Taxation

Reason Politicians Promise Tax Cuts	
To help me	15%
To help someone else	80%
Don't know	5%
More Likely To Vote for Congressional Candidate Who—	
Promises to cut taxes	23%
Balances the budget	72%
Don't know	5%

the corporation save on taxes, the corporate executives benefitted even more. Rewarded in terms of lowering costs, these executives are motivated regardless of other consequences to shareholders or, indeed, the U.S. Treasury. The words "greed," "unpatriotic," "corporate corruption," and "freeriding" began to enter the "Capital" vs. "State" strategic game. As this is being written, the "State" argument appeared to be gaining ground. The post-September 11 and post-Enron milieu was one of public anger at corporate America and its political supporters. An Associated Press poll (see Table 5.3) regarding taxation was revealing:[30]

While this is an American debate, Caribbean leaders know very well that even as they have no influence over its eventual outcome, they surely will feel the consequences of the outcome of that game. This explains their strong lobbying efforts in favor of offshore banking. One such lobbyist wrote recently that the OECD efforts against tax havens were "a direct assault on [the] fiscal sovereignty [of] developing nations governed by people of color."[31] The combination of sovereignty and race used to carry a powerful wallop. This is less the case after September 11, 2001.[32]

Today there are more institutional channels for those arguing a sovereign right to operate an offshore business which is illegal in the U.S. In the first such move by a CARICOM country, Antigua has challenged U.S. policies on cross-border gambling and betting services before the WTO.[33] Whatever the outcome, the free ride for offshore businesses is over.

5.2   Smuggling: Guns and Drugs[34]

Despite its relative insignificance in the total scheme of U.S. geopolitical concerns, the Caribbean retains a certain *droit de regard*. Its location, the shared mutual interests, and its potential for causing a good deal of trouble for the U.S. all make it so. The Caribbean not only provides bridges between the producer and the consumer of drugs; in addition, its modern

Table 5.4 Amount of Cocaine in Transit at Any Time (1996) in Mexico, Central America, and Caribbean (Estimated Metric Tons)

Total Transiting at Any Time:	1,054 t
Transiting the Caribbean:	394 t (37.38% of total)
(a) Through Western Caribbean (toward Belize, Mexico, and, from there, also Cayman Island, Jamaica, Cuba, and Haiti)	60 t
(b) Through the Central and Eastern Caribbean	154 t
(c) Through the Caribbean to Europe	180 t
Transiting through Mexico, Central America, and Pacific:	660 t (62.61% of total)
(a) Through the Pacific towards Central America and Mexico	250 t
(b) In Mexico from Central America, Pacific, Western Caribbean, and own production	360 t

Source: U.S. Joint Interagency Task Force East, in UNDCP, *Focus on Drugs,* IV (January, 1997), pp. 1, 2.

banking system provides virtually impenetrable shelter for the profits and investments of that criminal industry.

By the mid-1990s a new upsurge in movements through the Caribbean became evident. As indicated in Table 5.4, the United Nations Office for Drug Control and Crime Prevention (UNDCP) calculated that the Caribbean handles close to 40% of the cocaine moving to the U.S. and Europe. Additionally, the shipments appear to be getting larger. In June 1996, officials on the French island of St. Barthelemy (25 square miles) discovered a cache of 863 kg, while officials in Suriname captured a shipment of 1,226 kg in a remote jungle village. By 2001, said a UNDCP official, U.S. $32 billion was passing through the Caribbean, 10% ($320 million) of which was paid in bribes.[35]

How can this resurgence in Caribbean routes be explained? One hypothesis is that the increasing power of the Mexican cartels has made it too expensive for the Colombians to use Mexico exclusively and has forced them to divert their routes to the Caribbean islands. It is calculated that the Mexican "surcharge" to the Colombians was 50% while the Dominican–Puerto Rican gangs charged them only 20%. Another is that the U.S. had moved many of its resources to the Mexican border, leaving the Caribbean relatively unpatrolled. A third is that organized crime in Brazil and Venezuela has sought outlets in the Caribbean using criminal connections established in the 1970s and 1980s which were still in place but now considerably enlarged and diversified. It is this diversification which provides

Table 5.5 Street Prices per Kilogram of Cocaine, Fourth Quarter, 1994 (US$)

Lesser Antilles	5,000–7,000
San Juan	10,500–13,000
Miami	16,000–22,000
North Florida	24,000–26,000

Source: DEA, Miami Field Division, January 1995.

the capacity to shift routes. A fourth, and most plausible, explanation is that of conjuncture: all three situations occurred virtually simultaneously, providing the move to the Caribbean with even greater impetus.

Whether the Caribbean shore is three tenths or four tenths of the trade, it has invariably represented big profits in the Caribbean. If one keeps in mind the small size of most of the islands, one realizes that even the relatively small amounts of drugs (usually packages weighing less than 200 kg) being transshipped from Colombia via Venezuela through the eastern Caribbean, for instance, have had dramatic consequences for each island, consequences which this study documents. Comparative street prices for a kilogram of cocaine (Table 5.5) make a fundamental point: no matter what the route, there is considerable value added in each stage of the movement from Colombia to Florida, and from there to points north.

There are various routes to Florida through the Islands. In fact, the Caribbean is akin to a series of bridges between producers and the higher-paying markets. It makes perfect economic sense to try to control and organize each of these bridges and so profit from the whole trade, from production to transshipment and sale in the U.S. The benefit is compounded if there is also control over the laundering of those U.S.-provided gains.

All this is to introduce our central research questions: (1) What is the degree of centralized organization in the drug trade in the Caribbean? (2) What are the forces favoring centralization or decentralization?

Once we have established that the Caribbean has become a traditional route for the trade, it is arguably less important to establish the precise tonnage of drugs intercepted in any particular year. First of all, establishing even an approximate figure is difficult. Then there is the reality that since the drug trade is a perfect example of opportunistic capitalism, its capacity to adapt in order to meet a variety of demands for its services is always present. This in turn provides it with a remarkable interest in continuity and incentives for engaging in imaginative maneuverability.

The key question, rather, has to be what does the trade do to the individual nation-states through which it operates? In this sense, there is no such thing as a "Caribbean" drug problem, but rather a Jamaican, Dominican and, indeed, even a Cuban problem. This question can be answered in terms of a set of generalizations followed by case-by-case analyses.

From a general perspective, the drug cartels will be successful in a particular country when the following conditions exist:

1. Preexisting milieus of generalized corruption in both the public and private spheres
2. Significant ethnic ties and loyalties along the transportation and transshipment routes, and in the overseas diaspora in the metropolitan market
3. The acquiescence or indifference of those nations with a major military and/or economic capacity in the region. In Colombia, Anthony Maingot was informed that the precursors necessary for processing cocaine powder came from the U.S. (50.96%), Trinidad and Tobago (28.44%), and Rumania (11.44%).

Space does not allow a country-by-country analysis of the impact of the drug trade. Two geographical "triangles" appear to be active in the movement on the Atlantic maritime side of the trade. Both have Colombian ports as their origin and multiple destinations but, very importantly, South Florida as their final destination.

1. San Andrés, Jamaica, and Miami
2. Coastal Colombia (Barranquilla, Santa Marta, and Cartagena), Dominican Republic, and Puerto Rico

A proper investigation of drug smuggling in these two "triangles" would require a detailed analysis of movements in each of the territories within those geographical spaces. This is not possible here. One approach is to trace the voyage of a captured drug ship, analyzing the situation in certain key stops. (see Table 5.6.) One value of this approach is that rather than selecting our case *a priori*, we let the criminal select it for us. The case is drawn from U.S. Drug Enforcement Agency (DEA) files and allows us to probe the probable levels of organization or localization as they existed in the mid-1990s.

This is obviously a very broad outline, but it is about as much information as researchers without clearance can access. Aside from the facts that some drugs were loaded off Jamaica and were discovered in Tampa, there is not much specific information. The challenge lies in adducing as many conclusions from such data as will help shed light on the central research problem: Did the voyage of the drug ship involve one business undertaking controlled by one organization, or was it a series of conspiracies, each maximizing its possible gain from the ultimate payoff—the sale of the drugs? The specific question makes it clear how difficult this area of research is. Did the ship arrive in Trinidad with the secret compartment in place and

Table 5.6 Tracing a Drug Shipment

1. February–July, 1994:
   M/V *Carib Coast* is docked for unspecified repairs in Trinidad. While there, the vessel changes ownership and is renamed M/V *Avior*.

2. July 28, 1994:
   Avior sails to Jamaica.

3. August 4, 1994:
   Avior sails to Honduras. Sets sail and claims to be adrift with mechanical problems somewhere in the Caribbean.

4. August 6, 1994:
   Avior Returns to Jamaica, where no mechanical problems are reported.

5. Sometime in August:
   Avior rendezvouses off Pedro Banks, Jamaica, with two Colombian "go-fast" boats known to have left from Canal del Dique, San Andrés Islands, Colombia. Ship returns to Jamaica and takes on a load of gypsum.

6. September 2, 1994:
   Avior unloads gypsum cargo in Santo Domingo, Dominican Republic. There the ownership of the vessel is again changed, and it is renamed M/V *Inge Frank*.

7. September 9, 1994:
   Inge Frank sails into Tampa Bay, FL, and schedules dry dock repairs similar to repairs done in Trinidad.

8. September 16, 1994:
   U.S. Coast Guard boards the *Inge Frank* and locates secret steel and cement compartments containing 1,948 kg of contraband cocaine.

Source: Anthony P. Maingot, "The Decentralization Imperative and Caribbean Criminal Enterprises" in *Transnational Crime in the Americas*, Ed. Tom Farer (New York: Routledge, 1999), pp. 143–170.

offload a cargo, or were the compartments added in Trinidad where it was taking on cargo? What do the changes of ownership imply—a subterfuge for a single owner or new owners at different legs or stages of the voyage?

We turn to two stops, San Andrés and the Dominican Republic.

5.2.1 San Andrés y Providencia

The archipelago of San Andrés y Providencia belongs to Colombia and is located some 110 kilometers southwest of Jamaica. It is inhabited by English-speaking people of West Indian descent, who, like the people of the Bay Islands, have long existed as fishermen, as crew on ocean and inter-island vessels, and as smugglers. Because San Andrés has always been a free port serving mainland Colombians, the smuggling business was always more important than it was in the Bay Islands. Yet San Andrés never brought in the kind of money and wealth that the Sanandresianos began to notice arriving in the late 1970s. The erstwhile bucolic existence of these islands has been replaced by high-rise hotels, fancy discos, shops with expensive clothing and merchandise, and yacht havens chock-full of vessels of every description and price.

The islanders know exactly to what this wealth is attributable and colorfully dubbed it the "lobster route." This is an operation which began with the Medellín Cartel and is said to be controlled today by the Cali Cartel. Drugs and fuel are flown in from the mainland, either delivered at the airport in San Andrés or dropped offshore and picked up by speedboats the islanders call *voladores.* These cargoes are delivered to larger vessels which ply the Caribbean. The word is that the "Mosquito Coast" of Nicaragua was once their principal destination; today it is the Bay Islands, Jamaica, and the Dominican Republic. According to a well-placed source, a Colombian police report called San Andrés the epicenter of the nation's drug exports. In addition to drugs, the archipelago trades in arms, precursor chemicals, and counterfeit dollars, and it provides the services necessary for money laundering. Another major service, according to a report of the Colombian Navy, is that "They can take an old ship, restore it to service, pack it with a ton of cocaine, and have it off the Jamaican coast, all in 30 hours." All these activities, noted the source, take place with brazen openness. Soon after that report was made public, the Colombian magazine *Cambio 16* reported that the "major" drug dealer on San Andrés had been arrested. The individual was said to be at the service of the Cali cartel and to have business associations with Italians and Jamaicans established on the island. On this critical launching point, there can be no doubt that the Colombian cartels, first the Medellín, then the Cali cartels, and now the so-called *Carteles de la Costa* are in full control.

One can also assume that the purpose of the ship in our study to pass in the vicinity of San Andres was to collect a cargo. The ship's next destination is now the Dominican Republic, part of the major route into Puerto Rico and the U.S. The Jamaican case will be treated at greater length later on.

5.2.2 Dominican Republic

The drug ship M/V *Avior* delivered its load of Jamaican gypsum and in the seven days it was in port in Santo Domingo, the ownership and the name of the ship changed. We know that when it left harbor as M/V *Inge Frank*, it was carrying a ton of cocaine. It should come as no surprise that the drug trade and the accompanying corruption of officials are today a major problem on that island. At the Technical Anti-Drug Summit held in Puerto Rico in May 1995, the head of Puerto Rico's DEA office spoke of the "Colombianization" of the region. He was not the first to so characterize it, but the characterization seems especially apt for the situations in Puerto Rico and the Dominican Republic. The most tragic evidence that this is indeed so is the increase in professionally executed murders by those in the trade of those combating the rot, and of those involved and soiled but "fallen from grace." There is also a real effort to influence the nation's politics. In late March 1996, Puerto Rican authorities seized $511,592 in $20 bills hidden in food cans. The destination was the Dominican Republic and there, according to Contraalmirante Julio Cesar Ventura Bayonet, then the Dominican drug czar, it was an attempt by Dominican "narcos" to influence the upcoming elections.

Today, the first point of contact for the Puerto Rican operators is the Dominican Republic. The rest of the Caribbean plays an essentially supporting role to this U.S./New York/Miami/Puerto Rico/Dominican Republic axis. The DEA claims that Colombians are directly organizing groups and routes in the Dominican Republic. It is, nevertheless, indisputable that the Dominicans have a formidable set of their own organizations. Michael Woods claims that the role of Dominican criminals has "dramatically evolved" as a result of their association with the Colombians. Previously, Dominicans were limited to acting as pickup crews and couriers assisting Puerto Rican criminals in drug-smuggling ventures. "Now," says Woods, "Dominican traffickers are smugglers, transporters, and wholesalers." Through their infrastructure support from Colombian traffickers, they have been able to dominate a significant portion of the market in U.S. East Coast cities.

Like the Jamaicans, the Dominicans have created truly binational societies between the U.S. and the Dominican Republic. The U.S.-based Dominicans are called "Dominicanyorks" and are resented in the Dominican Republic, for the most part because they have been stereotyped as drug dealers. They are not, of course, all drug dealers, but there is no doubt that there are powerful Dominican drug rings operating in New York with very tight contacts with the trade back home. Additionally, with no Dominican legislation against money laundering, the Dominican drug lords have literally flooded the island with dollars and in that way have penetrated the island's banking, business, judiciary, police, and even Congress. According to much of the growing literature on the subject, this penetration and corrupting of the Dominican system has taken place virtually unhindered and certainly with near-total impunity.

The establishment of a new Dominican National Directorate for Drug Control is part of the expansion of such local efforts throughout the Caribbean. This is one case, however, where the evidence does not warrant optimism about controlling the crime wave. One obstacle is the apparent absence of a mafia controlled by one or even a few *capos*. The state fights a hydra of decentralized and localized gangs without hierarchy or enduring central control, opportunistically engaging in whatever conspiracies are necessary to carry on the lucrative business. The drug ship we tracked could as well have been offloading a cargo for one group on the island and taking on the product of another for delivery to Tampa, where it was finally interdicted.

To be sure, there can be considerable and dramatic activities on small islands which would appear quite removed from the major routes. The 45,000 population, two-island nation of St. Kitts–Nevis is a case in point. It is not a matter of the frequent seizures of commercial amounts of drugs on board the many pleasure cruisers that ply the area. It is very difficult to unravel where these packages were loaded and which their final destination might be. During this author's nine-day stay in February 2001 in St. Kitts–Nevis, police seized 43 pounds of cocaine (value $1.2 million) on the England-based ship Sunbird. The ship had recently been in Dutch St. Maarten and was enroute to Barbados. Nothing further could be discovered about the incident.

More relevant was the fact that during that short stay, the author saw the following vessels moored on sequential days at the Basseterre dock: a U.S. Coast Guard cutter, a Canadian Navy frigate, and a French Navy cutter. There were ample reasons for this multinational armed presence. In June, 2000, the U.S. Department of the Treasury identified St. Kitts residents Noel Timothy Heath and Glenroy Vingrove Matthews as being among the major narco-traffickers in the world.

The director of the newly created United Nations Drug Control and Crime Prevention program (UNDCP) in the Caribbean relates a private conversation he had with a commissioner of police from the region. That commissioner was challenging the very rationale for establishing region-wide counternarcotics programs such as those being advanced by the UNDCP. In the commissioner's opinion, the drug problems of 29 different countries were like fingerprints: no two were identical, and, for that same reason, no two strategies to combat them could be identical either. The director of the UNDCP disagreed. He noted that "1996 has created a new awareness that the drug war can be won . . . if only we take up the challenge in a concerted manner." Which point of view provides the best starting point for a strategy?

The critical question, of course, is whether the sliver of reality we have analyzed here is representative of the larger Caribbean reality? The facts revealed in this study show that of the five ports used by the drug ship before reaching the U.S., two (Jamaica and the Dominican Republic) show very strong tendencies toward localization, two (Trinidad and Honduras) show mixed localization–centralization tendencies, and one (San Andrés) was clearly then under the central control of the Cali Cartel, and later the Carteles de la Costa. At least with respect to this slice of the overall drug trade in the Caribbean, there are no grounds to assume the existence of one organized—that is, centralized—criminal conspiracy (as defined in Table 5.6) that we can call "the Caribbean Mafia." There does not appear to be an organized hierarchy showing continuity over time and long-range planning. What appears to exist are Colombian-organized criminal syndicates or cartels that utilize the many local organizations, taking advantage of geopolitical opportunities (such as shifts in U.S. interests and emphases) and of the general milieus of corruption in which they operate. We are confronting many local gangs, mostly, like the Jamaican posses and the Dominicans, without a centralized hierarchical structure even in the islands themselves. All, without exception, seek, and get, guns. Guns provide protection, enforce loyalty, mete out punishment and, critically, are a major currency in the drug trade.

Sadly, the smuggling of guns is just as generalized as that of drugs. The big difference is that it is largely officially ignored.

5.2.3 Gun Smuggling

The United Nations calculates that in the year 2000 there were some 500 million small arms in the world. And fundamentally, contrary to the practice during the Cold War, there was little Great Power control over these weapons. The geopolitical and ideological reasons for supplying allies and surrogates with weapons has been replaced with a free-for-all "grand bazaar" in legal and illegal sales. The authoritative *Small Arms Survey* for 2002 details the dimension of the manufacturing and marketing of small arms in the world:

> More than 1,000 companies in 98 countries produce small arms.
> Nearly seven million commercial firearms were produced worldwide in 2000; nearly three quarters (four million or 74% of total) were produced in the U.S., and the European Union produced 1.1 million small arms.
> The value of this production was close to $3 billion in 2000.

The critical finding, however, was that licensed (i.e., legal) production "is an easy way to gain market share, evade strict export controls, or facilitate exports to prohibited destinations."[36]

It is the awareness of this frightening change which led to the signing of several conventions, including the June 1997 European Union Programme For Preventing and Combating Illicit Trafficking in Conventional Arms and the November 1997 OAS Convention Against the Illicit Manufacturing and Trafficking in Firearms, Ammunition, Explosives and Other Related Materials. In April 1998, 50 countries, including the G-7 and Russia, made an appeal to the UN to adopt measures to curb the illicit trade in arms.[37]

Despite all this, the U.S. has refused to join in the efforts to curb this trade. As *The New York Times* editorialized about the U.S.'s refusal to join the curtailment issue, it is "a shameless subordination of diplomacy to domestic political pandering."[38] Specifically, pandering to the powerful national rifle association (NRA) lobby. This is in a context of political decisions further deregulating controls on gun sales. In fact, in May 2002, the U.S. Administration further expanded the "right to bear arms" interpretation of the Second Amendment to the U.S. Constitution. Again, to cite another *New York Times* editorial, it hands dangerous criminals a potent new weapon, "a gift to pro-gun extremists, and a shabby deal for everyone else."[39]

The U.S. position is key to the continued proliferation of small weapons. According to the Congressional Research Service, in the year 2000 U.S. manufacturers sold somewhat over half of all the weapons sold on the world market. Nearly 70% of these went to developing nations.

As frightening as all this might be, it is only part of the story of this deadly trade, a trade which goes beyond the U.S. borders. As the *National Post* of Canada reports it: during the Cold War sympathetic powers could be counted on to supply the arms and funds to their surrogates, but "in the chaotic new global order" extremist groups have had to start paying their own way and criminal activities is one way they do that. Canada, said the newspaper, has become "a terrorists' supermarket."[40] But even as a dozen or so terrorist groups raise money in Canada, they buy their guns in the U.S. That is where the "weapons bazaar," to cite a *U.S. News* and CBS 60-Minutes program, is located.[41] Other than straightforward government sales to foreign governments, the legal sources of small arms in the U.S. are essentially three: (1) surplus Pentagon sales of supposedly "demilitarized" weapons (which are nothing of the sort) to private dealers, (2) private pawnshops which specialize in guns, and (3) gun shows. The former is a major source for the latter as the editors of the *U.S. News* discovered. Most of the high-tech weapons they ordered (viz., sophisticated missiles, night-vision weapons), "arrived within a week, courtesy of UPS."[42] One private California weapons company was stopped from shipping 14 seagoing containers full of top-secret encryption devices and other sophisticated military electronics. The entire cargo had been purchased legally.

Then there is the illegal market for guns legally manufactured. In February 14, 1993, *The New York Times Magazine* ran a special issue entitled "Street Guns: A Consumer Guide." It is these "ugly guns" (viz., Cobray M-11, Tec-9, various assault rifles, the "street sweeper") which are the preferred armaments of Caribbean criminal gangs. An interesting case of commercial manufacturing is Navegar, a Cuban-American run company in Miami (producer of the Cobray M-11 and Tec-9 machine guns) which closed shop in August, 2001. It was not the first time it had closed, reopened, and renamed its weapons. "Its market," said a story in *The Miami Herald*, "was people like criminals and soldiers of fortune. . . ."[43] Then there are the pawnshops and gun shows. Not only are the losses due to thefts of guns from pawnshops constant and substantial, guns used in crimes in Haiti, Puerto Rico, Dominican Republic, and Honduras were traced to just one pawnshop in Miami. Small weapons are shipped out of Miami in watermelons, frozen turkeys, the walls of refrigerators and dozens of other ingenious ways.

Even foreign weapons dealers find operating out of South Florida safe and profitable. Part of the sale of Argentine weapons to Ecuador, despite an OAS-mandated embargo, was arranged by a French arms dealer residing in Miami.[44]

In the Caribbean, criminals have taken advantage of the ready availability of guns on the open market in Miami and the ease of transportation to their island destination. This has taken a toll. The first, and most common use of weapons has been by international organized crime. The case of Dominica illustrates the collusion between corrupt local officials and a wide variety of international criminals.[45]

For two and a half decades after World War II, the sole peace-keeping force on the island of Dominica was the British-trained police force. Unarmed, they walked the beat and had direct contact with the civilian population. The Chief of Police was invariably a Britisher. In 1974 a Volunteer Defence Force was established in response to what was called a "rebellion" but which was really an outburst of localized violence by a group of local Rastafarians called "Dreds."

Upon being granted internal self-rule by Britain in 1975 (the usual step before full independence), the then-Premier, Patrick John, established a Defence Force. This process of change in the structure of the island's forces of law and order coincided with Premier John's entry into the perilous world of international skulduggery. John opened negotiations with one Sydney Burnett-Alleyne, a Barbadian international wheeler-dealer and arms merchant. Premier John announced that the government had signed an agreement with Burnett-Alleyne's "Dominica Development Corporation" to build an international airport, an oil refinery, a petrochemical plant, and a 1000-room hotel with marina. Funds were to be provided by the Alleyne Mercantile bank, one of 24 companies personally registered by Dominica's Attorney General. Virtually every member of John's government was a shareholder in the Dominica Development Corporation. In order to insure secrecy, the government passed legislation barring the disclosure of any details of the registration of foreign corporations. Thus, it was impossible for Dominicans, or anyone else for that matter, to know that the "headquarters" of the Dominica Development Corporation was a one-room office above a boutique in the English market town of Broadshaw, Cheshire.

In Barbados, Sidney Burnett-Alleyne had secured a government license for the Alleyne Mercantile Bank. This was, in a way, the beginning of Dominica's incursion into "offshore" banking. Leader of the Opposition and future Prime Minister Tom Adams charged in parliament that Burnett-Alleyne had been "subverting" important members of the Barbados government with guns and with gifts of from $600 to $20,000 for months before the license was granted. Whatever the truth of these allegations, it is a fact that the grandiose scheme in Dominica came crashing down when French intelligence in Martinique informed Interpol and British authorities of one of Burnett-Alleyne's other activities: attempting to overthrow the newly elected government of Tom Adams in Barbados. The evidence: a yacht, skippered by Burnett-Alleyne, loaded with weapons and heading towards Barbados. Three years later, and one month after independence, Burnett-Alleyne and the same John, now prime minister of independent Dominica, were at it again. This time Burnett-Alleyne promised John an incredible $11 billion development scheme in exchange for the right to use Dominica as a South Africa embargo-breaking transshipment depot. John also was once again to participate in a new plot to overthrow the Barbadian government. Once again, authorities intervened, and the scheme collapsed.

John was nothing if not persistent. In February 1979 he signed a 99-year lease for a 45-square-mile tract of prime land on the island with Texan supermarket magnate Don Pierson. Pierson's Dominica Caribbean Freeport Authority would be virtually sovereign in that free zone, including having control over immigration and security.

Threatened with massive demonstrations and public protests over the deal, Prime Minister John canceled the contract. John lost the next election, was tried in court, and was imprisoned on corruption charges. Despite all that, he continued his contacts with other international groups eager to "own" their own island. In early 1980 John contracted the New Orleans firm Nortic Enterprises for a daring job: overthrow the newly elected government of Eugenia Charles. Headed by white supremacists Michael Perdue and David Duke, former Imperial Wizard of the Ku Klux Klan (and later member of the Louisiana House of Representatives and candidate for the U.S. Senate), the firm also had contacts with neo-Nazi and underworld figures. The Americans established links with members of the Dominica Defence Force, the idea being to set up a "revolutionary" government headed by the still-incarcerated John. Michael Perdue would then control a 200-man army and have a free hand with any and all business deals on Dominica: tourism, banking, gambling, and a new airport. U.S. federal agents arrested the mercenaries and their arms-laden yacht just as they were to leave for Dominica. In Dominica, John's fellow conspirators in the Defence Force assaulted the prison in an attempt to free their leader, killing three guards in the process. After the trial and conviction of John and the others, only one received the death penalty and was hanged. John and the others got extended jail sentences which were commuted four years later. The Prime Minister of Dominica, Eugenia Charles, abolished the Defence Force and strengthened the police.

Unfortunately, the role of smuggled guns in the hands of the types of forces which threatened Dominica in the 1970s had not run its course. There existed too many small islands with the lethal mix of dire economic needs, political leaders eager to attract investment at whatever cost, and a network of offshore banks and "corporations" with seemingly inexhaustible amounts of money. Beside all this, and, critically, the "corporations" had virtually unhindered freedom to operate. The Cold War had so absorbed the preoccupation of the U.S. that the forces of international crime had what came close to being a *carte blanche*.

All this changed with the 1979 *coup d'etat* by the Marxist New Jewel Movement in Grenada. While this relatively small group of middle class revolutionaries would eventually become a significant factor in Cuban foreign policy (and, as such, supplied with thousands of guns), the initial *coup d'etat* was carried out with guns smuggled in from Miami in barrels marked "grease" and shipped directly to the home of a local Marxist. It was enough to arm the 45 men who overthrew the Gairy regime.[46]

If Grenada in 1979 was a case of an ideological, revolutionary movement, the cases of gun smuggling in Antigua and St. Kitts reflect pure greed and corruption. Antigua had long been reputed as being a major site for drug-related corruption in the region.

One of the most damaging blows to the Antiguan Government's legitimacy came in 1986. In a drug bust involving a sand barge owned by Sandco Ltd., three principals of this company, Lester Bird (now Prime Minister), Robin Yearwood, and Hugh Marshall—all government ministers—were forced to cool public suspicion by volunteering to take the now infamous public drug test. The fact that an individual can be involved in drugs and not use it personally, thus making any test useless, is not the worst part of this episode. What was most damaging was the fact public trust in these ministers was so low that the ministers felt obligated to prove their innocence. Such lack of public trust undermines the government's legitimacy, hence weakening its ability to perform its basic functions, most important of which is to maintain law and order.

Antigua had also been involved in the whole trade in weapons. It might have had its start in 1977 when artillery designer Gerald Bull settled there. The arrangement between the ruling Bird family and Bull was not revealed until a container being loaded onto a ship burst open and its load of howitzers spilled onto the dock. It turned out that the Birds and Bull, through his Space Research Corporation, were breaking the UN weapons embargo on South Africa. According to one author, the U.S. was fully aware of the happenings.[47]

The scandal did nothing to undermine the power of the Birds and their party. As in the Bahamas, the decolonization process with its strong racial overtones sustained the family and its interests. All this facilitated the penetration by international criminal syndicates. Antigua's most scandalous episode of corruption came in 1990 and 1991. Again, it involved smuggling guns and drugs. The Antigua case—as revealed by the Official Commission of Inquiry—exposes the depth and spread of corruption, indeed, its internationalization.[48] This inquiry led by Louis Blom-Cooper also clearly reveals the links between internationalized corruption and violence.

The charges were that 10 tons of arms were bought in Israel, the end-user to be the Antigua Defence Force (less than 100 men already armed by the U.S.), but the weapons ended up on the farm of Medellín Cartel henchman José Rodríguez Gacha. It was proven that some of the guns were used in the assassination of popular Colombian presidential candidate Luís Carlos Galán. Among the many terrifying details revealed by the Commission of Inquiry are the following:

1. While Antigua had "a heavy moral duty" to Colombia and the world to pursue this matter, its meager diplomatic and police capabilities meant that it could not alone pursue the investigations which had to cover over four continents.
2. Despite the wider conclusion that small Caribbean states cannot confront the cartels on their own, "Intellectual collaboration to elicit the truth about Israeli firearms finding their way into the hands of Colombian drug barons was not to be easily achieved." (p. 40). "The British government," said Blom-Cooper, "have turned a blind eye" to evidence that their nationals, operating as skilled mercenaries, "turned untrained killers into trained killers." (p. 34).
3. On the central role of the city of Miami: "This conspiracy was, in my judgment, hatched in Miami and developed from that city." (p. 37).
4. On the role of the banks: "I find it wholly unacceptable that banks in America, whose services were used to facilitate what can without exaggeration be described as a crime against humanity, should be permitted through the inaction of the American authorities to hide evidence of that crime behind the cloak of confidentiality." (p. 37).
5. Finally, and critically, the Report called attention to the role of the wider, more enduring corrupt relationships between the principals

in the scheme and high officials of the Antigua government, which called for "further investigation." (p. 83). Two questions in particular required urgent investigation: (1) what, if any, were the roles of Israeli and British mercenaries in establishing a training camp for terrorists in Antigua, and (2) were there plans to train Tamil guerrillas in that camp in exchange for access to the East Asian heroin trade?

These questions were answered by an investigation undertaken by the Permanent Sub-Committee on Investigations of the U.S. Senate. In a hearing held in February, 1991 the sub-committee established conclusively that (1) British and Israeli mercenaries, under contract to Colombian drug cartels, had been operating in Colombia since 1988, (2) that because of pressure from the Colombian government, they decided to shift operations to Antigua, (3) that Antigua would serve both as a training base and conduit of guns for the cartel, and (4) that the Antigua deal was only one part of a much deeper and wider operation. As the sub-committee noted:

> This transaction provides a case study of the multinational nature of arms trafficking. In this case, we had weapons made in Israel purportedly going to a Caribbean nation which wound up with the drug cartels in Colombia, financed through banks and individuals in Panama, the U.S. Israel, Antigua, and, probably, Colombia.

When government turns a blind eye or condones such activity, it serves to undermine democracy and political stability by essentially making Antigua a narco-terrorist state.

Again, the Birds survived to continue their corrupt ways. In 1995, Ivor Bird, the brother of the Prime Minster of Antigua, was convicted on drug charges. He was charged $200,000, a fine that was reportedly paid by his father, former Prime Minister, Vere Bird, Sr.

The roots of corruption do not go as deep in the case of St. Kitts (also known as St. Christopher). Once they took hold, however, the growth was fast and virulent.

It was during the late 1980s that St. Kitts came under increased scrutiny for being an area of trafficking and corruption. In 1994, William Herbert, St. Kitts-Nevis Ambassador to the United Nations, along with five other people, disappeared at sea. Dr. Herbert had been forced to resign his post as St. Kitts–Nevis Ambassador to the U.S. in 1987 under allegations that he was involved in drug-money operations. The Federal Bureau of Investigation (FBI) described Dr. Herbert as "a notorious money launderer for drug gangsters." Dr. Herbert's case was of even more concern when one considers the fact that he was a founder of the then-ruling party, The Peoples Action Movement (PAM). The involvement of such a high level political actor in such corruption necessarily had adverse implications, not just for the ruling party, but also for the state. And, so it came to be seen.

In the same year, Deputy Prime Minister Sidney Morris was forced to resign his post following charges against two of his sons for drugs and firearms offenses. These came after another of his sons and the son's girlfriend were found murdered in an apparently drug-related incident. There was widespread speculation that at least two of the people charged with Mr. Morris' son's murder were financial supporters of the then-opposition St. Kitts Labor Party. When these brothers were subsequently freed on bail, prisoners rioted and burned down the prison.

Anthony Maingot attempted in 2000 (6 years later) to uncover something more than what had been reported in the press, but was unsuccessful. Two official inquiries were conducted by the New Scotland Yard. The first, on the disappearance of the Kittisian diplomat, was published. The second, on the murders of 1994, was classified and unavailable.[49] The Scotland Yard Preface to the published report is itself revealing and goes a long way in explaining why nothing of substance was reported in the published report.

> *It should be stated that some difficulty was experienced when speaking to some people . . . there was little trust in the local police, generally . . . nothing new of any significance came to light, only their own personal disquiet of the local police.*

While the press in the English-speaking Caribbean reported that the New Scotland Yard Report concluded that "it is improbable that the disappearance is the result of a criminal act," (See press wire from CANA February 12, 2000) the report was a bit more cryptic than that:

> *However, if this was the result of criminal activity then it would require considerable resources . . . The only apparent possibilities, then, are limited to "The Mafia" or the drug barons of South America.*

How far off could the headline in the St. Kitt's opposition party's newspaper (*Labour Spokesman*, August 6, 1994) have been: "Colombians, Drug Runners, Money Launderers Behind Herbert Disappearance?" This same interpretation was suggested as plausible in an in-depth investigation by *The Sunday Times* of London, October 23, 1994. Duane Blake, historian of the Jamaican "Shower Posse," claims that it was Cecil Conner, a/k/a Charles Miller the "Don" of St. Kitts, who killed Ambassador Herbert.[50]

If a country's judicial system and law enforcement system are pillars of stability and order, then the increased pressure put on these institutions by the drug trade holds great danger for the future of eastern Caribbean political stability. Ivelaw Griffith, in a detailed analysis of the combination of drugs and arms smuggling, outlines how the very sovereignty of many a Caribbean state is "under siege." Corruption and intimidation work to paralyze efforts to combat the threat.[51]

Griffith clearly states the extent to which parts of the judicial systems in the region are compromised or, in other cases, have the potential of being compromised by drug-trafficking. Inherent in any properly functioning judicial system is the ability for law enforcement officials to carry out thorough and honest investigations. In St. Kitts and the rest of the eastern Caribbean this task was becoming increasingly difficult and dangerous. For instance, in October 1994 St. Kitts Police Superintendent Jude Matthew, an Englishman hired to be head of the island's Special Branch, was shot dead. At the time of his death, Commander Matthew was involved in the investigations of drug trafficking and murder cases which had ties to Jamaican *posses*. Commander Matthew's replacement, another Scotland Yard secondment, barely escaped with his life from an assassination attempt one week after taking over the job in St. Kitts.

The situation in St. Kitts had gone out of control, requiring an intervention by RSS forces based in Barbados. None of this could rid the society of the fear that the drug lords were having it their way. Several attempts to convict the major kingpin on the island failed when juries refused to return a finding of guilt. Efforts by the U.S. to have him extradited have also gone nowhere.

The changes wrought by the increasing U.S. awareness of the vulnerability of these small islands did nothing to stop the flow of small arms to the region. A classical case is the 1990 attempt by the Black Muslim Group, the Jamaat-al-Muslimeen, to take over the island of Trinidad. The 115 rifles used in the *coup d'etat* attempt were all legally bought at gun shows in Fort Lauderdale and shipped legally in a container to a known sympathizer of the Jamaat. Only the loyalty of Trinidad's small coast guard and the police prevented the creation of the first full-fledged Islamic government in the Caribbean.[52]

Nor did the failure of the first attempt stop the Jamaat from trying again, and hunting for the necessary guns in the same open market, South Florida. On May 30, 2001, federal agents arrested a Trinidadian–American who had contracted to buy 60 AK-47s and 10 Mach-10 machine guns. The individual involved was known to be an operative of the Jamaat in Trinidad and only 3 years earlier had been deported from the U.S. for trafficking in heroin. The critical point being that whether it was Marxist-oriented groups during the Cold War or Islamic Black Power groups in the post–Cold War era, the smuggling of small weapons out of Miami is relatively easy.[53]

None of this has brought to an end the smuggling of weapons through and to the region. If it was once the rogue BCCI which held the accounts of such known international weapons merchants as Adnan Khasoggi, Asaf Ali, and M.I. Bilbeisi, so now do the new merchants such as Vladimiro Montesinos of Peru operate out of bank accounts in the Cayman Islands. With tens of thousands of AK-47s left over from the Central American wars and with major Israeli arms dealers operating out of Miami and Panama,[54] there will be no shortage of weapons for groups as diverse as Colombian guerillas and paramilitary forces, Jamaican *posses*, and the garden-variety criminal.

The drug trade provides the money, the offshore secrecy havens hide and move the money, and the U.S. and other countries supply the guns. Miami is a favorite point of departure for many of these illicit operations, a fact to be kept in mind when we discuss that city's new role in the Caribbean.

CHAPTER 6

Transnational Complexities in U.S.–Caribbean Relations

6.1 The Positive: Migration and the Rise of Binational Societies

Among the spreading influences which make up what has become known as globalization, the global movement of people has been just as dynamic as the flow of goods, of capital, and ideas. The number of people emigrating, whether as displaced refugees or legal and illegal migrants, has been calculated at approximately 175 million people in the 1990s. This is 3% of the world population. Interestingly enough, as distinct from the movements of goods and capital, which are encouraged, there is no such open encouragement to the flow of people. Control over borders, who and what crosses them, is regarded as one of the most guarded prerogatives of sovereignty. Paradoxically, it is also one of the least enforceable of those prerogatives. The U.S. Census Bureau indicates that in 2000, in a total population of 291 million, 32 million were foreign-born. That is 11.5% of the total. Of these, 36% were Central American and Mexican, 10% Caribbean, and 6% South American. Europeans were only 14% of the foreign-born.

The Caribbean stands out among the regions where migration in search of work has such deep historical roots that it is now part of the cultural orientation. Indeed, one can speak of a Caribbean "culture of migration." Every nationality in the Caribbean has substantial percentages of their home populations living in the U.S. (see Table 6.1).

Proof of the historical roots of these populations in the U.S. are the figures in Table 6.2, showing a very high percentage of immigrants being sponsored by their relatives who are already citizens or permanent

Table 6.1ᵃ Migration to the U.S. from the Caribbean Islands

Country	Born Outside the U.S.	Illegal Population (Estimated)	Total	Total Population from Country	% of the Total Population Living in the U.S.
Cuba	913		913	10,440	9%
Dominican Republic	632	75	707	8,076	9%
Jamaica	506	50	556	2,574	22%
Haití	440	105	545	7,328	7%
Rest of the Caribbean	266	120	386	2,376	16%
Total from the Caribbean	2,757	350	3,107	30,794	10%

ᵃU.S. Immigration and Naturalization Service.
Source: Foreign Born Population, Jamaica, Haiti, and Rest of Caribbean Census CPS 1996; Foreign Born Population, Dominican Republic and Cuba Census CPS 1997.

residents in the U.S. The point is, of course, that most are now moving to the U.S. and, in increasing numbers, to South Florida.

The tables do not show Puerto Ricans because they are U.S. citizens, but by 1990 it was calculated that the percentage who migrated to the States was 75% of the home population. Other Caribbean groups with similar high percentages living in the metropolis are the Surinamese in the Netherlands (54%), Martinicans in France (48.7%), and Netherlands Antilleans in the Netherlands (30.5%).[2]

Table 6.2 Relatives-Sponsored Migration from the Caribbean Region (1996)

Country	Total Migrants	Sponsored by Relatives	%
Dominican Republic	39,604	39,107	98.7
Jamaica	19,089	17,893	93.7
Dominica	797	724	90.8
Other Caribbean Countries	3,285	2,807	85.4
Barbados	1,043	882	84.6
Grenada	797	635	79.7
Haiti	18,386	13,762	74.9
Trinidad and Tobago	7,344	5,377	73.2
Cuba	26,466	3,307	12.5
Total	116,801	84,494	72.3%

Source: 1996 Statistical Yearbook of the U.S. Immigration and Naturalization Service.

It must not be assumed that there is general scholarly agreement on either the origins or the consequences of this migration. In fact, there have been two dominant theoretical explanations of this periphery-to-metropolis migration, and they have been very specifically applied to Caribbean-to-U.S. migration.[3] First, there are theories based on some variant of "world system," Marxist, or "center-periphery" theories. Second, there are theories of rational choice.

The first group of theories invariably emphasizes the distortions in peripheral economies created by imperialism and colonialism, past and present. Occupations by the U.S. of Haiti and the Dominican Republic and interventions in Cuba and Nicaragua, according to this theory, have distorted local economies and their labor pools, forcing large numbers of persons to migrate to the metropolis where, in turn, they distort ("segment") the labor force. The results are poorly paid workers on the periphery and a dichotomized, poorly paid vs. highly paid work force in the center. The ongoing asymmetries of world trade guarantee that these distortions (and thus, migration) continue.

While this is not the occasion to debate the various strengths and short-comings of the model, there is nonetheless considerable merit and benefit to anyone looking at U.S.–Caribbean relations to review the historical emphases placed on macroeconomic conditions as they have affected migration. Yet, as theoretical explanations go, this approach is necessary but hardly sufficient. It looks perhaps a little too much at migration and not enough at the migrant. It should be complemented, especially for any understanding of U.S.–Caribbean relations, by a combination of exchange and rational choice theory, an approach which bridges both macro- and micro-sociological factors.[4] After all, the potential migrant, having chosen to come to the U.S., is revealing considerable knowledge about that destination.

It is a highly plausible assumption that the individual, or the household, makes a decision based on information about domestic (Caribbean) factors which are exercising a "pushing" influence on him or her, as well as those factors which are "pulling" him or her to the new destination, the U.S. In both instances, perceptions about the relative success, or lack thereof, of past migrations are taken into account. It is assumed that the individual makes an opportunity or alternative cost calculation, no matter how simply or crudely, before finally packing his bags.

Decision-making by individuals appears straightforward: they look at the difference between minimum wages here and there, availability of housing, possibility of purchasing a car and, very important, the education of the children. Returning to their home town in the Dominican Republic to "show and tell" is also an important incentive. It is assumed that

Dominican elites, assessing the macro-sociological and macro-economics picture, make a similar calculation regarding the national benefits of the migration of their working class compatriots to the U.S. While these considerations included imponderables and "externalities," generally they are quite specific concerning benefits to the sending country. Migration to the U.S., Portes and Bach argue, has three beneficial results: it relieves unemployment, in general, and among the restless young, specifically; it engenders an infusion of hard currency through remittances and repatriated capital of successful immigrant capitalists; and there is also a repatriation of human capital in the form of new attitudes, skills, and orientations. This position is defended despite charges that they are ignoring the fact that the human capital was initially educated and nurtured at considerable cost by the sending country. This is a charge heard throughout the Caribbean. These criticisms elicit two responses: first, they are irrelevant because there is no way to deny those who wish to migrate the right to do so, a sort of "law of necessity" approach especially in democracies and, second, that since there is no evidence that those who stay home have the same entrepreneurial initiatives, the critique is basically ideological, used by those who oppose the new capitalist "spirit" of many returning migrants.[5] This approach contains the right blend of macro-sociological and economic variables as well as micro-sociological variables such as community, family, and individual factors, including individual values and expectations. In other words, it assumes movement within an area with a long history of contacts and exchanges of knowledge and information.

What is absent in the more structural approaches are these micro-sociological variables, critical in the Caribbean, as we shall see. To cite but one aspect, a key part of these micro-sociological factors is the effect of remittances, invariably received by the family directly. These remittances play a crucial role in the fundamental transition from wanting to migrate but being financially unable to becoming the "genuine" migrant. According to the 60th CEPAL and the UN,[6] in 2001, Dominicans remitted $1.6 billion (6.8% of its GDP); Jamaicans, $789 million (10.9% of GDP); and Cubans, $720 million. All this, of course, implies the existence of networks or active communities in both the sending and the receiving societies. Not all Caribbean communities in the U.S. have the same history of movement, settlement, and engagement with the native country. English-speaking West Indians are the oldest, and Dominicans, the most recent. The latter is especially revealing of Cold War geopolitical dynamics. In fact, this Dominican migration was a child of the Cold War. The dramatic increase in Dominican migrants to the U.S. in the late 1960s lay in the fact that the U.S., concerned with the geopolitical threat from the Cuban revolution, actively encouraged Dominican migration. There was no crisis of man–land relations as in Haiti, nor did the migration result from a crisis in the Dominican state and political instability. Despite political and social turmoil in the early 1960s, there was no major push for emigration. In 1966, the Cortens concluded that the lack of desire to migrate reflected a deep-seated "patriotism" on the part of the Dominicans. Fully 70% of their middle-class sample expressed no interest in emigrating; only 3.7% wished that their children be born outside the Dominican Republic, although 70% would have liked their children to have studied abroad, preferably in the U.S. Only 20% of their sample had resided abroad for over a year and 51.6% of these had done so as students.[7]

When Dominican emigration increased, it was not in response to a labor recruiting program but, as already noted, originated from U.S. geopolitical considerations[8] and, subsequently, to the family reunification provisions in U.S. immigration legislation.[9] This explains the variation in motivation and social class origins. The first decade of significant migration (1964 to 1974) appeared to have been largely urban, educated, and middle class.[10] After 1975, migration tended to be essentially working class. As Max Castro noted, only Mexico and Italy among leading immigration countries have a proportionally higher working-class immigrant population than the Dominican Republic. Castro calls it "primarily a proletarian or proletarianizing migration."[11] Not that there was no professional component in that migration. Between 1969 and 1974, 5125 Dominicans were admitted to the U.S. with the intention of working in professional, managerial, administrative, or related jobs, equivalent to 45.8% of Dominican university graduates for the period.[12] Castro merely speculates that this "brain drain" affected development in the Dominican Republic, although the increasing output of university graduates was reducing the damage. The cost to Dominican development of this migration has not been calculated although it appears that these have been lower than in neighboring countries in part because the level of education and skills of Dominican migrants to the U.S. have been below that of other Caribbean countries, including Haiti.[13] In the case of skilled workers, for instance, Castro believes that their migration "would not seem to pose serious problems" to Dominican development needs.[14]

It is precisely the working-class origin of much of Dominican migration which makes the rapidity and relative success of their integration into American society so noteworthy. Occurring first in New York, it is now being replicated in other cities. The explanation lies in the capacity of these migrants to deal simultaneously with two national states. This capacity has two dimensions: first, institutional, i.e., neither the U.S. nor the Dominican Republic erected insurmountable barriers to migration; second, behavioral, i.e., the adaptability of the migrant, the capacity to hold multiple identifications even as their identity as Dominicans remains strong.[15] This is the essence of binationality. As Luis Guarnizo explains this binational citizenship: "They take advantage of every interstice in the power structure in both societies to gain the best of the two worlds."[16]

The speed with which this occurs is truly impressive. In 1994, the Dominican Lions Club of Miami adopted 10 rural schools in the Dominican Republic and provided school utensils and building repairs for each. It also started what was to become an annual clinic an annual clinic for indigent immigrants from the Dominican Republic. Given the well-known history of networks and community involvement, there is nothing extraordinary about this except that in 1996 the Lions Club of Miami was all of 2 years old and had only 12 members.[17] They are typical of the incipient organization which gives the equally incipient Dominican community in Miami shape and purpose. In 1990 there were 23,000 Dominicans in metropolitan Miami and in 2000, 39,000. Small numbers clearly do not stop these immigrants from organizing and mobilizing in the same way other Dominicans had done in New York, a community which, although considerably larger, is also recent in Caribbean terms. In New York as in Miami, the role of small businesses and of voluntary organizations has been critical. As Georges notes: "Leadership positions in one of these organizations, no matter how ephemeral, provide a platform of visibility and can potentially serve as a means of political promotions within the Dominican community, or even in the wider New York political arena and/or in the Dominican Republic."[18] Not surprisingly, Georges describes the binational relationship in terms of the lyrics of a popular Dominican merengue, "living with one foot here and the other there."

Dominicans have not been the only ones to adapt quite successfully to their new U.S. environment, virtually from the beginning of the movement. Early success and the social networks established by blacks from the English-speaking Caribbean broke many racial barriers which then allowed others to follow, even during periods of strident institutional and social racism. Their behavior was a combination of skills and attitudes developed back home, anticipatory socialization, (i.e., the enactment of expectations about what it took to be successful in the U.S.), and the existence of real material opportunities in their new land. But such a smooth and successful movement required more than personal attitudes and opportunities; it also required the background of a fairly high degree of cultural uniformity within the area of movement. In the case of the West Indies, the fact that both sending and receiving countries were at different times British gave them a similar language and somewhat similar legal and religious institutions. There is more cultural continuity between the U.S. and the English-speaking West Indies than with other parts of the Caribbean. The Haitians and Dominicans have not enjoyed this conjuncture of culture but the successes already described lead one to believe that they have engaged in sufficient "anticipatory socialization" as to overcome linguistic and other cultural barriers.

It therefore appears plausible to conceptualize the Caribbean and the U.S. as a sociocultural area,[19] keeping in mind Herskovits' admonition that the concept requires "fixing the eye on the broad lines of similarities and differences between cultures, not on the details . . ."[20] Thus, it is partly so because, as Portes indicated, capitalism operated generally within it, and as such, migration has taken place between units "articulated into the same system."[21]

By conceptualizing the Caribbean region as a sociocultural area with a high degree of shared values and norms and allowing considerable transferability of skills, one sees the region as something akin to one social structure. There is a logical inclination to see this as an expression of U.S. cultural hegemony. Before acceding to such an explanation, however, one has to inquire into the historical roots of certain cultural traits and complexes, such as respect for private property and the preference for profit-making enterprises. These cultural orientations have a profound historical legacy in the region.[22] One cannot fully understand the success of the Caribbean migrant as small capitalists in the U.S. without understanding their private-sector inclinations back home. As such, is it realistic to expect deep and enduring levels of anti-Americanism in such an area? We believe not. In fact, even as there might often be "resentment" over U.S. actions of a hegemonic type, the greatest body of evidence shows the presence of "binationality" among Caribbean people in the U.S. This, however, does not stop regional geopolitics from attempting to create formal barriers to U.S.–Caribbean relations.

In many ways the Association of Caribbean States (ACS), which was an act indicating a degree of anti-American resentment, was brought into being in Cartagena, Colombia, on July 24, 1994. The symbolism was not lost on any of the 25 states attending; that day marked the birthday of Simón Bolívar. And just as Bolívar had attempted to exclude the U.S. from the Congress of Panama of 1823, so the architects of the ACS excluded the U.S. from membership. The central idea was, on the face of it, admirable: to create a regional association that included only Caribbean states (and Cuba), strong enough to negotiate with the U.S. on a range of issues, including NAFTA.

Alas, this Caribbean post–Cold War initiative at confronting the challenges of globalization, in general, and U.S.-led initiatives such as NAFTA, specifically, was born with fatal flaws. Even understanding the sensitivities of the Cuba issue, one has to wonder about the exclusion of the U.S. by any region so closely tied to the U.S. by immigration and trade. Equally questionable was the adoption of an overarching ideology which perpetuated the statist developmental paradigm. As already noted in Chapter 3 above, important states in the Caribbean had already abandoned statism as national policy. This statism explains the bureaucracy-driven exclusion of the private sector from the ACS' initiatives and plans. Henry Gill, a noted consultant on economic development in the region, reveals that an earlier draft of the ACS convention did contemplate a role for the private sector, but the idea was eventually excluded. His interpretation is critical in light of the discussion in Chapter 5 above:

> Indeed, it could be argued that an important opportunity was missed for insti- tutionalizing private sector participation within the new organizational structure by not following the example of the MERCOSUR Industrial Council, which comprises representatives of the umbrella industrial organizations of the four member states (Argentina, Brazil, Paraguay, and Uruguay). Its aim is to evaluate the agreements being reached at the governmental level, to negotiate sectoral agreements, and to hold consultations on other integration process subjects. . . . In the present regional and global context, this would appear to be an important prerequisite for successfully implementing several objectives of the ACS convention.[23]

This was another instance where state officials who held office during the Cold War and during the ascendancy of "dependency" and other "Third World" theories, put hope over experience. It also reflects a certain incongruence in U.S.–Caribbean relations: excellent bilateral, i.e., one-to-one relations, often coexist with strained regional–U.S. relations. This is often a way of showing solidarity with Cuba and also an attempt to give substance to the oft-repeated rhetoric of "regional solidarity."

It is a fact that by the date of the founding of the ASC, not only was the growing commercial presence of the U.S. evident, so was that specifically of the state of Florida. Additionally, in Florida, it was the City of Miami's business elite which was spearheading the commercial drive towards the Caribbean and Latin America. This was given ample recognition when the Summit of the Americas launching the FTAA was held in that city in De- cember 1994. It was the 1990 Enterprise for the Americas Initiative of Pres- ident George H.W. Bush which brought to it fruition.

Given the previous discussion of size and viability, it is salutary to get a comparative sense of economic size when discussing relations between states. If one excludes the populations and the GDPs of Mexico, Venezuela, and Colombia, the remaining 22 full members of ACS have a total population of 66 million and a collective GDP of $114 billion. The state of Florida, the fourth largest in the U.S., has a population of 16 million but a GDP of $443 billion, four times that of the Caribbean. As one of the first economic analyses following the Summit of 1994 put it, "Florida, with half of all U.S./Central America trade, half of all U.S./Caribbean trade, and over 40%

of all U.S. exports to South America, is the leader in the U.S. for trade with these regions and will doubtlessly realize the highest gains of any area in the U.S. from hemispheric free trade."[24] Clearly, "Florida trade" means trade by private sector interests based in or operating out of South Florida. Not surprisingly, Florida sent strong delegations to the various Americas Business Forums which were specifically designated to give the private sectors from throughout the hemisphere direct input into the official decision-making.

It is a fact hardly to be countered by ideology that the Caribbean has to reckon with Miami. The Chilean magazine *América economía*[25] polled business executives in Latin America regarding the best venue from which to do business with Latin America and the Caribbean. The winner was Miami. Especially strong were its overall communication systems (telephones, Internet) and air and maritime transportation infrastructure. If Miami–Dade County were to be regarded as a separate state, consider the following features:

Population (2000)
2,140,000

Financial Institutions
As a financial capital of Latin America and the Caribbean, it has:
1. 121 national and international banks with $58 billion in total deposits
2. 13 Edge Act banks with $7 billion in deposits
3. 38 state licensed bank agencies with $12.5 billion in deposits
4. 59 commercial banks and 11 thrift institutions with 38.8 billion in deposits

Multinational Corporate Headquarters
Home to over 500 multinationals

Entertainment Center of the Hemisphere
About 3,000 entertainment companies based here, including Warner Bros., Sony, MTV, BMG Music, TV Colombia, and RTI Television

Trading Center
Handles $66 billion in trade through the following ports:
Miami International Airport
More than 33.8 million passengers in 1999
Served by 112 airlines; more passenger and cargo service to Latin America/Caribbean than all other U.S. airports combined
1,400 flights daily to more than 160 international cities

Port of Miami
Largest cruise port in the world: 3,112,355 passengers in 1999
Over 40 shipping lines connecting 362 ports in 132 countries

Medical Services
>   Health services employed some 4,000 new people in 2001, reflecting
>   the concerted effort to market its hospitals to Latin American and
>   Caribbean patients
>   "Salud Miami" is a consortium of seven hospitals with a Hispanic
>   marketing focus

One of the critical aspects of Caribbean migration to Miami is that it
has largely escaped the white (or Anglo)–black and Cuban–native black
antagonisms.[26] A telling case is that of the Haitians, arguably the poorest of
the Caribbean migrants to Miami and certainly the ones with the most
difficult immigration status. Interestingly enough, it was probably their
battle to achieve permanent residence which united the group and gave its
members focus and direction.

By the late 1970s and especially the 1990s the whole question of refugee
status as defined by national and international law was being submerged
by a flood of immigration and subsequent ethnic bargaining and lobbying.
The demographic of the area had changed dramatically, as Table 6.3
illustrates.

In Dade County it was not only Cubans and Haitians who were in the
streets demonstrating for refugee rights; 10,000 Nicaraguans were now
organized and marching, and thousands of Salvadoran, growing groups
of Guyanese, Guatemalans, and many other nationalities appeared to be
waiting in the wings. Claim to refugee status or to acquiring temporary
work permits (TWPs) appeared to have become a popular pitch of ethnic
lobbies, some legitimate and some not, but all equally impassioned.

The lobbying also had a feedback loop to the sending countries. By 1996,
the National Coalition for Haitian Refugees had changed its name to the
National Coalition for Haitian Rights. It could rightfully claim that its success
in securing the rights of Haitian refugees "helped establish a firmer foundation for future efforts to protect refugees fleeing persecution anywhere in

Table 6.3 Racial and Ethnic Composition, Miami–Dade County

Ethnicity	1990	2000
White Non-Hispanic	30%	21%
Hispanic[a]	49%	57%
Black	21%	20%
Other	—	2%

[a]Top six nationalities: Cubans (550,601), Puerto Ricans (80,327), Colombians (70,066),
Nicaraguans (69,257), Mexican (38,095), Honduran (26,820).
Source: U.S. Census Bureau, Census 2000, Summary, File 1.

the world." Reflecting the binational dynamics of population movements in the Caribbean, the U.S.-based coalition has added "the building of democratic institutions in Haiti" to its agenda.[27]

By the turn of the century, Haitians were buying many of the vacant houses in the Little River (Little Haiti) area of Miami–Dade and establishing businesses. Haitian businessman Ruly Ringo Cayard relates a story of material and professional progress in his community. "Education," he says, "is the key."[28] Whatever twists and turns take place in U.S. immigration policy, the Haitian community in Miami is now well established, skilled at the thrust and parry of U.S. pressure-group politics and, as such, is a new but quite permanent fixture of metropolitan Miami society.

Haitians were not the only ones seeking education in Miami. By 1998 there were 37,664 Caribbean-born students in Miami–Dade public schools, the largest numbers coming from:

Cuba 17,560 Bahamas 1,746 Dominican Republic 3,933 Haiti 5,744 Jamaica 2,901 Puerto Rico 4,289 That same year there were 6280 Caribbean students in the state university system, the largest group, at 1869, being Jamaican.[29]

The National Immigration Forum calls Miami "the cosmopolitan capital of the Americas" in their study of Miami–Dade as follows:

> . . . [It is] a growing center of international commerce, a dynamic urban area wrestling with its unique ethnic composition, and the breeding ground of a new generation of creative leaders committed to respecting pluralism. . . . Miami-Dade's ethnic mix is its greatest asset, and its multi-ethnic character is also good for business.[30]

The complex dynamics generating migration in the Caribbean socio-cultural area have been operating for about 100 years. Clearly, every Caribbean group and class participates in the culture of migration, and many have the wherewithal to actually move.

The sociopolitical dimension of migration, especially to Miami, is one of the fundamental characteristics of the area, and no decisions—by the receiving or sending societies—can be made without addressing it.

As if the concentration in Miami of commercial financial and immigration thrusts were not enough, in September 1997, Miami was chosen to be the center of military operations for a vast region, including the Caribbean. The implementation of the Panama Canal Treaty of 1977 led to the relocation of the U.S. Southern Command (Southcom) to Miami. While Miami is now not only the command center (since the Puerto Rican bases at Fort Buchanan and Roosevelt Roads are being downsized), it is also gaining some of the active military personnel who are being relocated. Interestingly, despite the virtual closing down of all major bases in the area, including those in Panama, the purview of Southcom has not changed. Southcom has 32 nations as its responsibility, 19 in Central and South America and 13 in the Caribbean. This represents an area of 15.6 million square miles, 1/6th of the landmass of the world.

Along with the tasks assigned to all U.S. regional unified commands, defending U.S. interests and assisting the militaries of friendly nations, Southcom responds to the following mission statement:[31]

> *USSOUTHCOM shapes the environment within its area of responsibility by conducting theater engagement and counterdrug activities in order to promote democracy, stability and collective approaches to threats to regional security; when required responds unilaterally or multilaterally to crises that threaten regional stability or national interest, and prepares to meet future hemispheric challenges.*

The critique that during the Cold War the U.S. was attempting to "restore its eroded regional hegemony" by militarizing the Caribbean had considerable validity.[32] In the post–Cold War era, however, even as U.S. military capabilities are greater than ever, there is little talk of the "militarization" of the region. Indeed, the discussions seem to concentrate on the inadequate level of U.S. military security in the face of the increasing threats of the drug trade, arms smuggling, and the activities of organized international crime. Further, even though Miami now houses the military command for the region, the area continues to be a virtual "open city" and locus of many illicit activities including drug running and gunrunning, alien smuggling, and money laundering, harboring vast sums of flight capital which Caribbean nations can ill afford to lose.[33]

Even in military terms, conventional U.S. hegemonic behavior has been modified, but the idea that this modification has insulated the sovereignties of Caribbean states is illusory. The fact is that the reduction of state involvement in a range of activities has provided greater operating space for licit and illicit activities alike. The sovereignty of the U.S. and of the Caribbean states is being challenged—clearly the latter much more than the former.[34]

Demographic trends make it highly likely that the historical patterns of Caribbean migration to the U.S. will continue. For one, despite the overall drop in rates of natural increase of population, the projections of Caribbean population growth should leave no one sanguine about the capacity of the small countries to sustain even present levels of development to provide an adequate number of jobs. The population (with migration) grew from 33 million to 37 million between 1990 and 2000. Without migration it is projected to be 49 million by the year 2050, or 54 million if there is zero migration after 2000. Clearly, keeping access to the U.S. is of vital national concern to every Caribbean nation.

If nothing else, these trends will continue to cement the transnational and binational links which shape this sociocultural area.

6.2 The Negatives: Violent Crime and Political Corruption Threatening Democracy and Sovereignty

Clearly crime, and especially drug-traffic-related crime, is one of the most contentious areas of U.S.–Caribbean relations. During the era of the Cold War there were often geopolitical reasons for sweeping aspects of this crime under the rug. In the post–Cold War era no such diplomatic niceties are in evidence. In fact, there is a very definite tendency on the part of Caribbean officials to portray the U.S. as the villain. Complaints about the number of criminal deportees and the flow of small arms have now joined the traditional complaints about the "brain drain" aspect of the wider criticisms of U.S. policy.

Addressing a joint sitting of the Jamaican Parliament, President Bharatt Jagdeo of Guyana chastised the U.S. for "aggressively" recruiting their nurses and teachers while at the same time "aggressively" deporting criminals and turning a blind eye to the export of small arms.[35] So bitter is the sentiment throughout the region about this deportation policy that a former ambassador of the Dominican Republic referred to it as a major part of the "Second Cold War."[36] Indeed, in September, 1999, the members of the Caribbean Regional Security System met in Roseau, Dominica, to formulate a common position vis-à-vis the U.S. in terms of the threats to sovereignty and security posed by the deportees. Nothing ever came of it.

There can be no doubt about the increasing number of deportees as Table 6.4 shows. There can be no doubt, either, that the sense of alarm about the presence of the "American-educated" criminals was regionwide and that regional leaders were struggling to cope with this crime wave.

The prime minister of St. Lucia was adamant: the island was facing a "new type" of criminal and would have to adjust its institutions accordingly.[37] By February, 1999 the island's home affairs minister was preparing new legislation to counter this crime wave. The specifics were not revealed but the minister's rhetoric left no doubt as to the new draconian mood, in St. Lucia and elsewhere in the Caribbean: "The people [criminals] we are dealing with have no scruples, no souls. . . . They are veritable animals, and animals must be hunted down and tamed."[38] From the Bahamas down the chain of islands to Guyana, jails are bursting at the seams.[39] In Trinidad it is kidnapping of businessmen, 8 in 2001, 29 in 2002, and 33 as of July 2003. No wonder the *Trinidad Guardian*, following the lead of the Chamber of Commerce, asked the minister of national security to resign.[40]

Table 6.4 U.S. Deportation of Criminals to Caribbean Countries by Year (1993–1998)

Country	1993	1994	1995	1996	1997	1998	Total
Antigua	14	13	19	14	18	26	104
Aruba	2	2	1	2	3	3	13
Bahamas	44	53	55	67	46	67	332
Barbados	27	28	23	33	43	46	200
Belize	83	72	53	76	90	109	483
Dominica	20	21	17	16	23	18	115
Grenada	12	7	12	12	9	15	67
Guyana	82	76	70	74	125	141	568
Haiti	193	125	245	213	260	309	1,345
Jamaica	870	844	921	990	1211	1203	6,039
Dominican Republic	1024	969	1165	1472	1952	1669	8,251
St. Kitts–Nevis	11	5	8	9	17	15	65
St. Lucia	12	8	7	12	13	22	74
St. Vincent and Grenada	5	9	13	12	18	13	70
Suriname	2	1	0	0	3	2	8
Total	2,401	2,233	2,609	3,002	3,831	3,658	17,734

Source: INS figures cited in Bernardo Vega, *Diario de una misión en Washington*, p. 500.

This sudden chorus of alarm and call for retribution might leave the uninitiated with the belief that the Caribbean jumped overnight from the days of praedial larceny as the most common crime, and of unarmed police providing society with protection, to what is today virtually open combat between heavily armed opponents. The reality is otherwise. Crime—and, specifically, drug related crime—has been on the increase for a very long time. But there has been for an equally long time an evident tendency towards relative passivity on the part of local authorities. Even after major outcries, and even with the local press literally pleading for action, there has been a tendency to shirk responsibility.

In May of 2002, *The Gleaner* of Jamaica ran a two-part series on the Kingston–London axis and the role of the "yardies" or gangs in the trade. The report noted something which, again, has been known for some time: Jamaican criminal gangs were part of "a single transnational network which operates simultaneously in the U.K., in Jamaica, and in North America."[41] Despite this reporting and planning, a week later the commissioner of police publicly expressed his frustration at not being able to dismiss policemen suspected of being involved in the drug trade. His comments elicited a sense of astonishment from *The Gleaner*. In an editorial entitled "Trapping Crooked Cops," *The Gleaner* brought into question the professionalism of the police force by arguing that,"Everybody on his/her veranda knows the criminals!"[42] The editorial went on to say the authorities should arrest the corrupt officials. One way to do this said the newspaper was to forge even stronger links with Scotland Yard.

Interestingly enough, that same week the commissioner of police in Trinidad and Tobago was complaining about the heavy criticism he was receiving for not doing more about the crime wave which was shaking the islands, especially the kidnapping of prominent business people. He could not make decisions, he said, because he was constantly stymied by the Police Services Commission.[43] The commissioner was surely responding to the repeated charges in the press about "rogue policemen" and general corruption in the forces of law and order.[44]

The state of denial in the Caribbean about the domestic causes of crime has existed for easily two decades. This also has been true about the corruption in official circles. The cant everywhere was the same: it is the North Americans and Europeans who use drugs. Caribbean people neither produce nor consume; they merely provide one function of the market— they transport the goods. Even a cursory overview of the contemporary drug scene in the Caribbean, however, reveals a problem of such enormous dimension it defies logic to believe that it is a new phenomena; it has to have had a long gestation. The problem clearly shows the "modern" aspect of these societies, i.e., societies which have always been an integral part of the developed world, its good and not-so-good sides.

In fact, in the Caribbean the threat of drugs and its extension into raging crime raises anew the question of viability, not as before in purely economic terms but in terms of sustaining democratic, law-abiding entities. Drugs, and the international cartels which handle them, are now perceived as a threat to the very foundation of civil society and to true sovereignty. This has turned the concept of a "war" into less of an analogy and more of a literal description of the Caribbean reality at the turn of the century. What is more, experts in intelligence fear that the war is at best in a stalemate and at worst in danger of being lost.

Jamaica is an excellent example of the long disconnect between growing crime, elite inattention, and lack of decisive action. Jamaica also demonstrates the slow shift of the focus of blame, from U.S. actions and inactions to domestic factors, including, very specifically, widespread political corruption.

6.2.1 The Jamaican Case

Jamaican authorities have had what can only be called a delayed or slow-motion way of acknowledging the depth and breadth of criminal activity on the island. Journalists and academicians have long been describing the growing links between Colombia drug-runners, Jamaican drug "dons," and the web of corruption which provides them with cover and protection. There is something frightfully repetitious in the warnings about crime and its effects and the inaction which tends to follow these warnings.

In August, 2002, the Report of the Police Executive Research Forum was released.[45] Crime and fear of crime, said the report, was "at the very top of people's minds." The very quality of life on the island was at stake:

> The economic viability of the country is being questioned as citizens talk openly about friends and business associates migrating off the island and the concomitant concern about an ongoing healthy tourist industry. So urgent is the issue of crime to the lives of Jamaicans that it is fair to say that unless there is a virtual sea change in the crime issue, the country's very existence is in danger.

This was certainly not the first alarming report about the dire situation the country was in. In 1996, when the murder rate had reached 889 (the same level as 1980, a year of terrible political violence), the Minister of National Security and Justice announced an emergency 20-point plan geared to drastically reducing the murder rate in 1997. Aside from a "zero tolerance" policy for minor offenses, there was to be a new high-tech center to investigate organized crime. In fact, it was promised that "the full glare of the police searchlight" would, from then on, be focused on organized crime and criminal gangs.[46] Part of the center's activities would be a database linked to a number of international agencies in countries in which Jamaican criminals were known to have contacts, even networks—the U.S., Canada, the U.K., and Colombia.

Just 2 months into 1997, however, Jamaicans were seeing an increase, not a decrease, in crime and were fearful for their nation. "It is idle to debate what is the most pressing problem facing the Jamaican society," said the editor of the major newspaper, " . . . clearly it is the ogre of crime that stands out. . . . The nation itself is at risk."[47] This editorial message would be repeated time and time again by this same newspaper. In March 2003 an editorial dealt with a survey of managers of businesses on the island, 92% of whom believed that crime was the main factor affecting both employment and investment. The editorial spoke of the "seemingly uncontrollable crime problem."[48]

Part of the problem was that not everyone appeared to share this level of alarm. Geoff Brown, criminologist at the University of the West Indies, noted that despite warnings, many important Jamaicans continued to be "purposefully blind, seeing no evil, hearing no evil and speaking not of the evil." This, he warned, is of concern because the power of Jamaican drug dons now parallels that of Mafia bosses in the U.S., and, worse, Jamaica "ain't seen nothing yet" as a Colombia-like situation appeared to be in the making.[49] Brown knew what he was talking about when he described what had already become a familiar pattern in the corporate Kingston area of Jamaica: police shoot an area's "drug don," then his followers declare war on the security forces and literally control certain "garrison" areas for a period of time, often exacting concessions from the politicians. The police, frustrated with the "pandering" of the politicians, take the law in their own hands and begin executing gang members.

In April 2000, the killing of the don of Vineyard Town led to the murder of two policemen and the subsequent calling out of the Jamaica Defense Force (army) to protect police stations. The murder rate by then was 260—in the month of April alone, 170. Absolutely no one was in doubt that crime was perceived as the gravest threat to Jamaica's society and its future development, economic, social, and even political.[50]

Interestingly, as the island's minister of national security and justice told a Miami audience in April, 2000, general crime in Jamaica was down by 20% in 1999 but not the murder rate. Contrary to historical patterns, only 30% of the murders were attributable to domestic violence; the rest had "substantially" to do with the influx of drugs and the availability of weapons, 99% "smuggled in various ways from the U.S." The minister then went on to talk about the role of organized criminal activities.[51] That same week of late April 2000, the island witnessed for the first time in its history, a judge being sentenced to prison for a criminal offense. No one seemed surprised that it had to do with a drug case.[52] Basic institutions were clearly being penetrated, a fact long recognized by authorities outside the island. The U.S. Department of State, for instance, reported in March 2000 that Jamaica's counter-drug cooperation is "good and improving." It also reported, however, that drug trafficking contributes to one of the island's gravest ills: corruption. "The GOJ arrested 6,718 drug offenders in 1999," says the report. "Nevertheless, no major drug traffickers were arrested or convicted during 1999, and they continue to operate with apparent impunity."[53]

A history of the origins and development of this situation of crisis in Jamaica helps bring home the point made in Chapter 1: stages, patterns, and causes of social change differ in various parts of the Caribbean. The history of crime has been no exception.

The Jamaica which became independent in 1962 had few of the characteristics which tended to attract organized crime to the Caribbean: no casinos as in Cuba, no offshore banks as in the Bahamas or history of deep corruption on the part of the political elites as was the case of Dominica. Jamaica's problem was violence between the two political parties organized for electoral and, thus, patronage purposes. In the decade between 1960 and 1970 there were 1,935 violent incidents with 746 deaths. Of the latter, 111 were killed and 188 were wounded by the police.[54]

Organized political violence was violence within, not against, the system, and it began well before there was public consciousness of the drug trade and the violence it spawned. It was this interparty violence which led to the first steps in the transformation of Jamaican institutions of law and order. It was the Left-leaning regime of Michael Manley which in 1972 introduced the Gun Court and special stockade for its convicts, and ordered a closer collaboration between the police and the army, the Jamaican Defence Force. There is no evidence that anyone other than "gunmen" were ever sent to that notorious stockade. What about the "money men?"

As early as 1966 the leading Jamaican newspaper, *The Gleaner*, asked "why it is the police never, ever, have sought and brought to justice any of the big wheels in the Western ganja [marijuana] trade; [crime and drugs] are related."[55] It took a major report in *The Financial Times*[56] of London, however, to force the reality of the Jamaica–U.S. crime connection home. In an article titled "Guns, Ganja and Gangsters," the *Times* estimated that over a ton of marijuana was exported to the U.S. every day from Jamaica.

Jamaican intellectuals, however, were completely enveloped in the "Left–Right" ideological struggles of the 1970s. It was capitalism and an "unjust international economic order" which were to blame for intrasystem violence. Crime was "epiphenomenal" or part of the "superstructure" of the Jamaican dependent capitalist system. This explains why Terry Lacey's major study of violence written in the 1970s ignores the drug trade throughout most of his analysis. It is only at the very end of a long treatise that Lacey addresses the drug trade and elite corruption, saying that it "can now be openly discussed."[57] "There is little chance," he concluded, "of coping with the problems of economic and social development in Jamaica if racketeers and gangsters are able to corrupt and undermine Jamaican society."[58]

In the late 1980s, after a number of years during which the Jamaican electorate had chosen many a new government without any serious debate or discussion of the Jamaican drug problem, a dramatically changed perception of the threat became evident. The drug dealers, wrote Carl Stone, the foremost pollster at the time, were "crippling Jamaica. . . . the very future and livelihood of this country and its people are at risk." Such was his sense of threat that he urged that steps be taken "in a hurry" to stop this trade, including making "any constitutional changes necessary."[59] What explains such a dramatic switch, and what does it say about the nature of the threat to the security of Caribbean countries? The answer is that it was a response to some very real challenges to the Jamaican state's control over its public health and economic activities.

While the word "posse" ("yardie" in the U.K.) was not widely used for gangs in the 1960s, the districts of origin and names of the gangs which later became notorious have a familiar ring: the Max, Blue Mafia, Dunkirk,

Phoenix, and Vikings. In the 1960s they were called "criminals" and "hooligans" and were known to be the "soldiers" of various leaders in both dominant political parties, the People's National Party (PNP) and the Jamaican Labour Party (JLP). It is precisely this native origin, their links with political parties, their deep roots in the local culture and networks of corruption and, fundamentally, their tight links with the Jamaican diaspora in the U.S. and the U.K. which explain their independence of action in the growing drug trade, and their capacity to shift from ganja to cocaine. According to Laurie Gunst, the first known and proven case of Jamaica's involvement in the international cocaine trade occurred in February 1975.[60] Although this involved a prominent businessman, the posses originally recruited in the slums of Kingston soon took control of the business. The sequence, according to Gunst, was as follows:

1. Party elites make use of gunmen to protect them and their constituencies.
2. With outlaws receiving outside sources of funding from marijuana trade, they begin to act independently of the politicians.
3. Politicians, feeling threatened by the crime and generalized violence, unleash the police on these posses. This "transformed the police force from a British-inspired constabulary into a tribe of killers in uniform." (39)
4. Gang members flee to the U.S., Canada, and Britain just as the crack trade is beginning. "Their timing was superb," says Gunst, "the Jamaican posses quickly proved themselves indispensable to the Colombians, Cubans and Panamanians who controlled the supply of cocaine and needed street-level dealers." (xv)
5. The U.S. begins to deport the Jamaicans; they unleash a new crime wave on the island.

This sequence certainly holds up to historical scrutiny. The capability to penetrate and operate in the American market has been one of the telling characteristics of the Jamaicans. In the decade of the 1970s, the U.S. became well acquainted with the violent Jamaican posses. Two in particular, the Shower Posse (originally with close ties to the JLP) and the Spangler Posse (originally close to the PNP), were operating with some 5000 members each throughout the U.S. By the end of the 1980s, the GAO calculated that there were some 40 posses in the U.S. with perhaps 22,000 members. An integral part of their trading scheme was smuggling guns. A new and sensationalist literature has given the dons of these posses near-legendary status.[61]

Despite all the evidence there was a continued reticence to openly confront the real situation. Certainly, the issue of the gangs' political ties, present or past, was a delicate one.[62] Then there was the issue of national reputation and a general penchant for sweeping drug-related crimes under the carpet for fear that it might affect both tourism and foreign investment. It took the writings of courageous journalists to fill the void. In October 1994, *Gleaner* columnist Dawn Ritch, drawing on police files, began revealing the links between crime, drugs, and politicians.[63] Despite the well-documented columns, in November 1994, the deputy commissioner of police skirted the issue, claiming not to have seen Ritch's columns. He gave the following "philosophical" (to use his own words) response to a journalist's querying, "Why do Jamaicans regard crime as the number one national problem?": "When social conditions exist which do not comfortably accommodate all social classes on an equal level, it is not uncommon for crime to increase . . ."[64]

There was plenty of evidence in the 1990s and later that the drug-related problems of so much concern in the 1980s had continued to grow. There was also evidence of decline in the integrity of the security forces. In 1994 the narcotics division of Jamaica's Police Services seized and destroyed J$1.3 billion worth of crack cocaine, ganja, and cocaine powder. Then, in October, 1995, Jamaican narcotics detectives intercepted an aircraft bringing J$111 million in cocaine. But in January 1996, it was reported that a significant part of the seized cargo had disappeared from the narcotics department's vault. Such was the distrust and lack of investigatory capabilities that three U.S. polygraph experts were brought in to help with the investigation. Officials were talking darkly about a possible "syndicate" operating in the police force.

The new cocaine contacts with the Colombians took various forms but some of the better known routes appear to be by "fast boat" from the San Andrés y Providencia Archipelago of Colombia and by air on any of the two airlines with Jamaican connections: SAM which flies from Medellín and COPA which flew, and still flies, from Panama. It was said that increasing numbers of Colombians were going to Jamaica on 30- to 60-day visas to organize multikilogram shipments by container and other commercial craft into the U.S.[65]

If this was going on in the 1990s, skeptical Jamaicans could not be faulted for asking why it took until June 2002 for the minister of national security to speak of something laymen had been noting for years: the large number of "fancy houses" rented by what the locals referred to as "South American" nationals in western Jamaica, especially Montego Bay. The police force, he said, intended to set up a National Intelligence Bureau to screen visas and keep track of these large numbers of "South Americans." The local paper felt compelled to editorialize that for quite a long time they had been reporting on the "go-fast" boats bringing cocaine and guns from Colombia and their contributions to the escalating drug wars on the island.[66]

Despite these frightening statistics and despite the increasing alarm in the high number of citizen complaints, there is no evidence that the society is ready to deal with a major contributor to the situation: official corruption. It is not that there have been no studies and warning as to the corrosive consequences of that corruption. The fact is that the political elites had let the corrosive forces of drug corruption operate for too long. They were focused on pursuing the common criminal, not the "money men."

In 1991, Jamaican pollster and university professor Carl Stone carried out a major survey of public attitudes towards the police and the court system.[67] The results were extremely discouraging: the public trusted neither the police, the courts, nor the justice system. The levels of support had dropped to where they had been in the violent 1970s; less than 40% believed the police could be trusted.

> *The police also get a low rating for their contribution to the fight against hard drugs because many citizens believe that the police are deeply involved in the drug trade.*

The court system fared even worse in terms of the public perception of their honesty. According to Stone, the strong perception that the courts were outright corrupt was a "carry over" from the strong perceptions that the police and the prison system were corrupt. Indeed, Stone continued, what he called "the alarming rate" of deterioration in the justice system stemmed from "a pervasive feeling among the public that all public institutions in the country are corrupt . . ."[68]

As early as 1986, Carl Stone had explained the rise in vigilante killings as resulting from people's impatience with and distrust of the criminal justice system. Because of these failings in the forces of law and order, citizens took the law in their own hands "and seek to establish their own 'balance of terror.'"[69]

In such an ambiance tempers tend to be short and patience scarce but the focus is on the easy target, the lowly gunman. The inclination from all sectors of the society to deal with this visible part of the problem, for "speedy justice," is great. Such impatience has been immortalized by the 1969 words of then Prime Minister Hugh Shearer:

> "When it comes to handling crime, in this country I do not expect any policeman, when he handles a criminal, to recite any Beatitudes to him."[70]

The prime minister's words were later repeated by the island's most read columnist, Morris Cargil, who observed in 1986 that "in the present circumstances" his only complaint was that the police "did not shoot enough criminals."[71] Dawn Ritch, fearing "anarchy," wrote an open letter to the prime minister: "If you do nothing else, please restore public order and cut the crime rate instantly. If you have convicted murders to hang, hang them."[72]

Predictably, none of these draconian vigilante actions or calls for the swift carrying out of hangings, indeed, not even the reintroduction of flogging, made much of a difference in the general climate. Neither did the over 20,000 private security guards on the island.

In 1998, Jamaica's murder rate was 42.53 per 100,000 inhabitants or, as *The Economist* observed in a story on the island's collapsing system of law and order, it was 20 times the murder rate in London. That year 15 policemen had been murdered. Flogging was reintroduced, and Jamaica was threatening to stop all appeals to the Judicial Committee of the Privy Council; several of its British members opposed capital punishment. Indeed, the push to create a Caribbean Court of Appeals to replace the Privy Council was the result of the rising popularity of capital punishment in the West Indies.

The official threats of "draconian responses" were interspersed with intimations that the island was descending into "chaos" and "anarchy." These words were used to describe everything, from the widespread failures in the banking and finance sectors, the harassment of tourists, and the "contamination" with drugs of merchandise containers to the increasing use of roadblocks to express collective discontent. As an editorial in the *Gleaner* put it, "The dilemma of this challenge to lawful authority has the seeds of anarchy."[73] Behind this perception of "anarchy" there might be aspects of a deep cultural orientation—the Victorian interpretations of drug users and criminals generally as cases of individuals "falling from grace" rather than as evidence of systemic problems. As one observer who has studied the Jamaican situation from a sociological perspective notes, the concept of culture violence finds its counterpart in the generalization that "respectable" Jamaican society "expects 'discipline' in social relations, in the sense of personal self-control as well as public order . . ."[74]

It would be a gross exaggeration to say that Jamaican society in 2003 is in a state of anarchy or that "chaos" has overtaken its institutions. On the other hand, what is quite clear is that the level of violence and crime has shown no sign of abatement. It was at 37 murders per 100,000 inhabitants in 2001, fourth in the world after South Africa (59), Colombia (56), and Namibia (45). Also quite evident was the further entrenchment of the garrison constituency. Perhaps most significant as a threat to democracy, however, is the dominant role of what a bipartisan committee on crime called the "nontraditional community leader."[75] The latter can neither be persuaded nor coopted by the state since he no longer depends on the prebends handed out by the politicians. Drugs provide him with financial independence. The ongoing "war" with the forces of law and order reveal that the state cannot successfully threaten him. He is as well, if not better, armed as they are. In short, he enjoys an independence which the politicians were now treating with marks of great respect, such attendance at his funeral and those of his relatives.

While the situation in the "alleys and gullies" of the various ghettos was slipping out of official control, things at the official level had a familiar ring to them. In July 2002, the government announced a special Anti-Narcotics Squad. It would be the first time, a government spokesman said, that such a specialized force would concentrate on counter-narcotics activities. Informed Jamaicans, of course, had witnessed such creations before. They were also skeptical of the optimism of former President Jimmy Carter who, with the greatest goodwill, has taken a special interest in Jamaica. Addressing the issue of corruption, Carter concluded that "With civil society, the private sector, and government cooperating toward a common goal, I am confident that Jamaica will be a model for others."[76] The situation on the ground appeared to be rather different. The following story appeared in *The Jamaica Weekly Gleaner* in late August 2003:

> *Highly mobile and well-organised criminal gangs are punching major holes in the Government's latest offensive on criminal activities in the country. On August 11, Police Commissioner Francis Forbes admitted that aspects of the crime initiative had failed and that it was necessary to return to the drawing board to come up with a new plan.*[77]

In fact, while there was a drop in overall crime in Jamaica in 2003, there was already by mid-2003 a 20% increase in murders.

Rather than serving as an example of the possible solution, the Jamaican case illustrates the dangerous consequences of countries, indeed whole regions, ignoring significant types of crimes while they address other "more important" issues—in this case, geopolitical reasons. During the Cold War the U.S. ignored the drug-related criminal activities of Cuban exiles and Bahamian leaders. There were straightforward political reasons: Jamaicans ignored the growing marijuana trade and the strengthening of the politically connected posses.

Patently evident, also, is the fact that after all the squabbles between the U.S. and Jamaica over the signing of the Shiprider Agreement, this extraterritorial extension of U.S. naval power, and concomitant concession of Jamaican sovereignty, has done little to reduce the traffic in drugs and the violence it engenders. It protected neither Jamaican sovereignty nor U.S. borders. Between October 2001 and April 2002—and as Jamaican democracy was under threat—it is calculated that the amount of cocaine entering through Miami went up 300%.[78]

In the final analysis, the Jamaican case is merely a somewhat extreme example of what is occurring throughout the region as the integration into the U.S. has increased. This is well stated by one who studied the situation in Jamaica from primary records and interviews. "Tighter integration in the U.S. drug trade," says Anthony Harriot, "has facilitated the importation of guns, the development of multiclass criminal networks, corrupt manipulation of the control agents of the state, and the corruption of whole communities and political institutions.[79] In Trinidad, it is kidnappings and murder. In Curaçao, a drug war between Colombian gangs openly operating there; 12 Colombians were murdered in the first 7 months of 2002.[80] In fact, there is not an island in the region where the threat of crime is not on the top of everyone's list of civic concerns.

Three critical links account for this situation throughout the region:

1. The cover which official corruption provides organized crime
2. The deep pockets of organized crime which gives it access to (a) criminal recruits, whether deportees or locals, and (b) an ample supply of guns
3. The links organized crime have in the islands with U.S.-based criminal activities and organizations

Predictably, Caribbean elites find it much easier to blame the U.S. for their predicament than root out the corruption which covers the criminals with a blanket of impunity. "An Imported Crime Problem!" screams an editorial in the *Trinidad Express*.[81] The reference is to the deportees, blamed for the kidnappings on the island and the crime wave "across the region."[82] They were, said the editorial, "a national security threat." In Jamaica, at a gathering of regional intellectuals, both the chancellor of the University of the West Indies, Sir Shridath Ramphal, and the prime minister of St. Vincent, Ralph Gonsalves, launched what the press called "a fierce attack" on the U.S. for ignoring the region. In Miami 55 Caribbean students refuse to substitute the word "resentment" for the word "hatred" to describe U.S.–Caribbean relations in mid-2002.[83]

A decade and a half after the end of the Cold War, U.S.–Caribbean relations are in a delicate state. A decade and a half after the end of the Cold War finds the Caribbean with agriculture in decline, with manufacturing facing stiff competition, with tourism buffeted by U.S. and world trends, and crime out of control. In the midst of all these dismal facts, there is a sliver of light: the Jamaican admission that they need international help. "We have collaborated," said the superintendent of the narcotics police, "with the British, Canadians, and the United States, and the French."[84]

CONCLUSION

By tracing U.S.–Caribbean relations before and after the end of the Cold War, this book highlights the continuities and changes across a range of areas of mutual interests. As such, it represents a case study in the complexity of international relations between one superpower and a large number of small states. The U.S.' capacity for an outright exercise of hegemonic power exists in the Caribbean as nowhere else in the world. The disparities of power have been a constant in these relations. This being said, the book also demonstrates that in international relations nothing is static. And so, changing world circumstances have brought about discernable changes in the way the U.S. uses its erstwhile hegemonic capabilities.

Two fundamentals have changed in the global context: the rise of new networks of sovereign nations willing to act in concert and of a new international network of transnational and international agencies, representing the attempt to create a new international order. The nations of the Caribbean have taken full advantage of both trends, using the instruments provided to negotiate with the superpower as well as the European Union. A comment regarding the failed WTO September, 2003 meeting in Cancun puts the operation on these global forces in context. "Only a couple of years ago," said *The Wall Street Journal*,[1] "the U.S. and the EU could largely dictate events at the global trade body." This is no longer so because "developing countries have become increasingly well organized and willing to throw their weight around." Among those carrying the message of the "developing" world was Jamaica's and CARICOM's spokesman, Ambassador Richard Bernal. "There is nothing for small countries in this (US/EU/Japan) proposal. We don't want any of this."[2] Whether such a stance, called "the harsh rhetoric of the 'won't do'" by U.S. Trade Representative Robert B. Zoellick, contributes to the welfare of the small nations remains to be seen. What is evident is the willingness of these small states to use the mechanism of the WTO to pry concessions out of the U.S., i.e., to modify the hegemonic relationship.

The ongoing case of Antigua and Barbuda vs. the U.S. affords a good example of some key aspects of this new context. In answer to a request by Antigua and Barbuda to appoint a panel to adjudicate a complaint against the U.S., WTO Director General Supachain Panitchpakdi last month appointed a three-man panel with B. K. Zuthshi of India as chairman. The other two panelists were Virachai Plasai of Thailand and Richard Plender, Queen's Council of the U.K. The case arises from a charge by Antigua and Barbuda that the U.S. Wire Act, generally, and the U.S. ban on the cross-border supply of gaming and betting services from Antigua and Barbuda to the U.S. violates U.S. commitments under the General Agreement of Trade in Services which seeks to create equal conditions of competition for domestic and foreign service suppliers. Antigua officials claim that over four and a half years from 1999, the government has lost EC$90 million (US$33.3 million) in license fees, and over EC$100 million (US$37 million) in wages and salaries as the number of Internet gaming entities were pushed out of business by U.S. actions.

Aside from what it says about the spread of the Internet and electronic commerce, two very critical aspects of this case tell us immediately that we are in the post–Cold War era. First, Antigua, far from arguing from some "Third World" or South vs. North paradigm, is pelting the hegemon with its own petards of "free trade" and the WTO as the final court on issues of trade. Second, further confirming that these two adversaries are on the same ideological arena in terms of governmental practices, Antigua has hired one of Washington's most influential law firms to argue its case. Clearly, Antigua will have many friends in court, including the U.K., since all it is doing is trying to cash in on the online gambling industry which is said to generate close to $50 billion a year.[3] On this score, the Antigua–Barbuda case reflects the Caribbean complaint that while they are small-fry in the world's offshore financial sector, they have been made targets of choice of the U.S. and the OECD. Whatever merit and logic there might be to such a reproach, and as much as it is used to rein in U.S. power, Antigua, as with most Caribbean states, should not lose sight of the limitations and modifications imposed on its own sovereignty by the development choices it makes. And, in that same vein, a realistic assessment of the opportunity costs can never come too early. The small state, not the large one, has everything to lose.

Small nations lean heavily on an international respect and regard for sovereignty. Not only does the emphasis reflect the collective expectations of the world community at the time they emerged as independent states, it also continues to be an eminently practical and realistic understanding of the vulnerabilities which might exist in the absence of such an emphasis. There are, however, limits, and in few areas are those limits more in evidence than in U.S.–Caribbean relations. It is a plausible thought that on small islands, the concept of *sovereignty* is intimately tied in with a keen sense of national identity and territorial control. The term "insularity," at least when stripped of its more pejorative psychological implications, adequately describes this relationship. All this explains why it is quite paradoxical that these small states, so nationalistic and so profoundly conscious of their sovereignty, should now be on development paths which are in many ways challenges to that sovereignty. The title of Chapter 5 puts it succinctly: they are small players in a global game. Whether it is creating financial "paradises," EPZs, or offshore gambling and pornographic telephone services, the state has to concede degrees of sovereignty in order to get the business. The Flags of Convenience businesses, so popular in the Caribbean, illustrate this reality. Of the 28 Flag of Convenience Registries listed by the International Transport Workers Federation, 11 are in the Greater Caribbean: Antigua/Barbuda, Aruba, Bahamas, Barbados, Belize, Bermuda, Cayman Islands, Honduras, the Netherlands Antilles, Panama, and St. Vincent.[4]

It is, of course, true that it was the U.S. which in 1940 began the business of registering their ships in Liberia as a means of skirting the U.S. Neutrality Act. That offshore service soon went from having a military–diplomatic function to serving tax benefit purposes. This, and low wages, explain the spread of the industry. Today, the misuse of the Liberian operation (in the words of one UN expert, it was "little more than a cash-extraction operation. . . ."[5]) and the concern over labor exploitation, have put the Flag of Convenience business under a microscope. Small Caribbean states will not escape the scrutiny.

What small countries are realizing is that they are easy targets for a worldwide revulsion against corruption in all its forms: bribery of public officials, trading in influence, accountancy fraud, money laundering, and bank secrecy. Indeed, these were some of the topics of the first global anticorruption convention held in Vienna in July, 2003[6] and were "the biggest stumbling block" at the WTO meeting in Cancun.[7] Stumbling block or not, these concerns are sure to remain on the table in all international negotiations.

Despite the brave front put up within the WTO, it is evident that there is increasing competition among all nations, North or South, for a wide array of business opportunities from markets to capital investments to offshore businesses. In this sense, again, there is no firm and enduring North–South divide or South–South cooperation. Indeed, the list of conflicting national interests among developing nations is a long one.

Logically, so are the negotiating strategies they use to gain national advantages. As noted in Chapter 4, such is the financial dependence among Caribbean countries on tariffs that it becomes very difficult to abolish them in the name of free trade even as this free trade is within the region and to the ultimate benefit of the region. And the Caribbean is not alone. While in no way justifying the hypocrisy of the massive subsidies in the industrial states, it is a fact that some of the main reasons for continued anemic South–South trade are the barriers they erect themselves. Tariffs serve as a source of funds and also to protect the interests of the most influential economic sectors in individual countries. U.S. Trade Representative Robert Zoellick is empirically correct when he notes that "About 70% of the tariffs that developing country exporters pay are imposed by other developing countries." This, of course, begs the questions as to, first, which practice—rich country subsidies or poor country tariffs—does the most harm to world free trade and, second, which group is in the best position to cut the Gordian knot of subsidies vs. tariffs. In the final analysis it boils down to the cliche that all international politics is ultimately domestic politics, as described in this book. It can be summarized in four broad generalizations which are directly relevant to future U.S.–Caribbean relations.

First, despite what occurred in Cancun, the days of an enduring Third World solidarity are gone. Evidence of this is the fact that the same WTO Settlement Body which agreed to hear the Antigua–Barbuda case also agreed to hear a challenge to the EU export subsidies on sugar. The request came from three major sugar producers: Australia, Brazil, and Thailand. Clearly, a judgment in their favor will negatively affect the CARICOM countries. It is, in a way, a repeat of the "banana wars" (discussed in Chapter 4) which pitted several Latin American countries against the Caribbean.

Second, the Caribbean is well aware that among the industrial countries, the U.S. is still attentive to their particular concerns. Certainly, the U.S. willingness to abide by WTO rulings reflects its use of "soft power," i.e., modifying its hegemonic instincts. It is not a trivial matter that the U.S. trade representative should consider that small countries—in his words, "particularly in the Caribbean"—face unique challenges from free trade, and that longer time frames for liberalization will be required.[8] When put within the context of the totality of U.S.–Caribbean exchanges, from immigration and the remittances they send to assistance with national security concerns such as the threats of organized crime and to funds for combating the escalating HIV/AIDS pandemic, issues of subsidies and tariffs are but a minor part. In the area of crime, the Greater Caribbean faces the problem of organized crime in the form of gangs, which is taking on frightening proportions. Their corrupting power is widely recognized. Says Jamaica's deputy superintendent of police, "They hire the best accountants, the best lawyers, financial controllers . . . the best of everything."[9] Their links to U.S.-based gangs is evident, which means that the need for close cooperation with U.S. agencies is urgent. The responsibility is shared, the solutions have to come from shared efforts. In terms of health issues, Caribbean statesmen should know that when the U.S. confronted its own powerful pharmaceutical industry in order to offer poorer nations access to life-saving medicines, it was grasping the nettle in ways not often understood by those less informed about the workings of U.S. domestic politics. Again, the situation is a regionwide tragedy; it requires collective action, and U.S. assistance is simply indispensable.

Third, there is some encouragement to be derived from the thought that despite the fact that the goal of completing the Doha Development Agenda in 2005 will not be met, the Caribbean has other opportunities for negotiating free trade agreements with the U.S. in its immediate future, bilaterally at first and in a NAFTA agreement eventually. And negotiate they will because they must. Isolation is not an option and, as distinct from the days of the Cold War, there are no alternative blocs to turn to. Even Brazilian Foreign Minister Celso Amorin, a leading voice in the Group of 22 "won't doers" at Cancun, has reiterated that globalization forces, such as common markets, carry with them compromises on absolute sovereignty. "The logic of international negotiations, and especially those that involve many countries," he told the Associate Press, makes the option of not joining an accord very costly."[10] If this is so for mighty Brazil, how much more so for the small states of the Caribbean. It is an interesting comment that no Caribbean country (except Cuba which is not a WTO member) was represented on the G-22. They opted to speak for the ACP countries, a reflection of the continuity of post-colonial arrangements.

Finally, there is the vital matter of the democratic values the Caribbean shares with the U.S. In Chapter 2 we demonstrated that it was more the value attached to democratic practices and less U.S. hegemonic imposition which gave backbone to the region's resistance to the "totalitarian temptation." Today that shared set of values will resist the opportunistic and irrational calls to take strident and unbending appeals to a new type of "anti-imperialism." Those days are gone. It is widely accepted that democracy, whether at home or in the international arena, involves the ongoing interplay of cooperation, competition, and conflict. The region can expect to see all three processes occur on-again and off-again in its relations with the U.S. It takes creative and courageous statesmanship to make sure that the cooperative periods outlast the inevitable occasional conflict. It takes even more of those sterling qualities of leadership, however, for the heads of small states and those of the superpower to know how to handle competition. This book has dealt at length with the paradoxes and dilemmas posed by the extraordinary asymmetry in power between the parties. We concluded that after a lamentable period of U.S. hegemonic muscle flexing, there followed tense but mutually beneficial relations during the Cold War and after. It is not excessive optimism which leads us to believe that the future will also be characterized by such mutually beneficial cooperative relations.

Endnotes

Chapter 1

1. Warren Zimmerman, *First Great Triumph* (New York: Farrar, Straus and Giroux, 2002), p. 464.
2. Frederick Merk, *Manifest Destiny and Mission in American History* (New York: Random House Vintage Books, 1966), p. 232.
3. Dana G. Munro, *Intervention and Dollar Diplomacy in the Caribbean, 1900–1921* (Princeton: Princeton University Press, 1994).
4. Albert J. Beveridge, cited in Merk, *Manifest Destiny,* p. 232.
5. For the very large number of U.S. military interventions see George Black, *The Good Neighbor* (New York: Pantheon Books, 1988).
6. William Appleman Williams argues this point in several books but most relevantly for our purposes in William Appleman Williams, *The Tragedy of American Diplomacy* 2nd ed. (New York: Dell, 1972).
7. See Lester D. Langley, *The Banana Wars: An Inner History of American Empire, 1900–1934* (Lexington: University Press of Kentucky, 1983).
8. On this see Bryce Wood, *The Making of the Good Neighbor Policy* (New York: W.W. Norton, 1967).
9. On the worldwide reach of Caribbean Sephardic Jewish financiers, see Isaac and Suzanne A. Emmanuel, *History of the Jews of the Netherlands Antilles* 2 Vols., (Cincinnati: American Jewish Archives, 1970). For the enormous influence of Freemasonry in the Dominican Republic see Frank Moya Pons, *The Dominican Republic* (New Rochelle: Hispaniola Books, 1995), pp. 109–110. And H. Hoetink, *El pueblo dominicano, 1850–1900* (Santiago: Universidad Católica Madre y Maestra, 1971).
10. Further on this see Anthony P. Maingot, *The U.S. and the Caribbean* (London: Macmillan, 1994).
11. Frederick Merk, *Manifest Destiny and Mission in American History* (New York: Random House Vintage Books, 1966), p. 237.
12. See Niall Ferguson, *Empire* (New York: Basic Books, 2002), pp. 163–220.
13. See Anthony P. Maingot, National identity, instrumental identifications and the Caribbean's culture of "play," *Identity*, 2: 2, (2002), 115–124. See the case of Belize.
14. Heraldo Muñoz, "Goodby USA?" in *Latin America in the New International System*, Eds. Joseph S. Tulchin and Ralph H. Espach (Boulder, Co.: Lynne Rienner, 2001), p. 74. Muñoz hastens to add that his thesis applies to South America, and does not apply to Mexico, Central America, and the Caribbean.

15. It was Abraham Lowenthal who as early as 1977 argued that the U.S. presumptions of hegemony had ended. El fin de la presunción hegemónica, *Estudios Internacionales*, 37 (January–March, 1977), pp. 45–67.

16. Robert Kagan, *Of Paradise and Power* (New York: Alfred A. Knopf, 2003), pp. 85–103.

17. Statement of Principles, Project for the New American Century, June 3, 1997 at www.newamericancentury.com.

18. Joseph S. Nye, Jr., *Bound to Lead: The Changing Nature of American Power* (New York: Basic Books, 1991).

19. Donald Kagan, Comparing America to ancient empires is ludicrous, *The Atlanta Journal Constitution*, (October 6, 2002) online.

20. See James N. Rosenau, *The United Nations in a Turbulent World* (Boulder: Lynne Rienner, 1992).

21. Seymour Martin Lipset, *American Exceptionalism* (New York: W.W. Norton, 1996), p. 20.

22. See Edward Hallett Carr, *What Is History?* (New York: Alfred A. Knopf, 1963), pp. 80, 82.

23. Richard Wilk, Learning to be local in Belize: Global systems of common difference, in *Worlds Apart: Modernity through the Prism of the Local,* Ed. Daniel Miller (London: Routledge, 1995), p. 130.

24. William J. Jorden, *Panama Odyssey* (Austin: University of Texas Press, 1984), p. 554. This is the most complete account of the whole process.

25. William L. Furlong and Margaret E. Scranton, *The Dynamics of Foreign Policy-Making: The President, the Congress and the Panama Canal Treaties* (Boulder: Westview Press, 1983).

26. Ronald Reagan, Introduction in *Surrender in Panama: The Case against the Treaty,* Ed. Honorable Philip M. Crane (New York: Dale Books, 1978), VIII.

27. Crane, *Surrender in Panama*, p. 105.

28. See George D. Moffett III, *The Limits of Victory: The Ratification of the Panama Canal Treaties* (Ithaca: Cornell University Press, 1985).

29. William J. Jorden, *Panama Odyssey* (Austin: University of Texas Press, 1984), p. 621.

30. Quoted in Jorden, *Panama Odyssey,* p. 564.

31. Quoted in Thomas, *Cuba,* p. 455.

31. Kagan of Paradise and Power, p. 87.

32. Agreement between the Government of Trinidad and Tobago and the Government of the United States Concerning Maritime Counter-Drug Operations. Done at Port-of-Spain, March 4, 1996.

33. *Trinidad Express* Port-of-Spain (March 5, 1996), p. 1.

34. Stephan Vascianvie, Political and policy aspects of the Jamaica/United States Shiprider negotiations, *Caribbean Quarterly,* 43: 3 (1997).

35. Courtney Clarke, *Jamaica Gleaner* (October 16, 1996), p. 19.

36. See the very well argued analysis of Sue Smith, We Will Not grovel: Drugs and Jamaican Sovereignty, Paper, Caribbean Studies Association Conference, Antigua (May 1998), p. 16.

37. Forum on Sovereignty, University of the West Indies, St. Augustine, Trinidad, June 7, 1997.

38. Kathy Brown, Now that the ship has docked: A postscript to the Shiprider debate, *CARICOM Perspectives,* 67: (1997), p. 49.

39. Elliot Abrams, The shiprider solution: policing the Caribbean, *The National Interest,* 30:1 (1996). Abrams was a signatory to the New American Century "Statement of Principles" of June 3, 1997.

40. *The Jamaican Weekly Gleaner* (March 6–12, 1996), p. 1.

41. Peter M. Haas, Epistemic communities and international policy coordination, *International Organization,* 46: 1 (1992), 1–36.

Chapter 2

1. Charles D. Ameringer, *The Democratic Left in Exile* (Miami: University of Miami Press, 1974).

2. The section is taken from Anthony P. Maingot, The difficult road to socialism in the English-speaking Caribbean, *Capitalism and the State in U.S.–Latin American Relations,* Ed. Richard R. Fagen (Stanford, CA: Stanford University Press, 1979), pp. 254–289.

3. Perhaps the most detailed account of this ideological struggle, of which the Caribbean was but one chapter, is Cheddi Jagan, *The West on Trial* (London: Michael Joseph, 1966), 170–221.

4. See Forbes Burnham, *A Destiny to Mold* (New York: Africana, 1970), p. 5.
5. Robert Alexander, *Communism in Latin America* (New Brunswick: Rutgers University, Press, 1957), p. 354.
6. *Washington Post*, (February 18, 1963), 1. CIA participation in the overthrow of Arbenz is plainly described by the then head of the CIA, Allen W. Dulles, *The Craft of Intelligence* (Illinois: Harper and Row, 1963). Kagan, 27.
7. U.S. Department of State Bulletin, 31 (July 12, 1954), pp. 43–44.
8. U.S. Department of State Bulletin, 43 (August 1, 1960), pp. 170–171.
9. Samuel Flagg Bemis, *The Latin American Policy of the United States* (New York: Harcourt Brace, 1943), p. 355.
10. Bernardo Vega, *Trujillo y las Fuerzas Armadas Norteamericanas* (Santo Domingo: Fundación Cultural Dominicana, 1992).
11. Arthur M. Schlesinger, Jr., *A Thousand Days* (New York: Fawcet Premier, 1965), p. 704.
12. Alleged Assassination Plots Involving Foreign Leaders, *An Interim Report. Select Committee to Study Governmental Operations, United States Senate* (N.Y.: W.W. Norton, 1976), 191–215. See also the documents from the CIA, Department of State and Dominican Agencies in Bernardo Vega, *Los Estados Unidos y Trujillo, Los dias finales, 1960–61* (Santo Domingo: Fundación Cultural Dominicana, 1999).
13. Arthur M. Schlesinger, Jr., *A Thousand Days* (New York: Fawcet Premier, 1965), pp. 704–705.
14. Alleged Assassination Plots Involving Foreign Leaders, *An Interim Report. Select Committee to Study Governmental Operations, United States Senate* (N.Y.: W.W. Norton, 1976), p. 209.
15. John Bartlow Martin, *Overtaken by Events* (New York: Doubleday, 1966), p. 82.
16. U.S. envoys such as John Bartlow Martin did perceive a communist and Cuban threat in the Dominican Republic. One who does not believe that the 1965 "constitutionalists" were either communists or bent on establishing another Cuba is Piero Gleijeses, *The Dominican Crisis* (Baltimore: The Johns Hopkins University Press, 1978), pp. 282–301.
17. Theodore C. Sorensen, *The Kennedy Legacy: A Peaceful Revolution for the Seventies* (New York: Macmillan, 1969).
18. Theodore C. Sorensen, *The Kennedy Legacy: A Peaceful Revolution for the Seventies* (New York: Macmillan, 1969) p. 182.
19. Arthur M. Schlesinger, Jr., *A Thousand Days* (New York: Fawcet Premier, 1965), p. 700.
20. Letter of March 17, 1997 cited in John Lewis Gaddis, *Strategies of Containment* (New York: Oxford University Press, 1982), p. 181.
21. Eric Williams, *From Columbus to Castro—The History of the Caribbean, 1492–1969* (London: Andre Deutsch, 1970), p. 502.
22. Eric Williams, *From Columbus to Castro—The History of the Caribbean, 1492–1969* (London: Andre Deutsch, 1970), p. 503.
23. Eric Williams, *From Columbus to Castro—The History of the Caribbean, 1492–1969* (London: Andre Deutsch, 1970), p. 510.
24. International perspectives for Trinidad and Tobago, *Le Monde Diplomatique* (August 1963) reprinted in *Forged From the Love of Liberty*, selected speeches of Eric Williams (Port-of-Spain: Longman Caribbean, 1981), pp. 365–367.
25. See Anthony P. Maingot, *The United States and the Caribbean* (London: Macmillan, 1994), pp. 113–139.
26. Eric Williams, *From Columbus to Castro—The History of the Caribbean, 1492–1969* (London: Andre Deutsch, 1970), p. 510.
27. Speech by A.N.R. Robinson, September 27, 1967 reprinted in A.N.R. Robinson, *Caribbean Man* (Port-of-Spain: Inprint, 1986), p. 102.
28. See Anthony P. Maingot, Perceptions as realities: The United States, Venezuela, and Cuba in the Caribbean, in *Latin American Nations in World Politics*, Ed. Heraldo Muñoz and Joseph Tulchin (Boulder, CO: Westview, 1984), pp. 63–84.
29. Deryck R. Brown, The coup that failed; the Jamesian connection, in Selwyn Ryan, (ed.) *The Black Power Revolution* (St. Augustine Trinidad: ISER, 1995), pp. 543–578.
30. Herbert L. Matthews, *The New York Times* (March 4, 1976), p. 31.
31. A good overview can be had from Anthony Payne, Paul Sutton, and Tony Thorndike, *Grenada, Revolution and Invasion* (New York: St. Martin's, 1984), and Jay R. Mandle, *Big Revolution, Small Country: The Rise and Fall of the Grenada Revolution* (Lanham, MD: North–South, 1985).

32. Yuri Pavlov, *Soviet–Cuban Alliance, 1959–1991* (Miami, FL: North–South Center, 1996), p. 98.
33. See *Report of the Trinidad and Tobago House Paper No. 2 of 1965* (1965), 19.
34. Michael Manley, *The Search For Solutions* (Ontario: Maple House, 1976), p. 205.
35. Michael Manley, *The Politics of Change* (London: André Deutsch, 1974), p. 31.
36. Michael Kaufman, *Jamaica under Manley* (Westport, CT: Lawrence Hill, 1985), p. 146.
37. Anthony Payne, *Politics in Jamaica* (New York: St. Martin's, 1988), p. 58.
38. See Destabilization diary in Michael Manley, *Jamaica: Struggle in the Periphery* (London: Third World Media, 1982), pp. 223–237.
39. On this, see Evelyne Huber Stephens and John D. Stephens, *Democratic Socialism in Jamaica* (Princeton, NJ: Princeton University Press, 1986), pp. 318–319.
40. See Michael Manley, *Up the Down Escalator* (London: André Deutsch, 1987).
41. José A. Moreno, *El pueblo en armas: Revolución en Santo Domingo* (Madrid: Editorial Tecnos, 1973), pp. 109–124. Moreno was studying in the city's working class neighborhoods when the rebellion broke out.
42. Brian Meeks, *Caribbean Revolutions and Revolutionary Theory* (London: Macmillan Caribbean, 1993), p. 4.
43. George Lamming, December 14, 1981, quoted in Stephens and Stephens, *Democratic Socialism in Jamaica*, p. 33.
44. *Foreign Affairs* 60: (Summer, 1982), 1042. A confidential report by Philip C. Habib still stressed social and economic conditions, but emphasized that Cuba was using these as "targets of opportunity" and thus military assistance was called for. *Washington Post* (June 15, 1980), 1, 18.

Chapter 3

1. *The Nation*, Editorial, June 4, 1990.
2. This section owes much to the analysis in Robert Cassá, *Modos de producción, clases sociales y luchas políticas en la República Dominicana, Siglo XX* (Santo Domingo: Alfa y Omega, 1986).
3. See the analysis in Jacqueline Jimenez-Polanco, Los Partidos Politicos en la República Dominicana. Ph.D. dissertation, Universidad Complutense, Madrid, 1994.
4. Jonathan Hartlyn, *The Struggle for Democratic Politics in the Dominican Republic* (Chapel Hill: The University of North Carolina Press, 1998), pp. 114, 125, 249, 265.
5. Rosario Espinal and Jonathan Hartlyn, Las Relaciones entre Estados Unidos y República Domincana: el tema de la democracia, in *Cambio Político en el Caribe: Escenarios de la Post Guerra Fría, Cuba, Haití y República Dominicana*, Ed. Wilfredo Lozano (Caracas: Editorial Nueva Sociedad, 1998), p. 143.
6. For a detailed analysis of the Dominican foreign policy see: Secretaría de Estado de Relaciones Exteriores 1997, in *La Nueva Política Exterior Dominicana y Temas de Relaciones Internacionales, Tomo I* (Santo Domingo, República Dominicana, 1997); Secretaría de Estado de Relaciones Exteriores 1999, in *La Nueva Política Exterior Dominicana y Temas de Relaciones Internacionales, Tomo II* (Santo Domingo, República Dominicana, 1999); Wilfredo Lozano, *Cambio Político en el Caribe: Escenarios de la Post Guerra Fría, Cuba, Haití y República Dominicana* (Caracas: Nueva Sociedad, 1998), p. 198.
7. Bernardo Vega, La cambiante Agenda Dominico-Americana in Secretaría de Estado de Relaciones Exteriores, in *La Nueva Política Exterior Dominica y Temas de Relaciones Internacionales, Tomo I* (Santo Domingo, República Dominicana, 1997).
8. Bernardo Vega, *Diario de una misión en Washington* (Santo Domingo: Fundación Cultural Dominicana, 2002), pp. 11–12.
9. Bernardo Vega, *La Segunda Guerra Fria* (Santo Domingo: FLACSO, 1999).
10. Bernardo Vega, *En la Decada Perdida* (Santo Domingo: Fundación Cultural Dominicana, 1991).
11. See Vega, *Diario*, p. 412.
12. See the detailed study on this issue in Centre of Ethnic Studies, *Ethnicity and Employment Practices in Trinidad–Tobago*, Vol. 1 (St. Augustine: University of West Indies, nd.).
13. Government of Trinidad and Tobago, *White Paper on Public Participation in Industrial and Commercial Activities* (Port-of-Spain: Government Printery, 1972).

14. Government of Trinidad and Tobago, *White Paper on Public Participation in Industrial and Commercial Activities* (Port-of-Spain: Government Printery, 1972).
15. Government of Trinidad and Tobago, *White Paper on Public Participation in Industrial and Commercial Activities* (Port-of-Spain: Government Printery, 1972).
16. Leslie H. Scotland, The impact of the 1970s Black Power revolution on banking, in *Power: The Black Power Revolution*, Eds. Selwyn Ryan and Taimoon Stewart (St. Augustine: ISER, 1995), pp. 66–67.
17. Speech by Dante B. Fascell, American Assembly–University of Miami Conference on the Caribbean, Miami, FL, April 28, 1973.
18. Commission on U.S.–Latin American Relations, *The Americas in a Changing World* (New York: Center for Inter-American Relations, 1974).
19. *Weekly Compilation of Presidential Documents*, 13: 6 (Washington, D.C.: Government Printing Office, 1977), pp. 523–528. It was a sign of the Caribbean leadership's keen interest in what Washington officialdom was thinking that in Trinidad the speech was carried in its entirety by the *Trinidad Guardian*, (April 15, 1977), 2, 6, 16.
20. *The New York Times* (August 14, 1977), 15.
21. *The New York Times* (August 18, 1977), 3.
22. See Anthony P. Maingot, *Global Economics and Local Politics in Trinidad's Divestment Program* (Miami: The North–South Agenda, No. 34, 1998).
23. On this issue see Selwyn Ryan and Lou Ann Barclay, *Sharks and Sardines: Blacks in Business in Trinidad–Tobago* (St. Augustine: Multimedia Productions, 1992).
24. Selwyn Ryan and Lou Anne Barclay, *The Muslameen Grab for Power* (Port-of-Spain: Imprint Caribbean, 1991), p. 19.
25. Ryan and Lou Ann Barclay, *Sharks and Sardines: Blacks in Business in Trinidad–Tobago* (St. Augustine: Multimedia Productions, 1992).
26. Ryan and Lou Ann Barclay, *Sharks and Sardines: Blacks in Business in Trinidad–Tobago* (St. Augustine: Multimedia Productions, 1992). p. 203.
27. Anthony P. Maingot was given access to a collection of unpublished speeches of Basdeo Panday, Port-of-Spain, May 1997.
28. Clemes J. Bibo, The Business Climate in Trinidad and Tobago Through the Eyes of the Private Sector, unpublished manuscript. Port-of-Spain: Economic Commission for Latin America and the Caribbean, July 8, 1994.
29. David Nicholls, *From Dessalines to Duvalier: Race, Colour and National Independence in Haiti* (Cambridge: Cambridge University Press, 1979).
30. On the 1915–1934 occupation, see Ludwell Lee Montague, *Haiti and the U.S. 1714–1938* (Durham: Duke University Press, 1940), p. 276. Hans Schmidt notes the stimulus given to a new black middle sector but also agrees that even the substantial material accomplishments "proved to be largely ephemeral"; *The U.S. Occupation of Haiti, 1915–1934* (New Brunswick: Rutgers University Press, 1971), p. 233. See also David Healy, *Gunboat Diplomacy in the Wilson Era* (Madison: University of Wisconsin Press, 1976), p. 229.
31. Former Secretary of State Dean Rusk, 1978, cited in Robert Debs Heinl and Nancy Gordon Heinl, *Written in Blood* (Boston: Houghton Mifflin, 1978), p. 622.
32. Aristide Says He'd Support Surgical Strike to Oust "Thugs," *The Miami Herald* (January 5, 1994), 1.
33. Tom Farer, Reconstructing sovereignty in a democratic age, in *Beyond Sovereignty: Collectively Defending Democracy in the Americas*, Ed. Tom Farer (Baltimore: The Johns Hopkins University Press, 1996).
34. Michael Manley, No existe solución rápida para Haiti, *El Nuevo Herald,* (November 26, 1993), 14.
35. Heraldo Muñoz, Haiti and Beyond, *The Miami Herald* (March 1, 1992), 6C.
36. See The Hammer That Failed in Cuba, *The New York Times* (November 8, 1993).
37. Leslie F. Manigat, *Haiti of the Sixties, Object of International Concern* (Washington Center of Foreign Policy Research, 1964), 89–93.
38. OAS Ambassador Muñoz's position that these sanctions "have apparently hurt the average citizen without threatening the putschists' control." See Heraldo Muñoz, *The Future of the Organization of American States* (New York: The Twentieth Century Fund Press, 1933), p. 83.
39. See these arguments in Tom Farer, Introduction in *Beyond Sovereignty*, p. 9.
40. Farer, *Beyond Sovereignty*, p. 9.

41. See *UN Development Program, Human Development Report, 1993* (New York: Oxford University Press, 1993).

Chapter 4

1. Commonwealth Secretariat, *Vulnerability: Small States in the Global Society*, (London: Marlborough House, 1985), p. 15.

2. William G. Demas, *The Economics of Development in Small Countries* (Montreal: McGill University Press, 1965).

3. P. Bachr, Small states: A tool for analysis? *World Politics*, 27: 3 (1975).

4. See the positions outlined in *Size, Self-Determination, and International Relations: The Caribbean*, Ed. Vaughan A. Lewis (Mona: Institute of Social and Economic Research, 1976).

5. Lewis, *Size, Self-Determination, and International Relations: The Caribbean*, Ed. Vaughan A. Lewis (Mona: Institute of Social and Economic Research, 1976), p. 341.

6. Lewis, *Size, Self-Determination, and International Relations: The Caribbean*, Ed. Vaughan A. Lewis (Mona: Institute of Social and Economic Research, 1976), p. 229.

7. *Amigoe*, (Curaçao), August 15, 2003, p. 1. Anthony P. Maingot was in Curaçao for the elections in May, 2003.

8. For an indepth analysis of this Dutch conundrum see Gert Oostindie and Inge Klinkers, *Decolonizing the Caribbean: Dutch Policies in a Comparative Perspective* (Amsterdam: Amsterdam University Press, 2003.)

9. Commonwealth Secretariat, *Vulnerability: Small States in the Global Society*, (London: Marlborough House, 1985), p. 97.

10. *The New York Times*, August 15, 2003.

11. *The Financial Times*, August 14, 2003.

12. *Jamaica Observer*, (September 9, 2003), 1.

13. Further on this in Darren L. Nicholas, CARICOM Participation in the FTAA: The Difficult Issues, unpublished thesis, Florida International University, July 2003.

14. Quoted in Paul Sutton, The Banana Regime of the European Union, the Caribbean and Latin America, unpublished manuscript, University of Hull, n.d., 2.

15. Henry Gill and Anthony Gonzales, Economic Consequences of a Banana Collapse in the Caribbean (May 1995). Although sponsored by the Caribbean Banana Exporters Association, this report by two respected economists draws plausible conclusions from hard data.

16. Quoted in James Ferguson, A Case of Bananas, *Geographical*, January 1998, p. 50.

17. Quoted in Sutton, The Banana Regime of the European Union, the Caribbean and Latin America, unpublished manuscript, University of Hull, n.d., 19.

18. Quoted in Sutton, The Banana Regime of the European Union, the Caribbean and Latin America, unpublished manuscript, University of Hull, n.d., 19.

19. Quote in the *Cincinnati Enquirer*, May 3, 1998.

20. David Sanger, Dangerous Selectivity about Rules of Global Trade, *The New York Times*, March 21, 1999, Business, 4.

21. Caribbean Community Secretariat, Issues Relating to the Marketing of CARICOM Bananas, Georgetown, Guyana, June 24–27, 1996.

22. Caribbean Community Secretariat, Issues Relating to the Marketing of CARICOM Bananas, Georgetown, Guyana, June 24–27, 1996, 14.

23. The whole series was consulted by this author under http://www.enquirer.com.8-/edition/1998/05/28.

24. U.S. Trade Representative, Press Release, July 1, 2001.

25. Caribbean Export Development Agency, *Tradewatch*, June 23, 2003.

26. Office of the U.S. Trade Representative, Joint U.S.-EU Release, April 11, 2001.

27. On the early development of upscale tourism in Barbados, see Edsill Phillips, The Development of the Tourist Industry in Barbados, 1956–1980, in *The Economy of Barbados*, Ed. DeLisle Worrell (Bridgetown: Central Bank of Barbados, 1982), pp. 107–140.

28. Perhaps typical of the over-ideologized objection to any type of foreign presence in the Caribbean is the analysis by Tom Barry, Beth Wood, and Deb Preusch in *The Other Side of Paradise: Foreign Control in the Caribbean* (New York: Grove, 1984). This point of view was also, in the 1970s and 1980s, that of the bimonthly *NACLA Report on the Americas* and its Canadian twin, *Latin American Working Group Letter*. In the Caribbean, the journal of the Caribbean Conference of Churches, *Caribbean Contract* (Bridgetown), was

generally critical of the tourist and assembly industries. In the U.K., the publications of the Latin American Bureau have been systematically critical of foreign investment, from oil to bananas.

29. Gordon K. Lewis, *Puerto Rico: Freedom and Power in the Caribbean* (New York: Monthly Review, 1963), p. 312.

30. See DeLisle Worrell, *Small Island Economies* (New York: Praeger, 1987), pp. 119–120.

31. *Caribbean Insight,* May 28, 1999, 2.

32. The Planning Institute of Jamaica, *Jamaica Five-Year Development Plan, 1990–1995* (Kingston: The Planning Institute of Jamaica, 1990), pp. 80–81.

33. Planning Institute of Jamaica, *Economic and Social Survey, Jamaica 1999* (Kingston: Planning Institute of Jamaica, 2000), Section 15.1.

34. Krista Carothers, The Caribbean Plays Catch-Up, *Conde Nast Traveler* (July 1999), p. 40.

35. Data provided by John Collins of *Caribbean Business,* interview, Nassau, Bahamas, May 30, 2002.

36. *Wall Street Journal,* July 12, 2002, W-6.

37. Bob Dickinson and Andy Vladimir, *Selling The Sea: An Inside Look at the Cruise Industry* (New York: John Wiley & Sons, 1997), pp. 24, 145.

38. George Ritzer, *Enchanting a Disenchanted World* (Thousand Oaks: Pine Forge Press, 1999), p. ix.

39. *The New York Times,* September 13, 1998, 6.

40. *The Miami Herald,* March 18, 1999, 1B.

41. *The New York Times,* September 13, 1998, 6.

42. ECLAC, *Latin American and Caribbean Lobbying for International Trade in Washington, D.C.* (Washington, D.C., June, 1990). Based on data from the U.S. Department of Justice.

43. See the detailed analysis provided by the Jamaican Ambassador Richard Bernal to the U.S. Trade Representative, July 15, 1996.

44. Major Shippers Report, U.S. Department of Commerce, Office of Textiles and Apparel: *U.S. Imports of Textiles and Apparel Under the Multilateral Fiber Arrangement: Annual Report of 1994* (U.S. International Trade Commission, Publication No. 2884, April 1995).

45. Fundación APEC de Crédito Educativo (FUNDAPEC): *Encuesta nacional de mano de obra* (Santo Domingo, 1992).

46. Comisión Económica para América Latina (CEPAL): Centroamérica, México y la República Dominicana: *Maquila y Transformación Productiva* (Estudios e Informes de la CEPAL No. 95, Santiago de Chile, 1998).

47. Caribbean Export Development Agency. *Tradewatch* (June 23, 2003.)

48. Michael Mortimore, Industrializatión a base de confecciones en la cuenca del Caribe: ¿Un tejido raido?, in *Revista de la CEPAL,* 67: Abril de 1999.

49. Secretaría de Estado de Relaciones Exteriores: *La Nueva Política Exterior Dominicana y Temas de Relaciones Internacionales, Tomo I* (Santo Domingo, República Dominicana, 1997).

50. The information comes from the Dominican EPZs Association (ADOZONA–Asociación Dominicana de Zonas Francas). See also Fernando Alvarez Bogaert (Minister of Finance), El entorno económico internacional y la coyuntura económica dominicana," Speech to the American Chamber of Commerce, Santo Domingo, December 12, 2001.

51. Comisión Económica para América Latina (CEPAL): *Centroamérica, México y la República Dominicana* (Santiago de Chile, 1998).

52. *Centroamérica, México y la República Dominicana.* Comisión Económica para América Latina (CEPAL): *Centroamérica, México y la República Dominicana* (Santiago de Chile, 1998).

53. Constantino Vaitsos, *Opciones dominicanas en tiempos de globalización* (PNUD, Santo Domingo, 1994).

54. Bernardo Vega, *Diario de una misión en Washington* (Santo Domingo: Fundación Cultural Dominicana, 2002), p. 449.

55. This section draws heavily from CARICOM Secretariat, *Caribbean Trade and Investment Report, 2000* (Kingston: Ian Randle, 2000).

56. Paul Chen-Young, *With All Good Intentions: The Collapse of Jamaica's Domestic Financial Sector* (Washington, D.C.: The Center For Strategic and International Studies, November 1, 1998), p. 14.

57. See for example, Julio Santana, *Estrategia Neoliberal, Urbanización y Zonas Francas. El Caso de Santiago* (República Dominicana, Programa FLACSO-República Dominicana, 1994); Oscar Ugarteche, *El falso dilema. América Latina en la economía global, Nueva Sociedad* (Caracas, 1997); Constantino Vaitsos, *Opciones Dominicanas en Tiempos de Globalización* (PNUD, Santo Domingo, 1994).

58. Mary King, The Trinidad and Tobago Economy, *Caribbean Investor*, 1: 1, (First Quarter 2001), 72.

59. Bernardo Vega, *En la decada perdida* (Santo Domingo: Fundación Cultural Dominicana, 1991), pp. 47–50. The Poll first appeared in *Listin Diario*, August 13, 1986.

60. *The Jamaican Observer*, July 13, 2001, 1.

61. C. James Hospedales, HIV/AIDS Epidemic in the Caribbean, in *Caribbean 2000 Plus: A Vision for Health and Ecology in The New Global Economy* (Grenada: St. Georges University, 2000), p. 45.

62. According to *The New York Times* this program that was so well received initially "has been underfinanced by Congress, with the White House's encouragement." (Editorial, September 9, 2003), A-30.

Chapter 5

1. Fundamental sources for this chapter are: (1) O.E.C.D., *Harmful Tax Competition: An Emerging Global Issue* (Paris: OECD, 1998); Oxfam Policy Papers, *Tax Havens*. (London, June, 2000); UN ECLAC, CDCC, *Offshore Financial Centres in the Caribbean*, March 31, 1995.

2. On Blum's role in bringing it down, see Jonathan Beaty and S.C. Gwynne, *The Outlaw Bank* (New York: Random House, 1993). See also, Senate Subcommittee on Terrorism, Narcotics and International Operations, *The BCCI Affair: A Report To The Senate Committee On Foreign Relations*, September 30, 1992.

3. Interview with Anthony P. Maingot, San José, Costa Rica, July 15, 1997.

4. Jack A. Blum, Offshore Money, in *Transnational Crime in the Americas*, Ed. Tom Farer (New York: Routledge, 1999), p. 62.

5. Permanent Subcommittee on Investigations of the Senate Committee on Governmental Affairs "Crime and Secrecy: The Use of Offshore Banks and Companies," Senate Report No. 130 (49th Congress, 1st Session, 1985), 83.

6. R. Thomas Naylor, Drug money, hot money, and debt, *European Journal of International Affairs*, 2: 3 (1989), 62.

7. See Jack A. Blum, Michael Levi, R. Thomas Naylor, and Phil Williams, Financial Havens, Banking Secrecy and Money Laundering, UN Office for Drug Control and Crime Prevention (UNDCP) Technical Series, No. 8, 1998.

7. *Financial Times*, January 15, 1997, 4.

8. *The Wall Street Journal*, September 27, 1996; see also story in *The Sunday Times*, U.K., September 29, 1996.

9. Carol L. Loomis, Lies, Damned Lies, and Managed Earnings, *Fortune*, August 2, 1999, 74–92.

10. Nick Cohen, *The Observer*, (London, August 1, 1999, 29).

11. *The Observer*, (London, July 18, 1999, 12).

12. Michael M. Phillips, Taking Shelter, *The Wall Street Journal*, August 4, 1999, 1, 8.

13. *The New York Times*, July 9, 2002, 11.

14. <www.1-offshore-banking-off . . . >

15. *Offshore Financial Freedom 1998–2002*, cited by *Money Laundering Alert* Website, May 28, 2002.

16. See Theda Skocpol, *Protecting Soldiers and Mothers: The Political Origins of Social Policy in the United States*, (Cambridge: The Belknap Press of Harvard University Press, 1992).

17. Ira Katznelson, Knowledge about what? in *States, Social Knowledge, and the Origins of Modern Social Policies*, Eds. Dietrich Rueschemeyer and Theda Skocpol (Princeton, N.J.: Princeton University Press, 1996), pp. 17–47.

18. PL 107-56 (October 26, 2001), "Uniting and Strengthening America by Providing Appropriate Tools Required to Intercept and Obstruct Terrorism." For the American Bar Association's

response (and support) of the legislation, see John Gibeaut, Show them the money, *ABA Journal* (January 2002), 46–51.

19.   *The New York Times*, March 26, 2002, 1.
20.   *The New York Times*, January 17, 2002, C-8.
21.   *The New York Times*, June 28, 2002, C-1.
22.   *The Wall Street Journal*, June 26, 2002, C-1; to cite *The New York Times*, June 28, 2002, C-1.
23.   *The New York Times*, June 1, 1997, 8.
24.   *The New York Times*, April 28, 1999, C-1.
25.   Ronen Palan, *The Offshore World* (Ithaca, N.Y.: Cornell University Press, 2003), p. 44.
26.   *The Miami Herald*, July 7, 2001, C-1.
27.   *The New York Times*, June 9, 2001, C-1.
28.   *The New York Times*, May 20, 2002, Letter. This position is supported by *The Wall Street Journal* (Editorial, May 16, 2002), opposed by *The New York Times*, (Editorial May 13, 2002) and *Newsweek* (April 15, 2002).
29.   *The Miami Herald*, April 3, 2002, 3C.
30.   Daniel Mitchell, *Foreign Policy*, (July/August, 2002). Mitchell is described by *Offshore Finance USA*, (November/December, 2002) as "lobbying to rally opposition to plans . . . to enforce punitive measures against the so-called tax havens."
31.   See Anthony P. Maingot, Taxing Free Riders, *Foreign Policy*, (September/October, 2002), 6.
32.   Caribbean Export Development Agency, *Tradewatch*, (April 16, 2003), 1.
33.   This chapter draws heavily from Anthony P. Maingot, The illicit drug trade in the Caribbean, *International Security and Democracy*, Ed. Jorge I. Dominguez (Pittsburgh: University of Pittsburgh Press, 1998), pp. 188–210; The decentralization imperative and Caribbean criminal enterprises, *Transnational Crime in the Americas*, Ed. Tom Farer (New York: Routledge, 1999), pp. 143–170.
34.   *The Jamaican Observer*, July 30, 2002, 2.
35.   Graduate institute of international studies (Geneva), *Small Arms Survey 2002: Counting the Human Cost* (Oxford: Oxford University Press, 2002), p. 13.
36.   On this see especially, Michael J. Klare, Light weapon diffusion and global violence in the post-Cold War era, *Light Weapons and International Security*, Ed. Jasjit Singh (Delhi: Indian Pugwash Society, 1995); Edward J. Laurence, *Light Weapons and Intrastate Conflict* (New York: Carnegie Corporation, 1998).
37.   *The New York Times*, Editorial, July 10, 2001.
38.   *The New York Times*, Editorial, May 14, 2002.
39.   *National Post*, October 21, 2000, B-1.
40   *U.S. News and World Report*, December 9, 1996, 26.
41.   *U.S. News and World Report*, December 9, 1996, 32.
42.   *The Miami Herald*, August 17, 2001, 3-C.
43.   *The Miami Herald*, May 22, 1999, 1.
44.   *The New York Times*, June 9, 2002, 15.
45.   This section draws heavily from Anthony P. Maingot, *The United States and the Caribbean*, pp. 142–162.
46.   Tony Thorndike, *Grenada: Politics, Economics and Society* (London: Frances Pinter, 1985), p. 54.
47.   See Robert Coram, *Caribbean Time Bomb: The United States Complicity in the Corruption of Antigua* (New York: William Morrow, 1993), pp. 44–53.
48.   See Guns for Antigua, report of the commission of inquiry into the circumstances surrounding the shipment of arms from Israel to Antigua . . . en route to Colombia (London, November 2, 1990).
49.   The report by officers from the organized crime group New Scotland Yard on the "Maxi II" disappearance, No date, no publisher indicated, but picked up by the author at the Prime Minister's Office, Basseterre, St. Kitts, February 25, 2000.
50.   Duane Blake, *Shower Posse* (New York: Diamond, 2002), pp. 385–390.
51.   Ivelaw Lloyd Griffith, *Drugs and Security in the Caribbean: Sovereignty under Siege* (University Park, PA: Pennsylvania State University Press, 1997).
52.   Selwyn Ryan, *The Muslimeen Grab for Power* (Port-of-Spain: Inprint, 1991).

53. For a comparative analysis of the two gun smuggling attempts and the ultimate aims of the groups see, Anthony P. Maingot, Transnacionalización de identificaciones raciales y religiosas en el Caribe, *Nueva Sociedad*, No. 177 (enero-febrero, 2002), 161–171.
54. On the Israeli involvement in the arms trade see *El Nuevo Herald*, June 4, 2000, 1; *The Miami Herald*, June 14, 2002, 1; *El Tiempo* (Bogota), April 21, 2002, 1.

Chapter 6

1. Ramon Grosfoguel, Colonial Caribbean migrations to France, the Netherlands, Great Britain, and the United States, *Ethnic and Racial Studies*, 20: 3 (1997).
2. This section draws heavily from Alejandro Portes and Rubén G. Rumbaut, *Immigrant America: a Portrait* (Berkeley: University of California Press, 1996).
3. Alejandro Portes and Robert Bach, *Latin Journey: Cuban and Mexican Immigrants in the U.S.* (Berkeley: University of California Press, 1984), pp. 6–7.
4. A persuasive case study illustrating this point is Alejandro Portes and Luis Guarnizo: *Capitalistas del Trópico. La inmigración en los Estados Unidos y el desarrollo de la pequeña empresa en la República Dominicana* (Facultad Latinoamericana de Ciencias Sociales (FLACSO)–Programa República Dominicana and The Johns Hopkins University Press, 1991).
5. See United Nations Department of Economic and Social Affairs, *International Migration Report, 2002* (New York: UN Publication, 2002), *passim*.
6. Andre Corten and Andrée Corten, *Cambio Social en Santo Domingo* (Rio Piedras, P.R.: Instituto de Estudios del Caribe, 1968), p. 128.
7. On this see Sherri Grasmuck and Patricia Pessar, *Between Two Islands: Dominican International Migration* (Berkeley: University of California Press, 1991).
8. Christopher Mitchell, U.S. foreign policy and Dominican migration to the U.S., *Western Hemisphere Immigration and U.S. Foreign Policy*, Ed. C. Mitchell (University Park, PA: The Pennsylvania State University Press, 1992), pp. 89–123.
9. Antonio Ugalde, Frank Bean, and G. Cardenas, International migration from the Dominican Republic: findings from a national survey, *International Migration Review*, 13: 2 (1979), 235–254.
10. Max Castro, Dominican Journey: Patterns, Context, and Consequences of Migration from the Dominican Republic to the U.S., Unpublished Ph.D. dissertation, Department of Sociology, University of North Carolina, Chapel Hill, 1985, p. 132.
11. Max Castro, Dominican Journey: Patterns, Context, and Consequences of Migration from the Dominican Republic to the U.S., Unpublished Ph.D. dissertation, Department of Sociology, University of North Carolina, Chapel Hill, 1985, p. 140.
12. For a comparison of the Haitian and Dominican cases see Anthony P. Maingot, Emigration dynamics in the Caribbean: the cases of Haiti and the Dominican Republic, *Emigration Dynamics in Developing Countries*, Vol. 3, Ed. Reginald Appleyard (Aldershot, U.K.: Ashgate, 1999), pp. 178–231. In a study realized by Wilfredo Lozano in 1997 (published in 1998) about informal economy, the process of urbanization and urban poverty in the city of Santo Domingo, it was detected that the emigration of the urban poor's relatives in this city who had emigrated abroad, not only were going to New York but to other cities such as Miami, Boston, Chicago, Madrid, Rome, Berlin, Estocolmo, and Athens, among other cities. *La urbanización de la pobreza* (Programa FLACSO–República Dominicana, Santo Domingo, 1998b).
13. Max Castro, Dominican Journey: Patterns, Context, and Consequences of Migration from the Dominican Republic to the U.S., Unpublished Ph.D. dissertation, Department of Sociology, University of North Carolina, Chapel Hill, 1985, p. 146.
14. See Anthony P. Maingot, National identity, instrumental identifications and the Caribbean's culture of "play," *Identity*, 2: 2 (2002), 115–124.
15. Luis Guarnizo, Los Dominicayorks: the making of a binational society, *The Annals of the American Academy of Political and Social Science*, 533 (1994), 83.
16. *El Nuevo Herald*, May 10, 1996, 3.
17. E. Georges, *Dominicanos ausentes*, Ed. E. Georges (Santo Domingo: Fundación Friederich Eberts, 1989), p. 198.
18. See Sidney Mintz, The question of Caribbean peasantries: a comment, *Caribbean Studies*, 1: 3 (1961), 31–34. Anthony P. Maingot, Political implications of migration in a socio-cultural area, *Migration and Development in the Caribbean: The Unexplored Connection*, Ed. R.A. Pastor (Boulder: Westview, 1985).

19. Melville Herskovits, *Life in a Haitian Valley* (New York: Octagon Books, [1934] 1968), p. 198.

20. Alejandro Portes and J. Walton, *Labor, Class and the International System* (New York: Academic, 1981), p. 16.

21. See Anthony P. Maingot, The Caribbean: the structure of modern-conservative societies, *Latin America: Its Problems and Promise*, Ed. Jan K. Black (Boulder: Westview, 1984), pp. 362–380.

22. Henry S. Gill, The Association of Caribbean States: Prospects for a "Quantum Leap," Miami: The North-South Agenda Papers No. 11, University of Miami, 1995, p. 14.

23. Charles I. Jainarain, *Annual Report on Trade, 1995–1996*, Miami: Summit of the Americas Center (FIU), 1996, Foreword.

24. Terry McCoy, *The Free Trade Area of the Americas Opportunities and Challenges for Florida* (Gainesville, FL: Latin American Business Environment Program, March, 2001).

25. *América economía*, 10 agosto 2000, 36–40.

26. On the various levels of ethnic conflict in Miami-Dade, see Guillermo J. Grenier and Max J. Castro, The emergence of an adversarial relation: Black–Cuban relations in Miami, 1959–1998, *Research in Urban Policy*, 7 (1998), 33–35; Guillermo J. Grenier and Max J. Castro, Triadic politics: ethnicity, race, and politics in Miami, 1959–1998, *Pacific Historical Review*, 68: 2 (1999), 273–292.

27. *The New York Times*, March 3, 1996, 1 (National Coalition For Haitian Rights, letter).

28. *The New Americans*, 25.

29. Greenheart International, Florida/Caribbean Assessment, Policy Options Unpublished ms., Miami, FL, 2000.

30. The National Immigration Forum, *The New American Miami* (Washington, D.C., 1998), Letter from the editor.

31. Cited at www.southcom.mil/PA/Facts/History.htm

32. Jorge Rodríguez Beruff, "Prologo" in *La estrategia de los Estados Unidos y la militarización del Caribe*, Ed. Humberto García Muñiz (Rio Piedras: Institutio de Estudios del Caribe, 1988).

33. Further on this, see Anthony P. Maingot, Laundering the gains of the drug trade: Miami and Caribbean tax havens, *Journal of Inter-American Studies and World Affairs*, 30: 2, 3 (1988), 167–187.

34. See Anthony P. Maingot, Offshore secrecy centers and the necessary role of states: bucking the trend, *Journal of Inter-American Studies and World Affairs*, 37: 4 (1995), 1–24.

35. *The Weekly Gleaner*, August 15, 2001, 5.

36. Bernardo Vega, La Segunda Guerra Fria, (Santo Domingo: Flacso, 1999).

37. British Broadcasting Corporation (BBC), Caribbean Report, December 18, 1998, 6:00 A.M.

38. *The Miami Herald*, February 22, 1999, 1.

39. Ivelaw L. Griffith, The Drama of Deportation, *Caribbean Perspective*, January 1999, 12.

40. *Trinidad Guardian*, July 18, 2003, 1.

41. *The Gleaner*, Website, August 12, 2002.

42. *The Gleaner*, Website, Editorial, August 19, 2002.

43. *Trinidad Express*, Website, August 21, 2002.

44. *Trinidad Express*, Website, Editorial, August 6, 2002.

45. Executive Summary of the Police Executive Research Forum (PERF) Study on Crime in Kingston in *The Gleaner*, August 2, 2002.

46. *Jamaica Gleaner*, December 31, 1996, 1.

47. Carl Windt, Ed., *Jamaica Gleaner*, February 11, 1997, 8.

48. *The Weekly Gleaner*, March 27–April 2, 2003, 7.

49. Geoff Brown, Myth versus Reality, *Jamaica Gleaner*, May 2, 1997, 9–10.

50. *Jamaica Gleaner*, April 20–May 10, 2000.

51. *The Weekly Gleaner*, May 4–10, 2000, 18.

52. *Jamaica Gleaner*, April 30, 2000, 1.

53. Bureau for International Narcotics and Law Enforcement Affairs, *International Narcotics Control Strategy Report*, 1999. (Washington, D.C.: U.S. Department of State, March 2000), 13.

54. Terry Lacey, *Violence and Politics in Jamaica 1960–1970* (Totowa, N.J.: Frank Case, 1977), p. 3.

55. Cited in Terry Lacey, *Violence and Politics in Jamaica*, p. 132.

56. *The Financial Times*, September 5, 1974, 5.

57. Terry Lacey, *Violence and Politics in Jamaica*, p. 160.

58. Terry Lacey, *Violence and Politics in Jamaica*, p. 162.

59. Quoted in Anthony P. Maingot, *The U.S. and the Caribbean*, (London: Macmillan, 1994), pp. 142–162.
60. Laurie Gunst, *Born Fi Dead* (New York: Henry Holt, 1995).
61. Aside from Laurie Gunst, *Born Fi Dead*, see also Andre M. Porter, *The Rise and Fall of a Jamaican Don* (Bloomington, IN.: First Books, 2002); Duane Blake, *Shower Posse* (New York: Diamond, 2002).
62. Note Gunst's assertion that [W]hether or not Seaga was feeding cocaine to his paladins, the JLP definitely controlled the trade . . . . and several of his government ministers were said to be involved in protecting its movement into and out of Jamaica. Gunst, *Born Fi Dead*, p. 117.
63. *Jamaica Weekly Gleaner*, October 12–19, November 25–December 1, 1994, 6.
64. *Jamaica Weekly Gleaner*, November 18–24, 1994, 4.
65. This section draws heavily from Anthony P. Maingot, Los procesos de cambio social y político en el Caribe de lá Posguerra Fría, in *Cambio político en el Caribe*, Ed. Wilfredo Lozano (Caracas: Nueva Sociedad, 1998), pp. 9–28.
65. *Jamaica Weekly Gleaner*, June 27–July 3, 2002, 1, 3.
66. *The Jamaica Gleaner*, September 9, 1991.
67. *The Jamaica Gleaner*, September 9, 1991.
68. *The Jamaica Gleaner*, October 15, 1986, 8.
69. Quoted in Terry Lacey, *Violence and Politics in Jamaica 1960–1970* (Totowa, N.J.: Frank Case, 1977), p. 138.
70. *The Jamaica Gleaner*, October 19, 1986, 8.
71. *Jamaica Weekly Gleaner*, January 21–27, 1999.
72. *Jamaica Weekly Gleaner*, October 22–28, 1998, 7.
73. Paul Chevigny, *Edge of the Knife, Police Violence in the Americas* (New York: The New Press, 1995), p. 205.
74. See the summary of this report in *Jamaica Weekly Gleaner*, June 20–26, 2002, 1, 2.
75. *Jamaica Weekly Gleaner*, July 11–17, 2002, 3.
76. Jimmy Carter, Foreword in *Fostering Transparency and Preventing Corruption in Jamaica*, Ed. Laura Neuman (Atlanta: The Carter Center, February, 2000).
77. *The Jamaica Weekly Gleaner*, August 14–20, 2003, 3.
78. *El Nuevo Herald*, August 28, 2002, 1.
79. Anthony Harriot, The Changing Social Organization of Crime and Criminals in Jamaica, *Caribbean Quarterly*, 42 (1996), 80.
80. Associated Press cable on Yahoo! News, September 4, 2002.
81. *Trinidad Express*, August 30, 2002.
82. *The Jamaica Weekly Gleaner*, September 5–11, 3.
83. *The Jamaica Weekly Gleaner*, May 29, 2003, 8.
84. Bernardo Vega, *Diario de una misión en Washington* (Santo Domingo: Fundación Cultural Dominicana, 2002), 11–12.

Conclusion

1. T*he Wall Street Journal*, September 15, 2003, A-18.
2. *The New York Times*, September 15, 2003, 4.
3. Interview with Sir John Saunders, High Commissioner of Antigua and Barbuda to the United Kingdom, in Ottawa, Canada, March 3, 2003.
4. At <www.itf.org.uk>.
5. *The Financial Times*, September 6–7, 2003, 24.
6. *The Financial Times*, July 21, 2003, 2.
7. *The Financial Times*, September 15, 2003, 1.
8. *The Wall Street Journal*, September 8, 2003, A-16.
9. *The Weekly Gleaner*, August 21–27, 2003, 7.
10. Quoted in *The Miami Herald*, September 13, 2003, 2C.

Index

161